NSW Targeting Maths

Year 2

Katy Pike

PASCAL PRESS

Contents

Term 1

Term 2

Term 3

Term 4

New Edition

Targeting Maths Australia's Favourite Maths Program

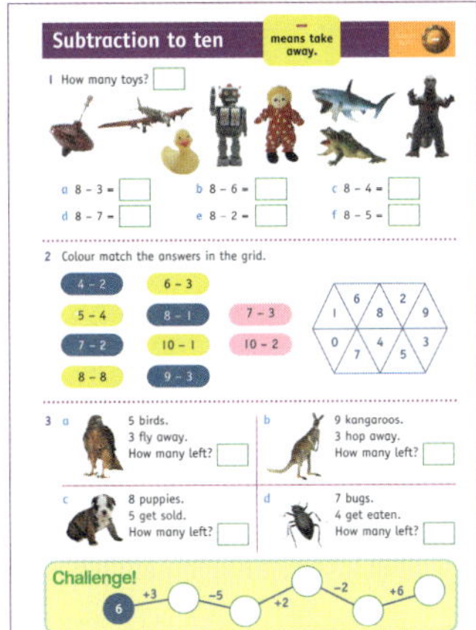

Australian Curriculum/NSW Alignment

This NEW Edition fully aligns each student page with both the new NSW Syllabus (2022) and the Australian Curriculum. The new NSW Syllabus outcome codes and content groups appear alongside the Australian Curriculum code and content descriptions on each student page.

iPad Apps

With an app for each year, from Kindergarten to Year 6, the Targeting Maths Apps include all the essential maths content that children need to know in an amazing app that makes learning maths fun, motivating and full of rewards. Look for it in Apple's App Store today! Made especially for the iPad and aligned to each student page in this book.

Integrated Problem-solving Program

Includes an integrated problem-solving program that actively builds students' problem solving capabilities.

In-stage Topic Alignment for Composite Classes

Great for composite classes too, the contents of each book in one stage, eg Year 1 and Year 2, match topic by topic.

Term Investigations

Each term includes an investigation that will get students planning and working through an extended problem.

Regular Revision

Revision pages appear both at mid term and at the end of each term to revise key concepts.

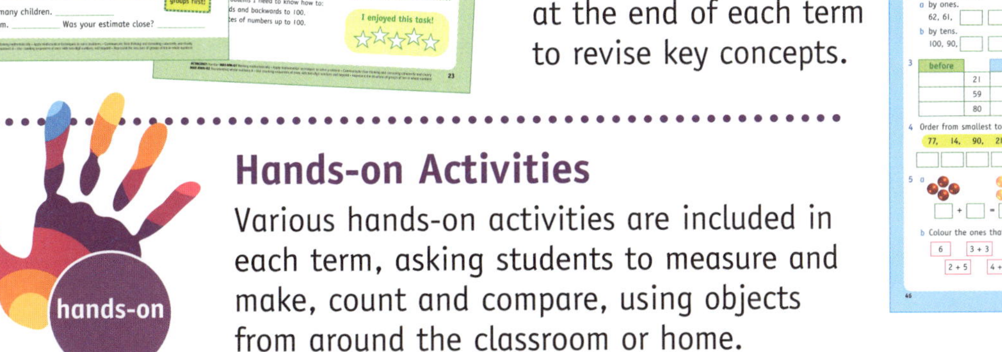

Hands-on Activities

Various hands-on activities are included in each term, asking students to measure and make, count and compare, using objects from around the classroom or home.

Year 2 Outcomes

	NSW Syllabus Outcomes	Student pages
Working Mathematically	**MA1-WM-01** develops understanding and fluency in mathematics through exploring and connecting mathematical concepts	pages 2 to 183
	MA1-WM-01 develops understanding and fluency in mathematics through choosing and applying mathematical techniques to solve problems	7, 14, 21, 22, 23, 35, 45, 53, 65, 66, 67, 74, 81, 84, 91, 100, 103, 107, 118, 119, 127, 144, 149, 155, 160, 161, 162, 163, 171, 175
	MA1-WM-01 develops understanding and fluency in mathematics through communicating their thinking and reasoning coherently and clearly	22, 23, 66, 67, 74, 84, 91, 118, 119, 162, 163, 175
Number and Algebra	**Representing whole numbers**	
	MA1-RWN-01 applies an understanding of place value and the role of zero to read, write and order two- and three-digit numbers	2, 3, 4, 5, 94, 95, 96, 97, 98, 99, 100, 140, 141, 142, 143
	MA1-RWN-02 reads numerals and represents whole numbers to at least 20	6, 22, 23, 94, 95, 96, 97, 98, 99, 100, 140, 141, 142, 143
	Combining and separating quantities	
	MA1-CSQ-01 uses number bonds and the relationship between addition and subtraction to solve problems involving partitioning	7, 15, 16, 17, 18, 19, 20, 21, 31, 32, 33, 34, 35, 48, 49, 50, 51, 52, 53, 58, 59, 60, 61, 62, 63, 64, 65, 118, 119, 122, 123, 124, 125, 126, 127, 150, 151, 152, 153, 154, 155
	Forming groups	
	MA1-FG-01 uses the structure of equal groups to solve multiplication problems, and shares or groups to solve division problems	40, 41, 75, 76, 77, 78, 79, 80, 81, 112, 113, 114, 115, 116, 117, 132, 133, 134, 135, 166, 167, 168, 169, 170, 171
Measurement and Space	**Geometric measure**	
	MA1-GM-01 represents and describes the positions of objects in familiar locations	88, 89, 90, 91
	MA1-GM-02 measures, records, compares and estimates lengths and distances using uniform informal units, as well as metres and centimetres	54, 55, 56, 57, 66, 67, 104, 105, 106, 107, 118, 119
	MA1-GM-03 creates and recognises halves, quarters and eighths as part measures of a whole length	38, 39, 42, 135
	Two-dimensional spatial structure	
	MA1-2DS-01 recognises, describes and represents shapes including quadrilaterals and other common polygons	8, 9, 10, 11, 12, 13, 14, 108, 109, 110, 111
	MA1-2DS-02 measures and compares areas using uniform informal units in rows and columns	101, 102, 103
	Three-dimensional spatial structure	
	MA1-3DS-01 recognises, describes and represents familiar three-dimensional objects	70, 71, 72, 73, 74, 176, 177, 178, 179
	MA1-3DS-02 measures, records, compares and estimates internal volumes (capacities) and volumes using uniform informal units	43, 44, 45, 156, 157, 158, 159, 161, 162, 163
	Non-spatial measure	
	MA1-NSM-01 measures, records, compares and estimates the masses of objects using uniform informal units	36, 37, 172, 173, 174, 175
	MA1-NSM-02 describes, compares and orders durations of events, and reads half- and quarter-hour time	26, 27, 28, 29, 118, 119, 128, 129, 130, 131, 145, 146, 147, 148, 149, 162, 163
Statistics & Probability	**Data**	
	MA1-DATA-01 gathers and organises data, displays data in lists, tables and picture graphs	30, 82, 83, 84, 136, 137, 180, 181, 182
	MA1-DATA-02 reasons about representations of data to describe and interpret the results	30, 82, 83, 84, 136, 137, 180, 181
	MA1-CHAN-01 recognises and describes the element of chance in everyday events	85, 86, 87, 180, 182

	Australian Curriculum Content Descriptions *Students learn to:*	Student pages
Number	**AC9M2N01** recognise, represent and order numbers to at least 1000 using physical and virtual materials, numerals and number lines	2, 3, 4, 5, 6, 22, 23, 94, 95, 96, 99, 140, 143, 144
	AC9M2N02 partition, rearrange, regroup and rename two- and three-digit numbers using standard and non-standard groupings; recognise the role of a zero digit in place value notation	96, 97, 98, 99, 100, 140, 141, 142
	AC9M2N03 recognise and describe one-half as one of 2 equal parts of a whole and connect halves, quarters and eighths through repeated halving	132, 133, 134, 135
	AC9M2N04 add and subtract one- and two-digit numbers, representing problems using number sentences and solve using part-part-whole reasoning and a variety of calculation strategies	15, 16, 17, 18, 19, 20, 21, 31, 32, 33, 34, 48, 49, 52, 58, 59, 122, 123, 125, 150, 151, 154
	AC9M2N05 multiply and divide by one-digit numbers using repeated addition, equal grouping, arrays, and partitioning to support a variety of calculation strategies	75, 76, 77, 78, 112, 113, 114, 116, 117, 166, 167, 168, 169, 170
	AC9M2N06 use mathematical modelling to solve practical problems involving additive and multiplicative situations, including money transactions; represent situations and choose calculation strategies; interpret and communicate solutions in terms of the situation	7, 17, 35, 50, 51, 53, 65, 81, 107, 119, 124, 127, 152, 155, 162, 171
Algebra	**AC9M2A01** recognise, describe and create additive patterns that increase or decrease by a constant amount, using numbers, shapes and objects, and identify missing elements in the pattern	64, 75, 79, 80, 115, 126, 142, 153
	AC9M2A02 recall and demonstrate proficiency with addition facts to 20; extend and apply facts to develop related subtraction facts	60, 61, 62, 63
	AC9M2A03 recall and demonstrate proficiency with multiplication facts for twos; extend and apply facts to develop the related division facts using doubling and halving	40, 41
Measurement	**AC9M2M01** measure and compare objects based on length, capacity and mass using appropriate uniform informal units and smaller units for accuracy when necessary	36, 37, 43, 54, 55, 56, 57, 66, 67, 104, 105, 106, 107, 118, 156, 159, 160, 161, 172, 173, 174, 175
	AC9M2M02 identify common uses and represent halves, quarters and eighths in relation to shapes, objects and events	38, 39, 40, 41, 42
	AC9M2M03 identify the date and determine the number of days between events using calendars	28, 29, 163
	AC9M2M04 recognise and read the time represented on an analog clock to the hour, half-hour and quarter-hour	26, 27, 119, 145, 146, 147, 148, 149
	AC9M2M05 identify, describe and demonstrate quarter, half, three-quarter and full measures of turn in everyday situations	12, 13, 14
Space	**AC9M2SP01** recognise, compare and classify shapes, referencing the number of sides and using spatial terms such as “opposite”, “parallel”, “curved” and “straight”	8, 9, 10, 11, 70, 71, 72, 73, 74, 108, 109, 110, 111, 176, 177, 178, 179
	AC9M2SP02 locate positions in two-dimensional representations of a familiar space; move positions by following directions and pathways	88, 89, 90, 91
Statistics	**AC9M2ST01** acquire data for categorical variables through surveys, observation, experiment and using digital tools; sort data into relevant categories and display data using lists and tables	30, 82, 83, 136, 137, 180
	AC9M2ST02 create different graphical representations of data using software where appropriate; compare the different representations, identify and describe common and distinctive features in response to questions	30, 82, 83, 84, 136, 137, 180, 181, 182

How to Solve a Problem

Read • Plan • Work • Check

Read the problem carefully. Underline the question. Circle the facts.

Plan What you will do: +, −, × (multiply) or ÷ (divide).

Work Write or draw a diagram to work it out. Write the answer.

Check your answer! Make sure that your answer makes sense.

Draw a diagram

Draw a simple picture.

Here are some pictures and what they mean:

take away	8 − 3 =	
add	6 + 7 =	
equal groups	4 × 4 =	
share	share 6 between 3	

Looking for patterns

If you can see a pattern, use it to help find the answer.

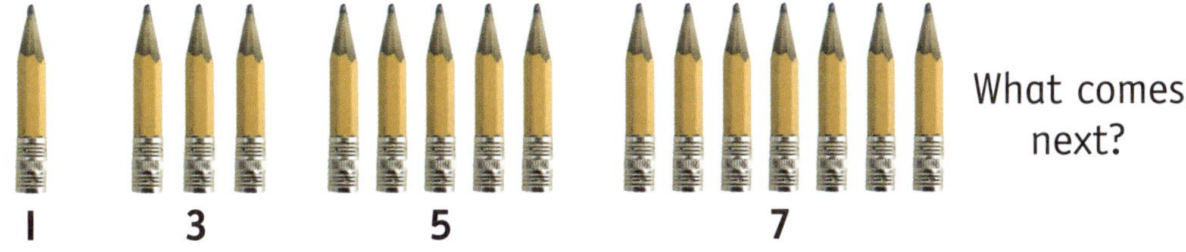

What comes next?

Act it out

Do something. You can use counters or blocks, cut things out, move things around.

Trial and error

Make a good guess and write it down. Check if it is right. If it's wrong, try again. Should it be higher or lower?

Dictionary

addition (+)

Six balls and two balls makes eight balls.

angle

An angle is made when two straight lines meet.

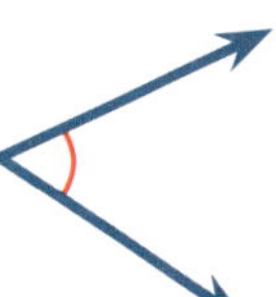

area

The amount of space something covers.

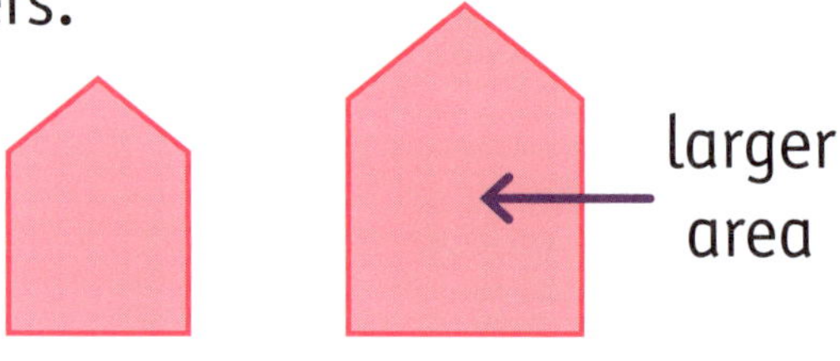

capacity

The amount it can hold.

The jug holds more.

clocks

half-past ten

analog

corner or vertex

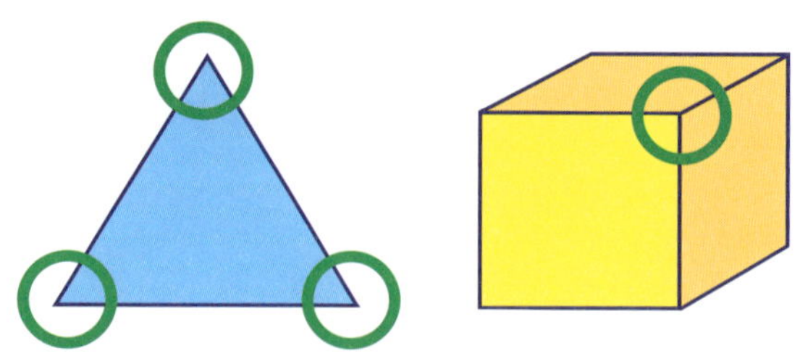

division (÷)

Sharing into equal groups.

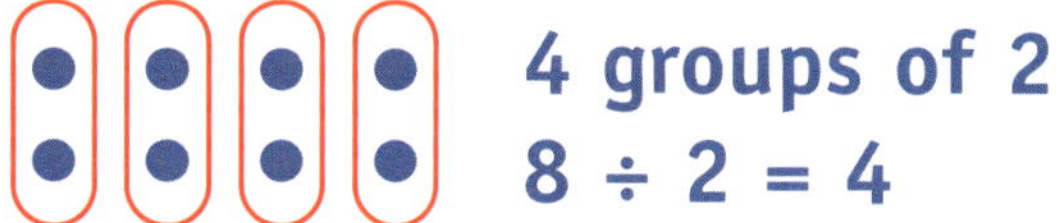

edge

Where two faces meet.

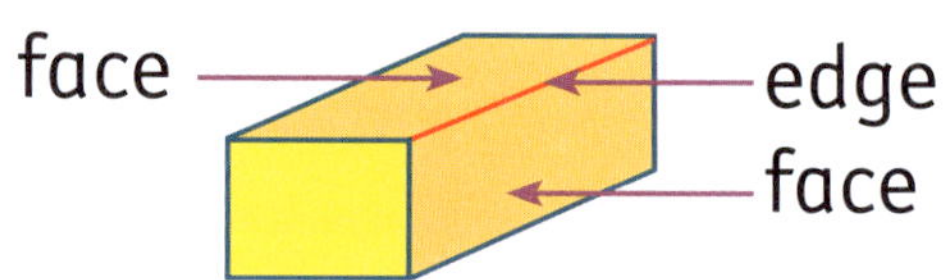

face

A flat surface.

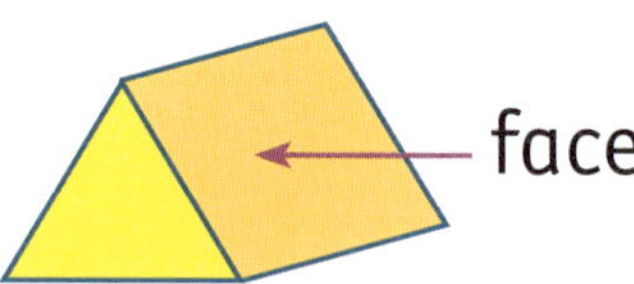

flip, slide, turn

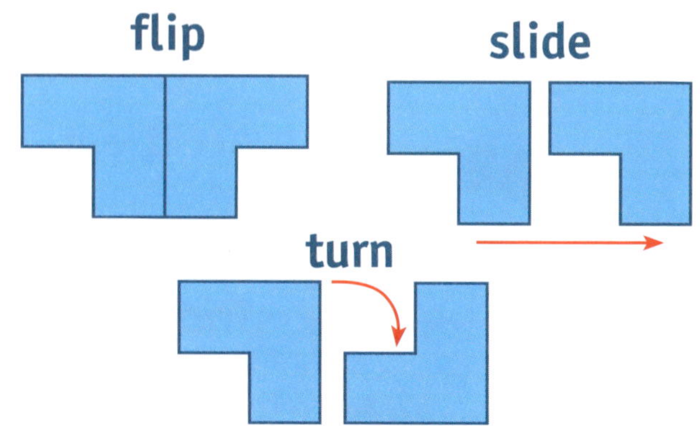

Dictionary

fractions

A part of a whole or of a group.

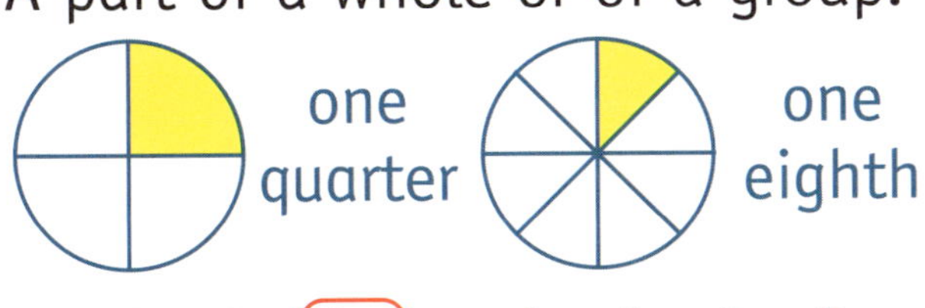

half a length

quarter lengths

eighths of a length

groups

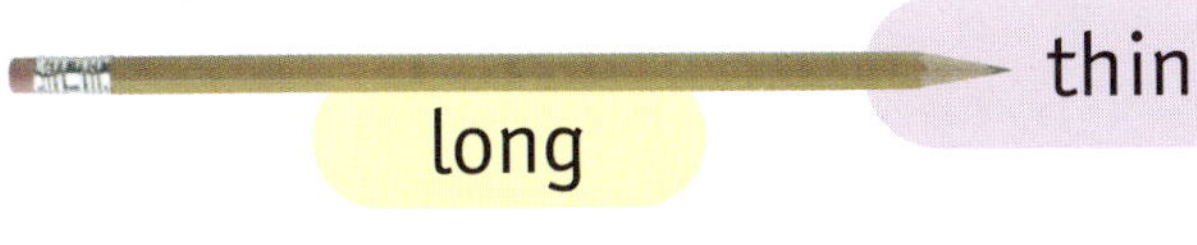

1 group of 5

3 groups of 7

length

line

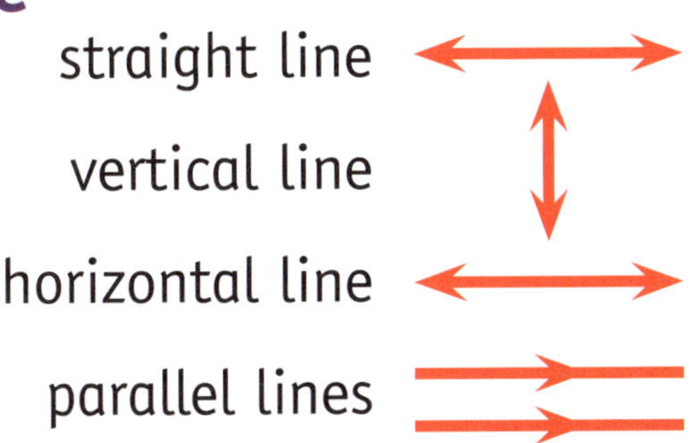

mass

money

coins

notes

Dictionary

months

January	May	September
February	June	October
March	July	November
April	August	December

multiplication (×)

To find the total in equal groups or rows.

5 groups of 3
$5 \times 3 = 15$

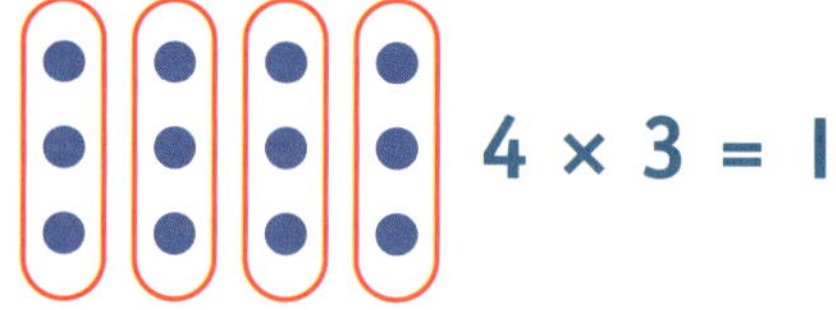

$4 \times 3 = 12$

numbers

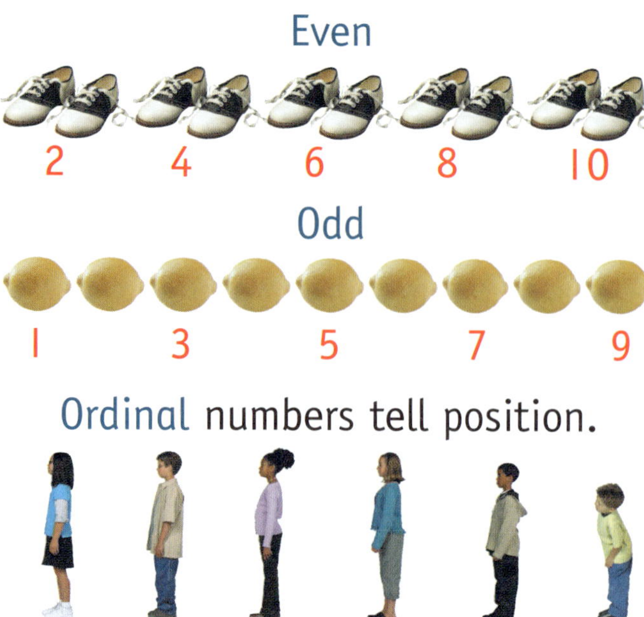

position

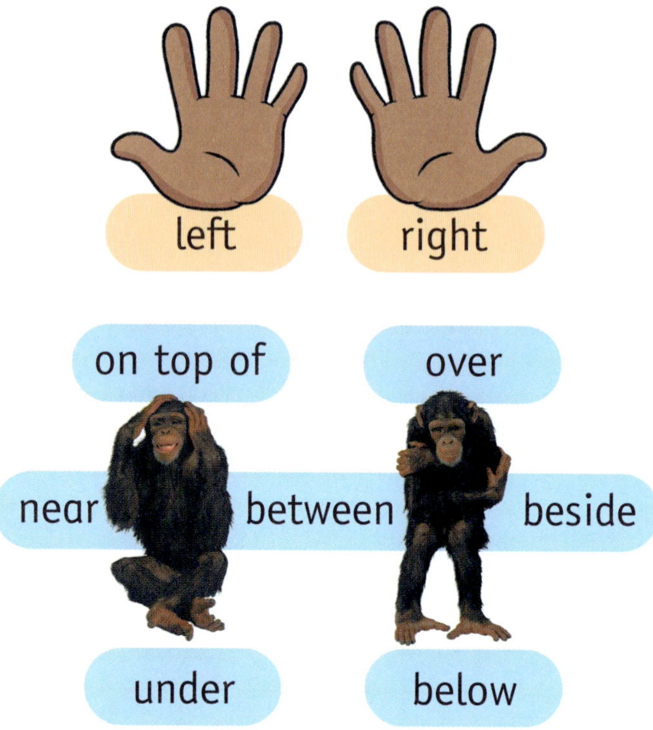

subtraction (–)

Nine rabbits take away three rabbits leaves six rabbits.

$9 - 3 = 6$

symmetry

Both halves match exactly when folded on the line of symmetry.

line of symmetry

Dictionary

tessellating shapes

Shapes that fit together without gaps or overlaps.

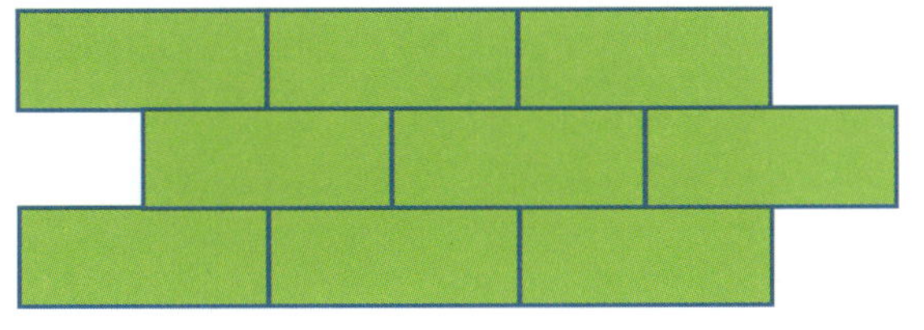

tally marks

Marks to help us count large numbers.

| = 1   𝍸 = 5

three-dimensional (3D) objects

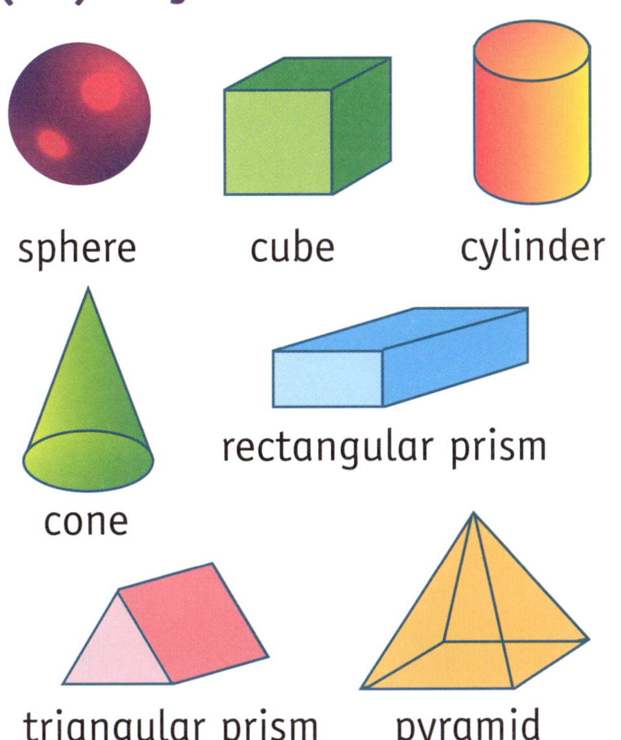

two-dimensional (2D) shapes

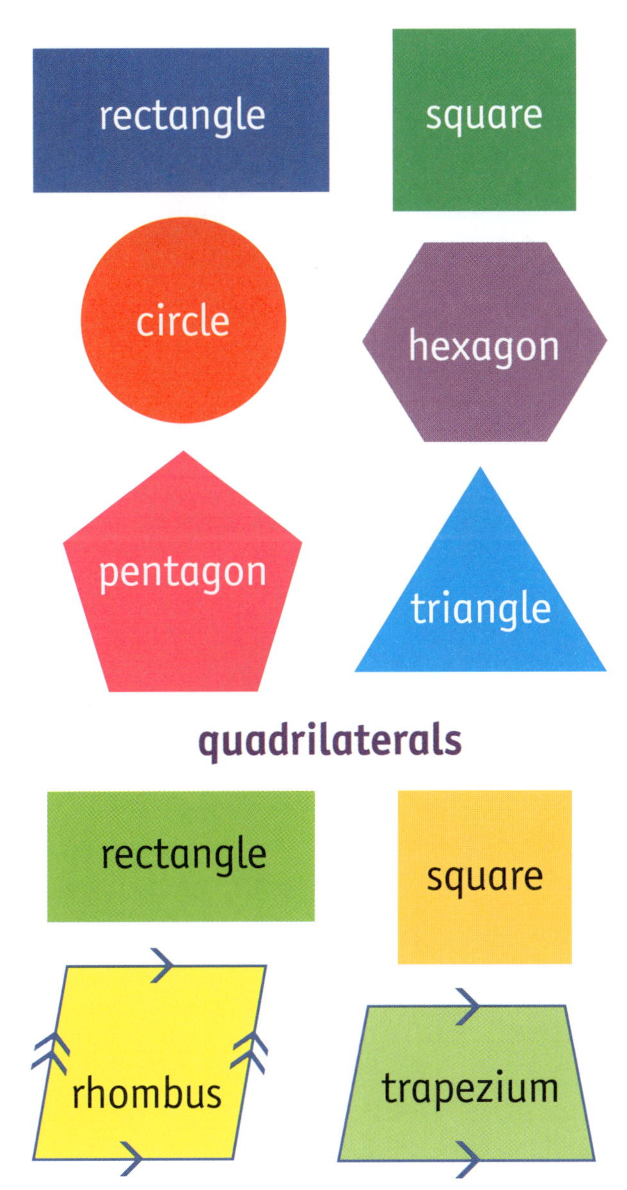

volume

The space it takes up.

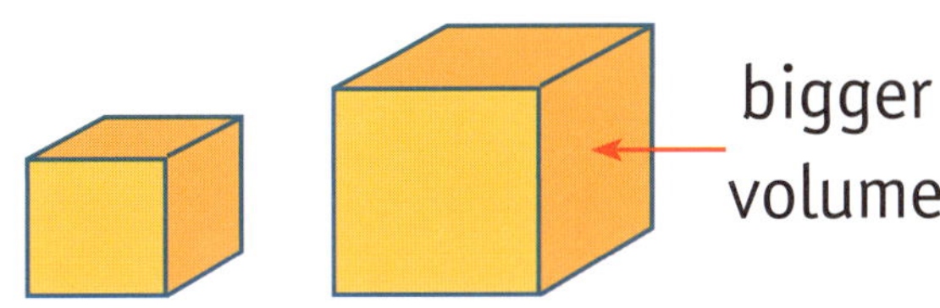

Numbers to 100

1 Which numbers are:

a more than 80? ☐

b less than 50? ☐

2 Write the number between

a 52 and 54 ☐

b 65 and 67 ☐

c 89 and 91 ☐

d 18 and 20 ☐

3 Order from smallest to largest.

smallest ☐ ☐ ☐ ☐ ☐ ☐ ☐ ☐ ☐ ☐ ☐ ☐ **largest**

Numbers to 100

Write the number:

1 one more than

a 44 **b** 52 **c** 97 **d** 89 **e** 91

2 one less than

a 29 **b** 67 **c** 88 **d** 81 **e** 20

3 ten more than

a 22 **b** 35 **c** 19 **d** 77  **e** 66

4 ten less than

a 26 **b** 82 **c** 77 **d** 100 **e** 89

5

	before		after
a		67	
b		31	
c		52	
d		70	

		between	
e			60
f			71
g			42
h	89		

6 Use   1 to make 2-digit numbers, eg 14.

smallest Write in order. **largest**

Challenge!

One rocket's number is double another's. Find the two rockets.

The hundred chart

1 Fill in the missing numbers.

1	2	3	4	5	6		8	9	10
11	12	13		15	16		18	19	20
				25	26		28	29	30
	32	33	34		36	37	38	39	40
	42	43	44						
51	52	53	54		56	57	58	59	60
61	62			65			68	69	70
71		73	74	75	76	77	78	79	
81		83	84	85	86	87		89	90
91		93	94	95	96	97	98		100

2 Count by tens.

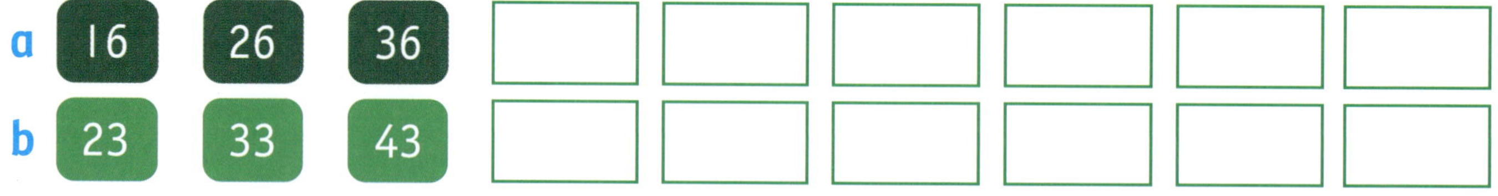

3 Count backwards.

a 54 53 52

b 81 80 79

c 90 80 70

d 86 76 66

Patterns in the hundred square

1 These are parts of a hundred square. Write the missing numbers.

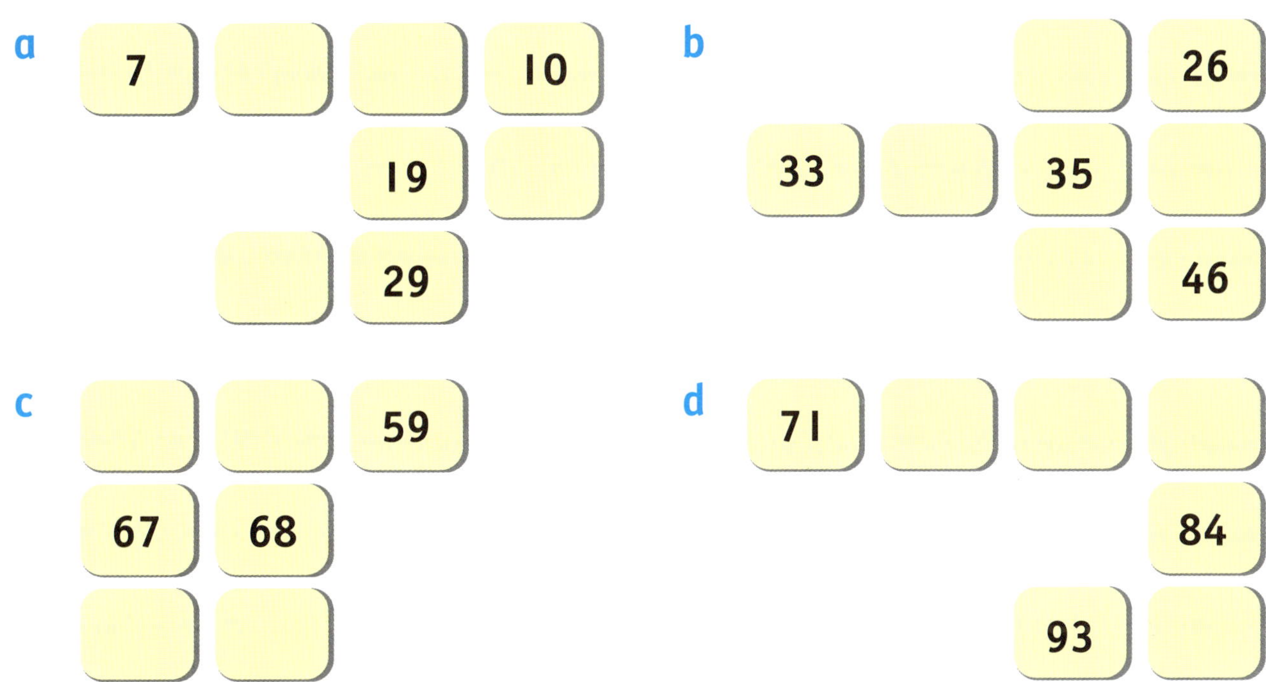

Hint! Use the 100 chart

2 The postman delivers letters to 20 houses. On Monday, every 2nd house got a letter. On Tuesday, every 3rd house got a letter. On Wednesday, every 5th house got a letter.

Which houses got no letters? ______________________

Which houses got 1 letter? ______________________

Which houses got 2 letters? ______________________

Looking for patterns

Jump back to zero. Use jumps of 2. Find different numbers in the hundred square that will take you back to zero.

Now try jumps of 5 and 10.
What patterns can you see?

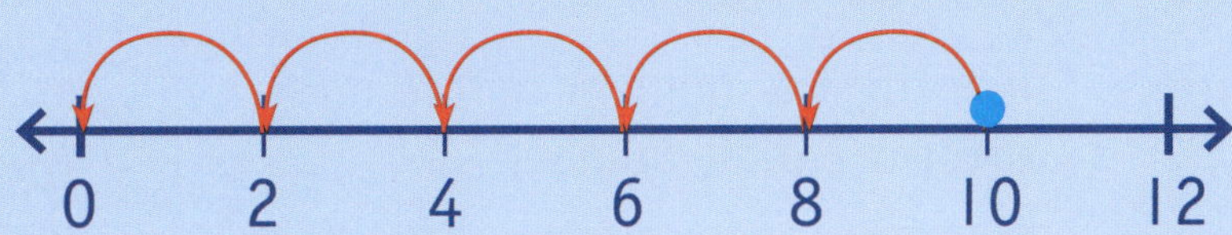

Estimation

Estimate
Make a good guess. Don't count.

Here are 20 flowers.

Don't count yet!

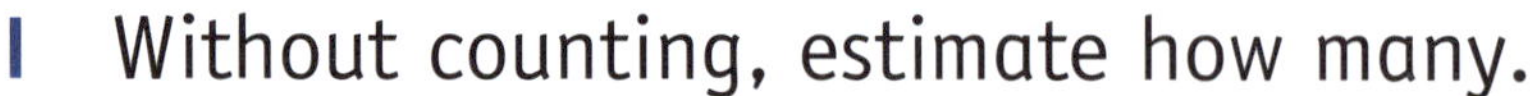

1 Without counting, estimate how many.

a

b

c

d

e

Here are 30 dots.

2 Estimate how many.

3 Count to check. Circle groups of 10. Were you close? ____________

Mastery Checklist

I can:
- ☐ identify the number before and after a 2-digit number.
- ☐ count by ones and tens to 100.
- ☐ estimate the number of objects in a group.
- ☐ count large sets of objects by grouping in tens.

Problem solving

You win a prize in a competition.

Each prize winner gets some notes. What could they be?

Choose a prize and work out which notes you could get.
Show as many answers as you can.

Extension What would you buy with the prize money?

I can solve a problem by:

☐ counting to 100. ☐ drawing a picture or writing an equation.

Sides and corners

A corner is where 2 straight lines meet.

1 How many sides has each shape?

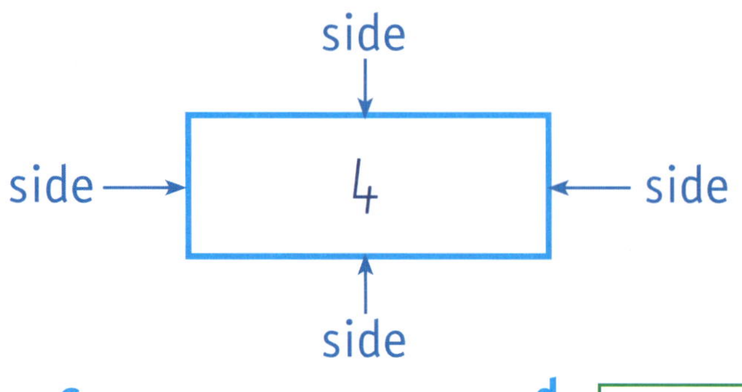

a 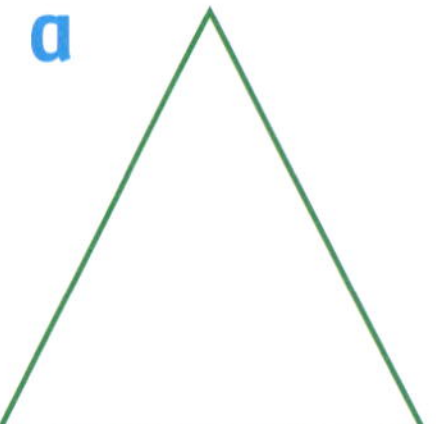

b 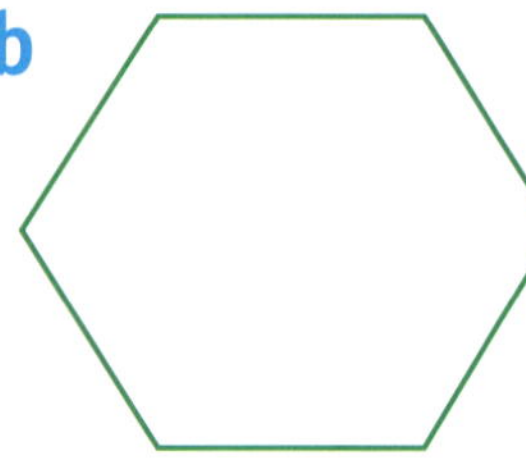

c 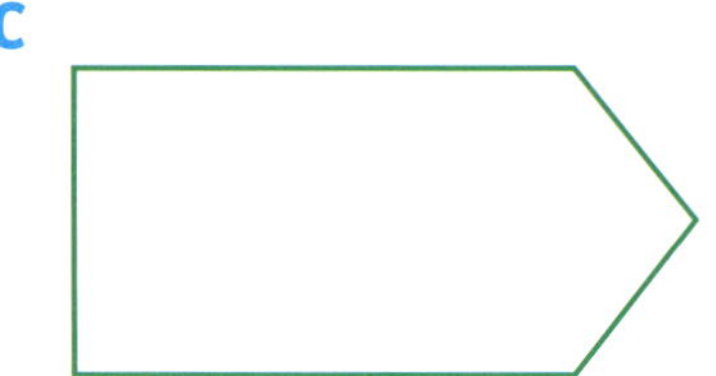

d 

e 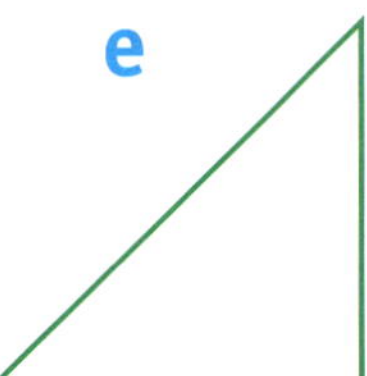

f

2 Circle corners.

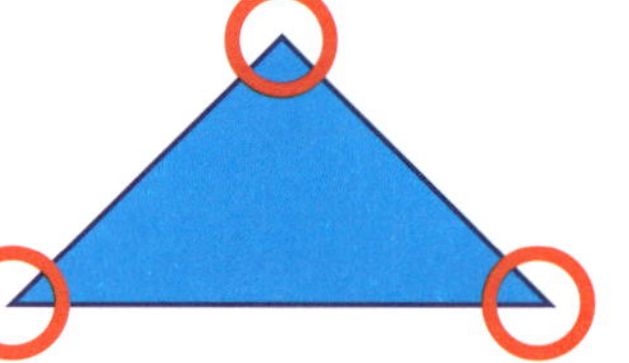

A corner is also called a vertex.

	Number of sides	Number of corners
a triangle		
b square		
c rectangle		
d pentagon		
e hexagon		

Looking for patterns

A shape with 4 straight sides has ☐ corners.

A shape with 5 straight sides has ☐ corners.

A shape with 6 straight sides has ☐ corners.

Trapeziums

Parallel lines are always the same distance apart and never meet.

Trapeziums have:

- 4 straight sides,
- 2 sides that are parallel and
- 2 sides that are not parallel.

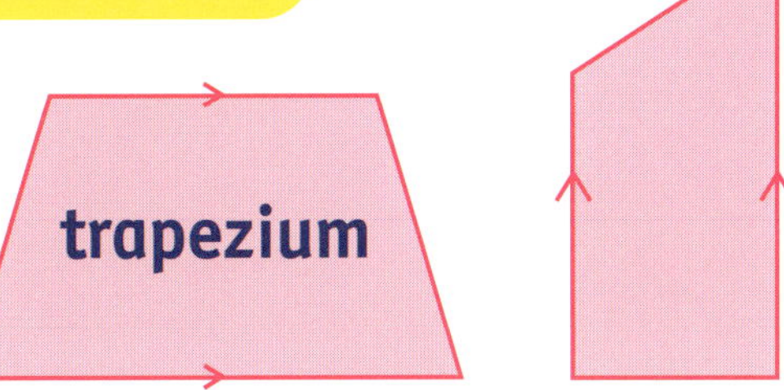

1 Circle the parallel lines.

2 Tick shapes with parallel lines. Colour the trapeziums.

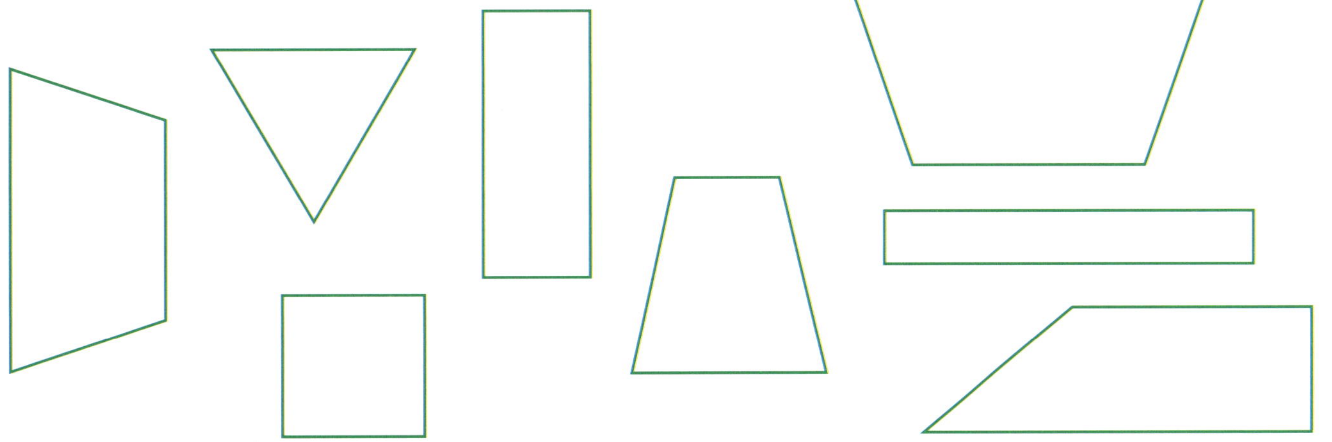

3 Draw 2 different trapeziums.

Symmetry

1 Draw a line of symmetry.

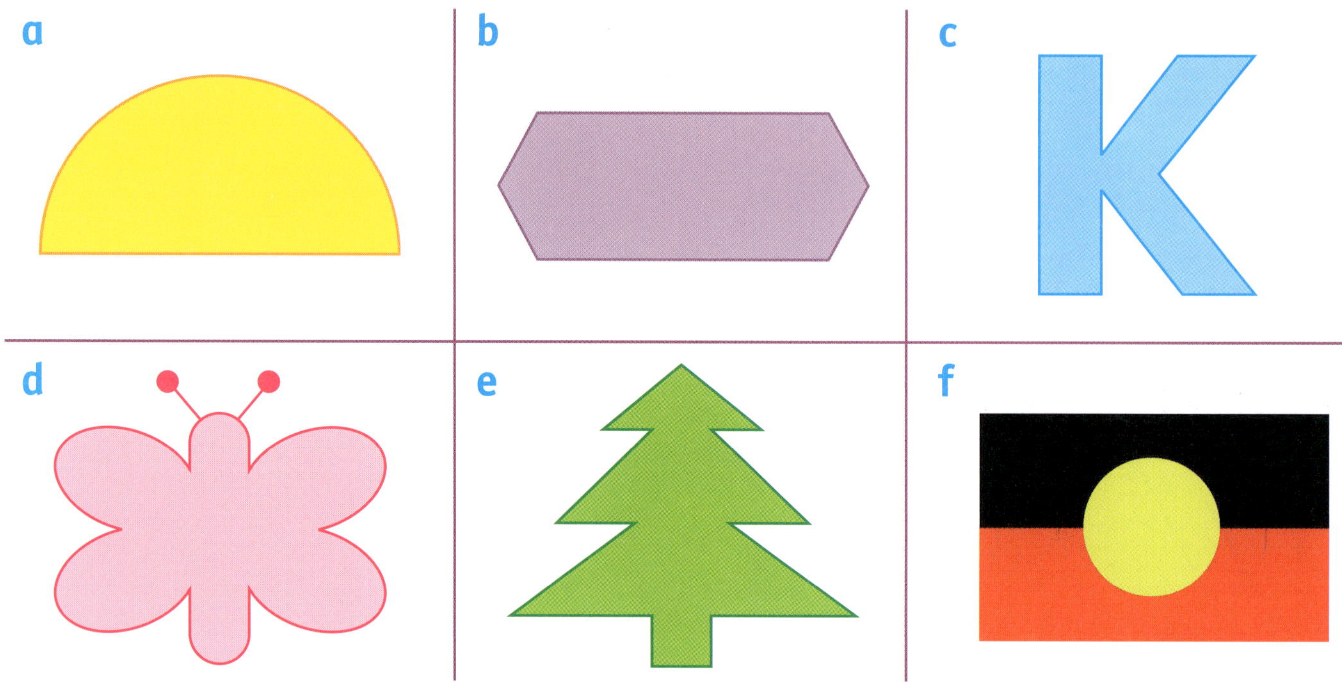

2 Colour to make each pattern symmetrical.

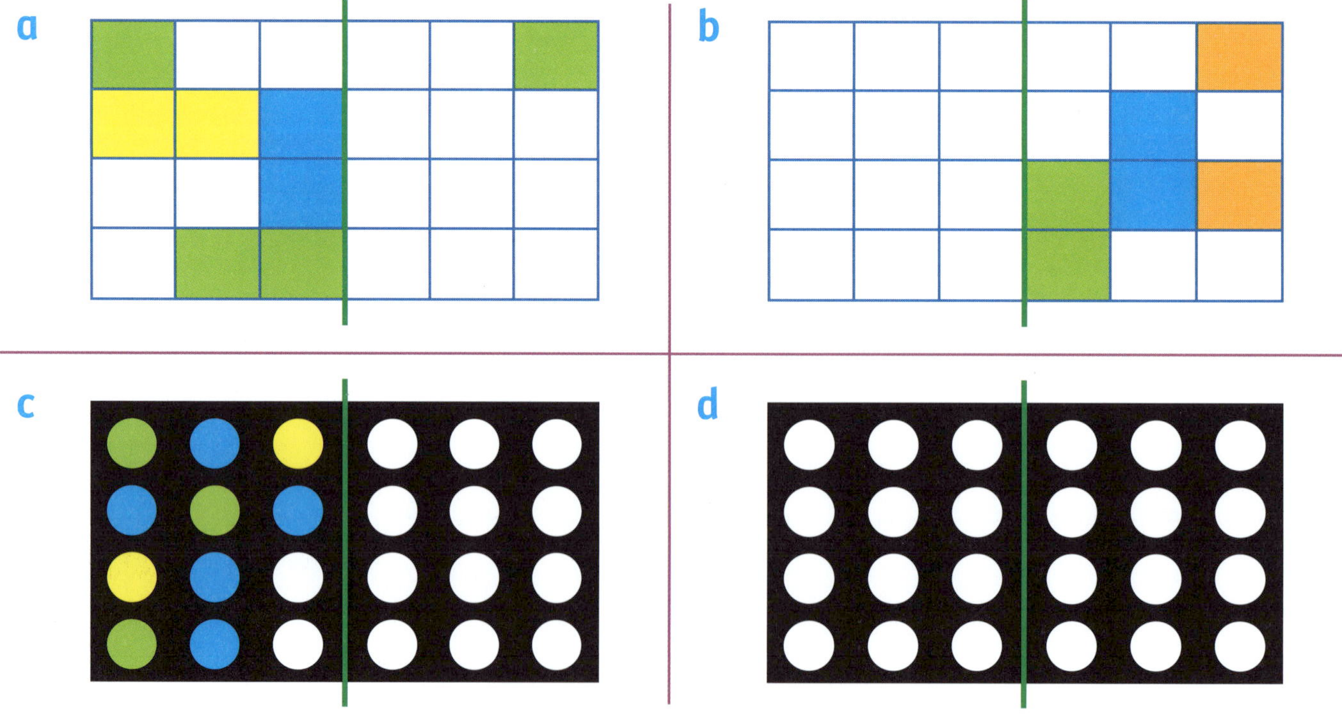

Challenge! Write two words using only symmetrical letters.

Rhombus

A rhombus has:

- 4 straight sides all the same length,
- and 2 pairs of parallel sides.

rhombus

Symmetry
Both sides match when folded on the line of symmetry.

1 Draw a rhombus. Draw a line of symmetry.
Draw another line of symmetry.

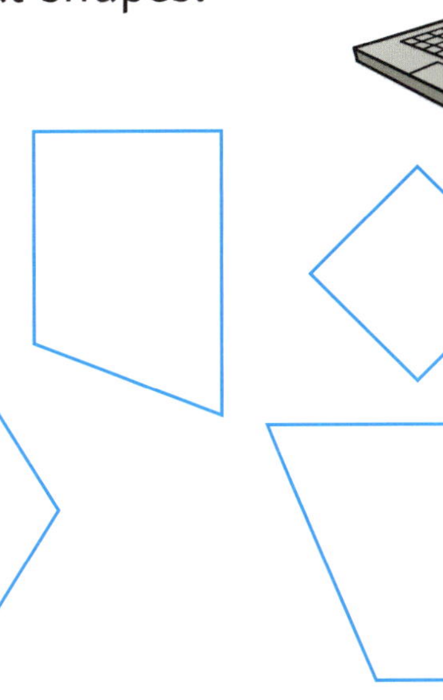

2 Colour each rhombus. Tick the symmetrical shapes.
Draw each line of symmetry.

Turns

1 Tick the shapes that show a quarter turn.

2 Circle the shapes that show a half turn.

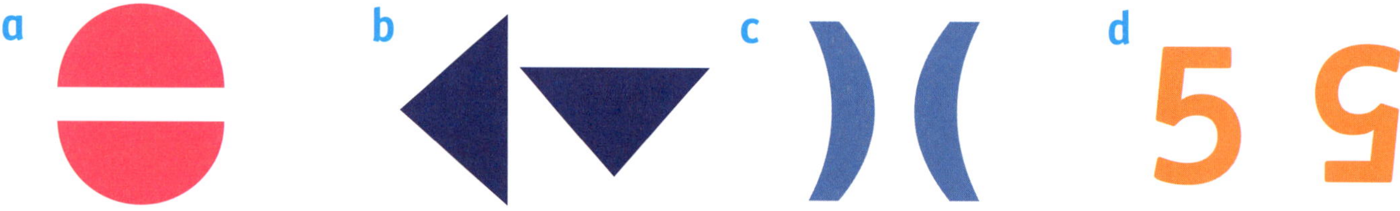

3 Draw this shape after a quarter turn and a half turn.

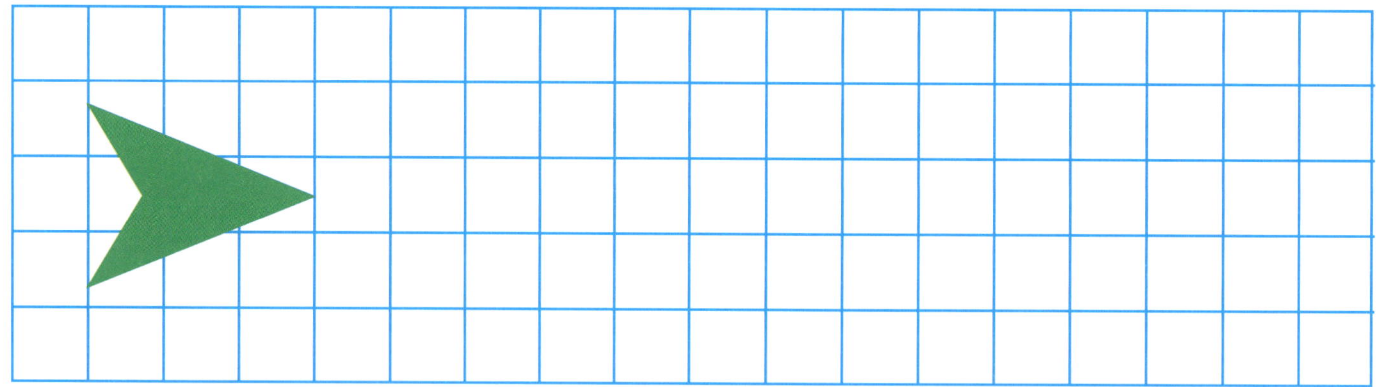

4 Draw this shape after a flip, a slide, a quarter turn and a half turn.

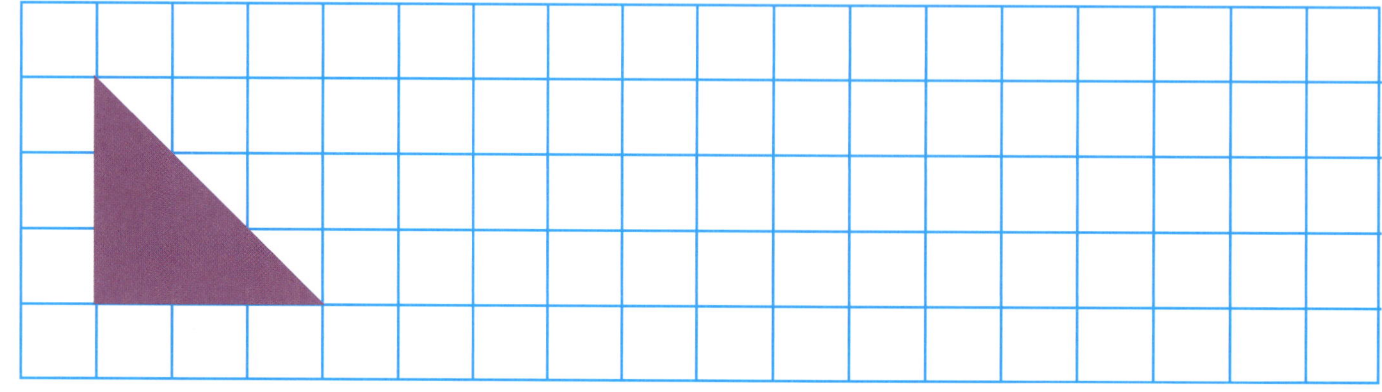

Turn direction

clockwise

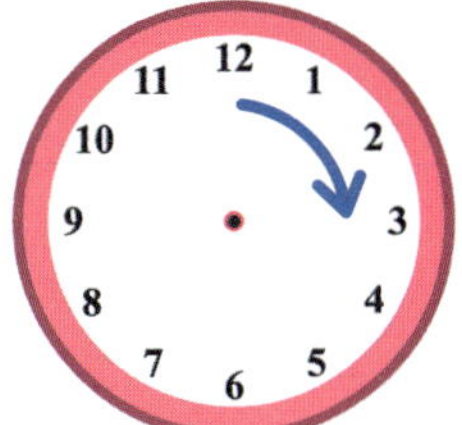

quarter turn

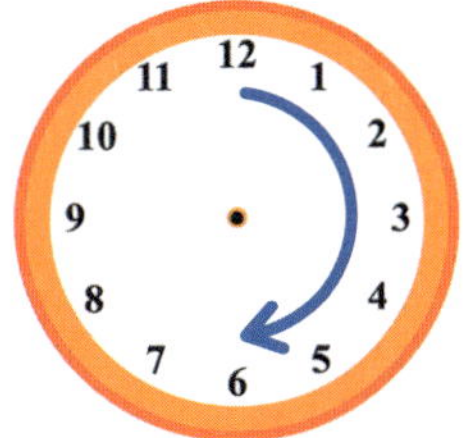

half turn

three-quarter turn

full turn

anticlockwise

quarter turn

half turn

three-quarter turn

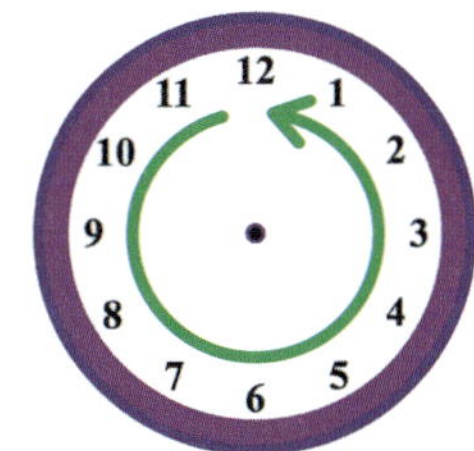

full turn

1 Name the turn. clockwise or anticlockwise
quarter or half or three-quarter or full turn

a ______________________

b ______________________

c ______________________

d ______________________

Mastery Checklist

I can:
- ☐ identify the features of 2D shapes.
- ☐ recognise a trapezium or rhombus.
- ☐ identify and create symmetry.
- ☐ identify and describe types of turns.

Challenge!

Rename the turns in question 1.
Clockwise turns become anticlockwise and anticlockwise turns become clockwise.

Problem solving

Patterns

Identify the turns. Complete the patterns.

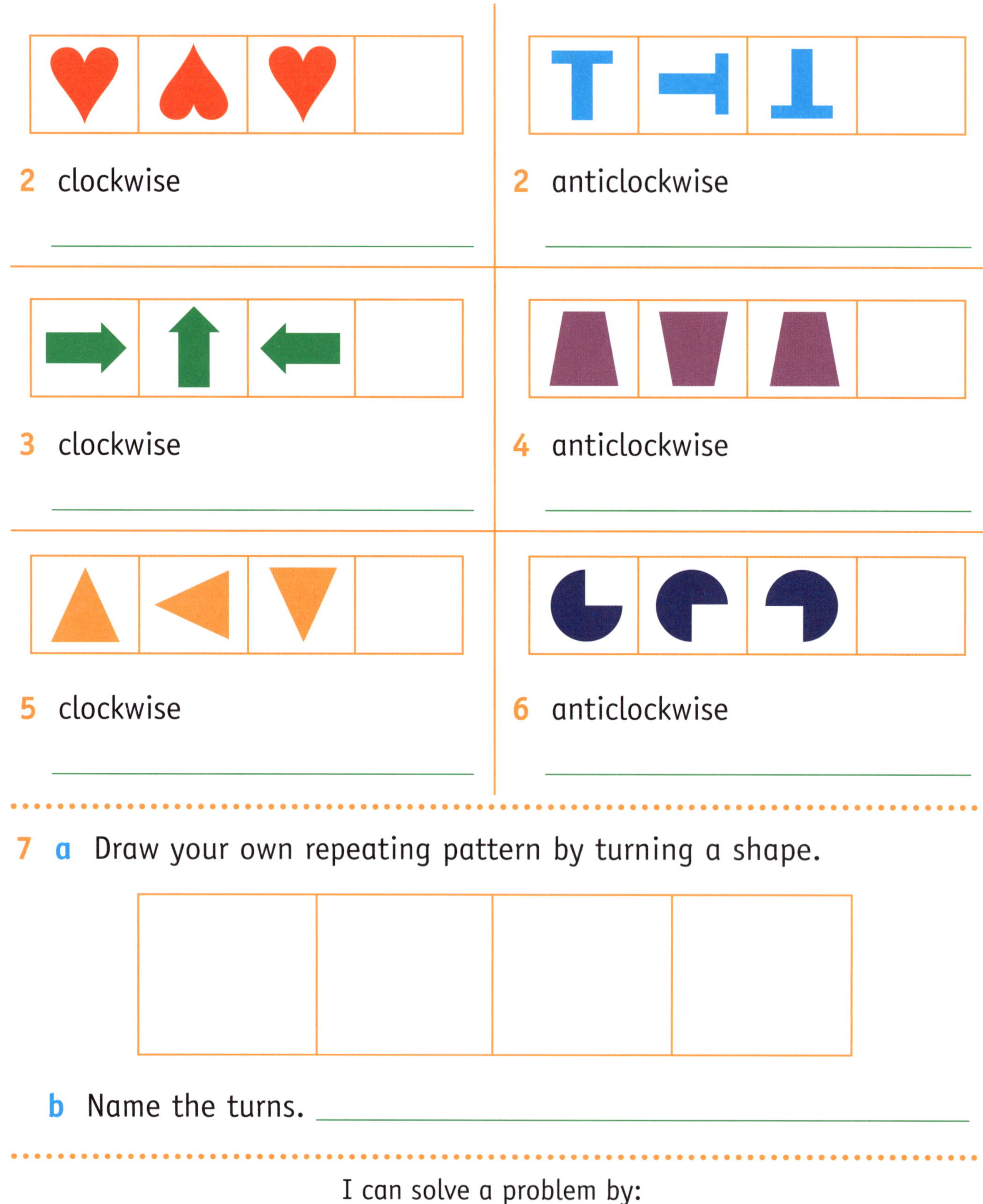

1 clockwise

2 anticlockwise

3 clockwise

4 anticlockwise

5 clockwise

6 anticlockwise

7 a Draw your own repeating pattern by turning a shape.

b Name the turns. ______

I can solve a problem by:

☐ identifying turns. ☐ making a repeating pattern.

AC9M2M05 Measurement **MA1-WM-01** Working mathematically • Apply mathematical techniques to solve problems
MA1-2DS-01 Two-dimensional spatial structure B • 2D shapes: Identify and describe the orientation of shapes using quarter turns

Make 10 to add

Add to 20

Make 10 to add.

1 $8 + 7 = 8 + 2 + 5 =$ $10 + 5 =$ ______

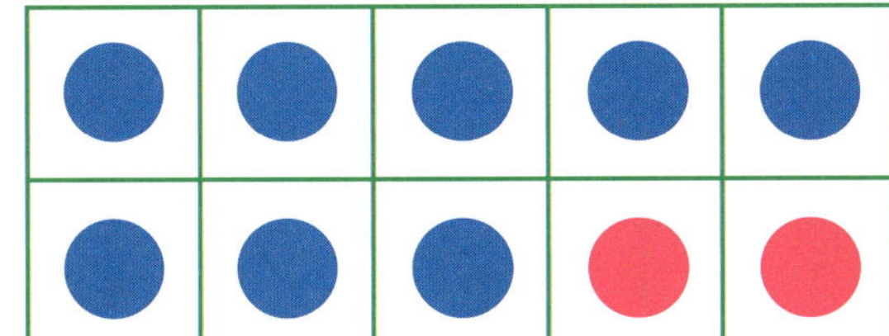
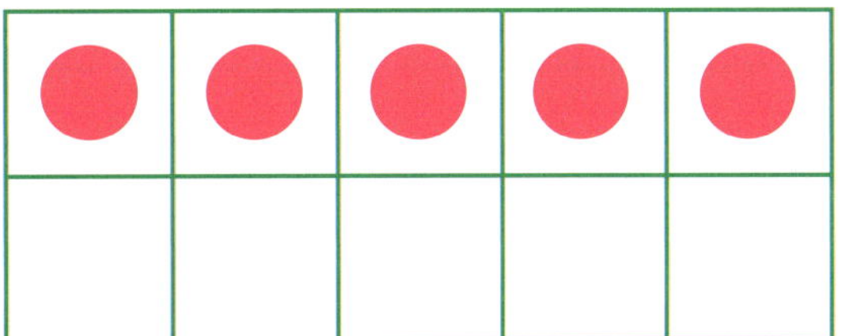

2 $7 + 5 = 7 + 3 + 2 =$ ______ + ______ = ______

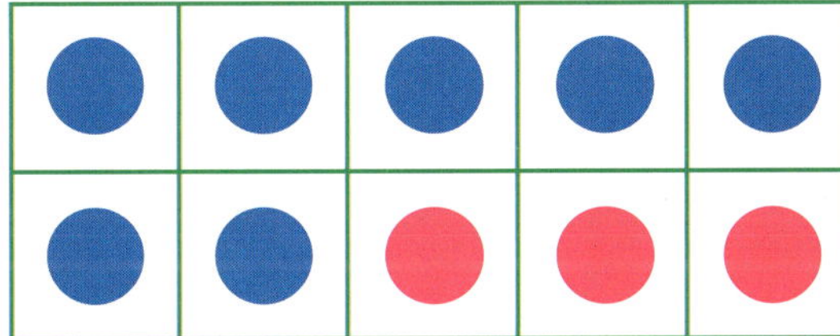
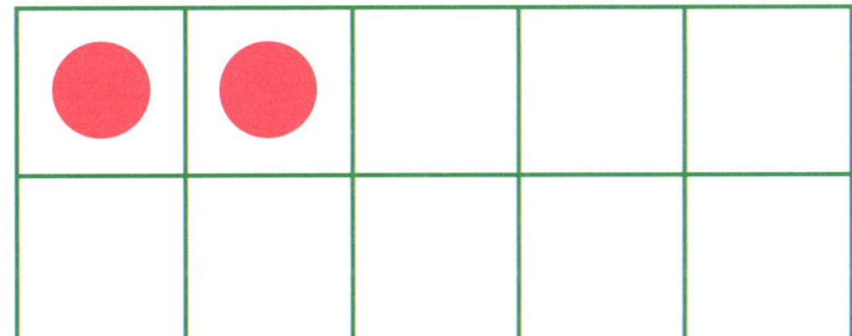

3 $9 + 6 =$ ______ ______

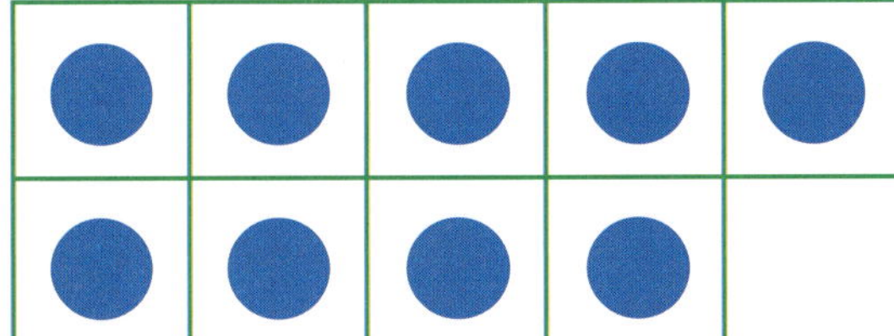
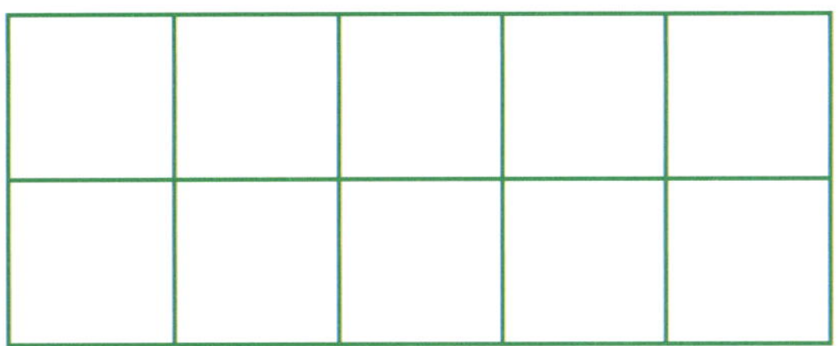

4 $8 + 5 =$ ______ ______

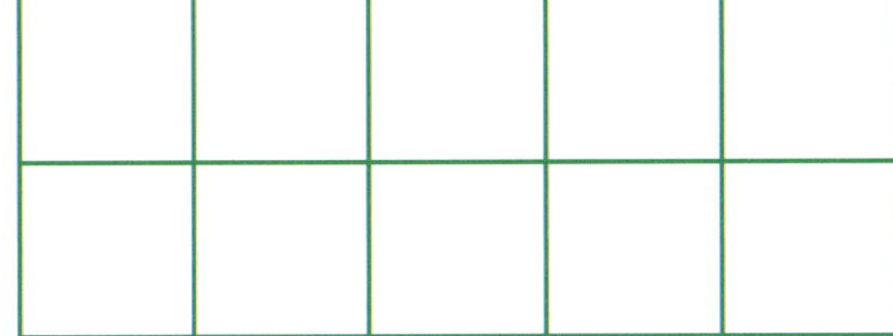
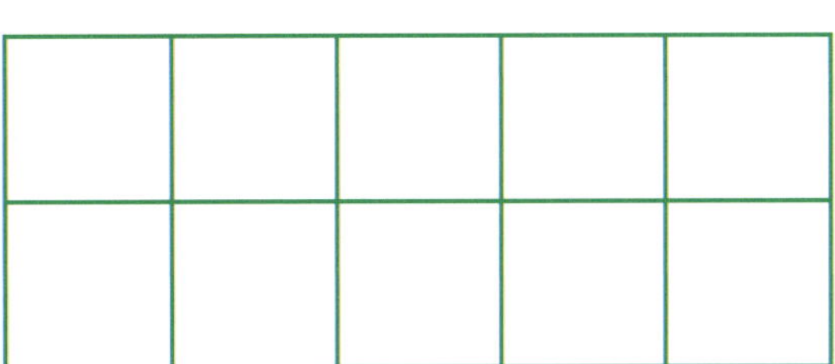

5 $9 + 7 =$ ______ ______

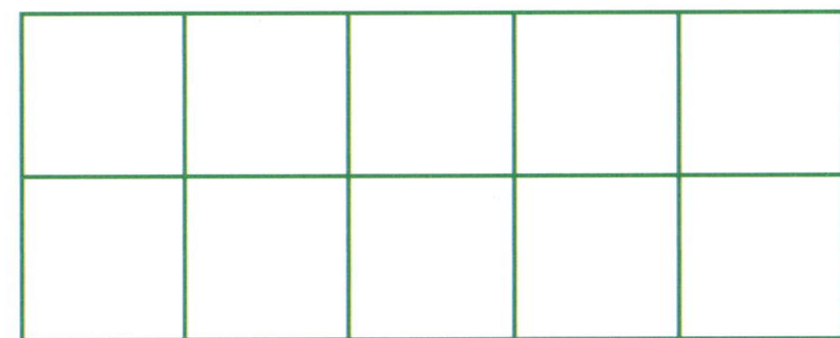
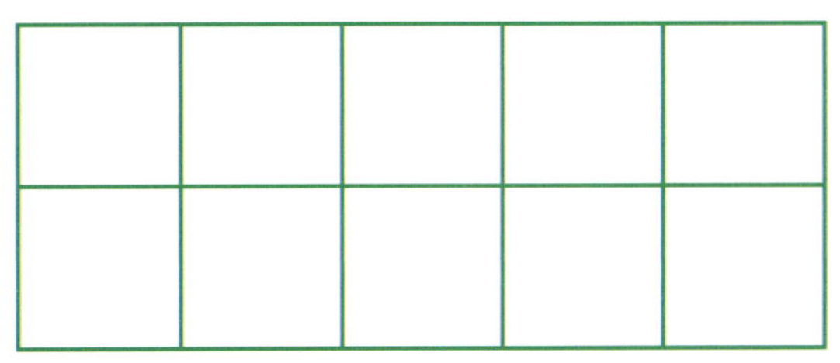

Addition on a number line

Jump strategy

When adding, always start with the biggest number.

Jump along the number line to add.

1

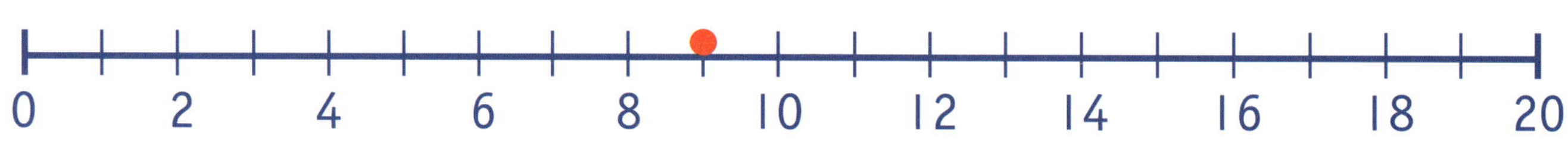

a 7 + 5 = ☐ b 14 + 3 = ☐ c 9 + 6 = ☐

2

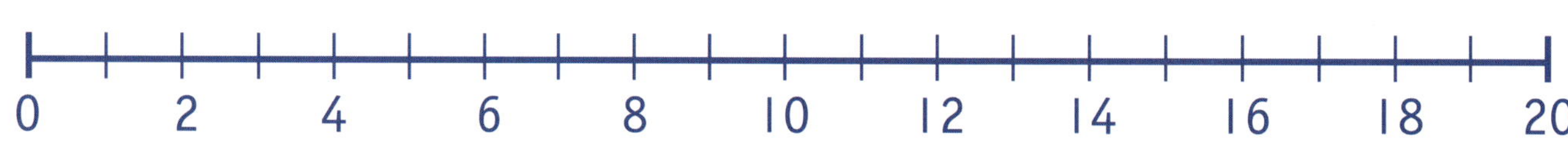

a 9 + 3 = ☐ b 15 + 4 = ☐ c 11 + 5 = ☐

3

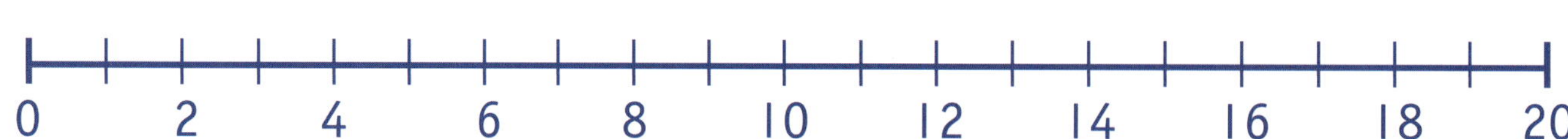

a 8 + 4 = ☐ b 13 + 5 = ☐ c 17 + 3 = ☐

4

0 2 4 6 8 10 12 14 16 18 20

Use the number line to help you.

a 7 + 4 = ☐ b 9 + 5 = ☐ c 8 + 6 = ☐

d 12 + 3 = ☐ e 13 + 7 = ☐ f 17 + 3 = ☐

g 14 + 5 = ☐ h 11 + 6 = ☐ i 15 + 3 = ☐

Challenge! Jump 3 times.

a 8 + 3 + 5 = ☐ b 6 + 5 + 3 = ☐ c 7 + 8 + 4 = ☐

Addition to twenty

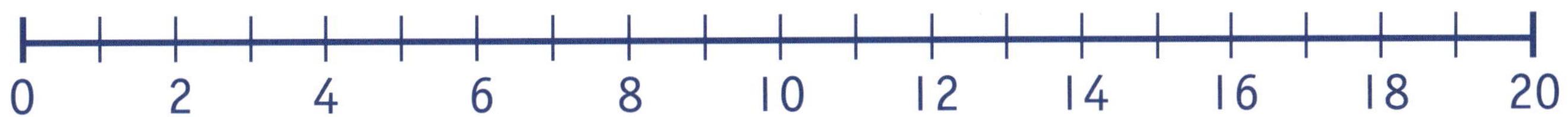

1 Write a number sentence. Then find the total.

a

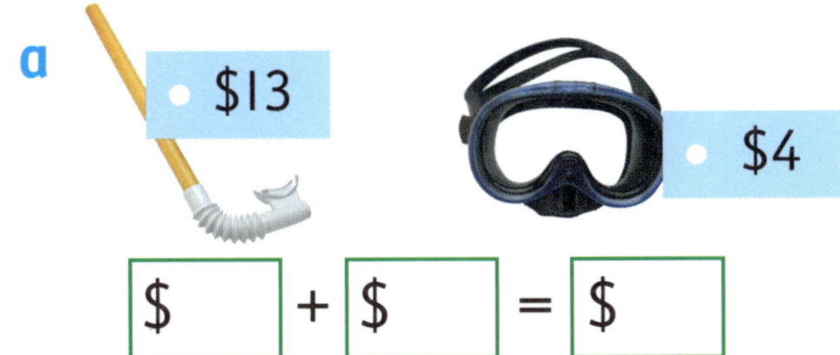

$ ___ + $ ___ = $ ___

b

$ ___ + $ ___ = $ ___

c

$ ___ + $ ___ = $ ___

d

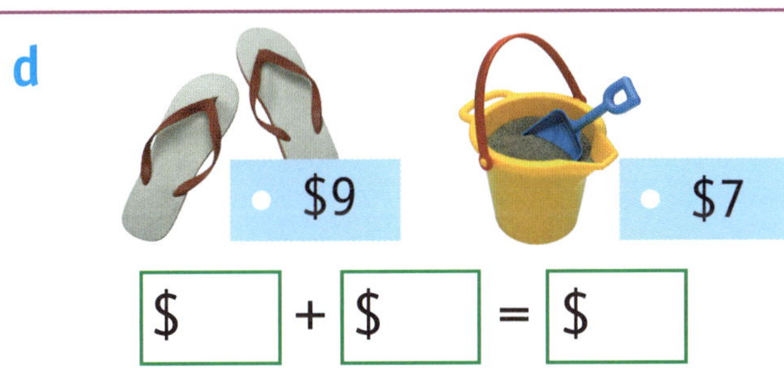

$ ___ + $ ___ = $ ___

2 How many altogether?

a John has 12 pencils.
Kate has 3 pencils.
___ pencils

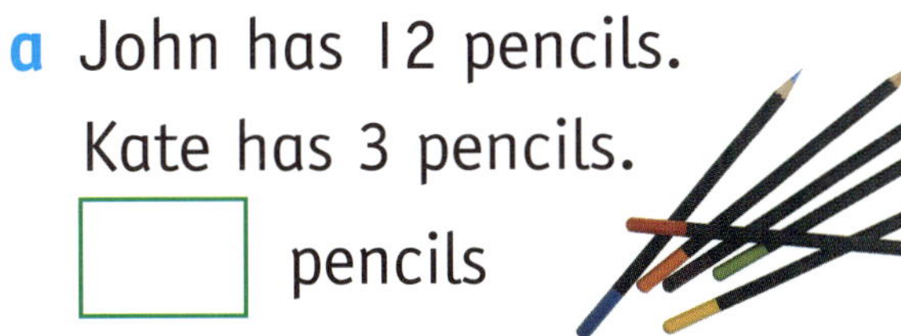

b Carmen read 9 books.
Shota read 6 books.
___ books

c Sue made 9 cupcakes.
Sam made 8 cupcakes.
___ cupcakes

d Jeff has 11 cards.
Sophie has 9 cards.
___ cards

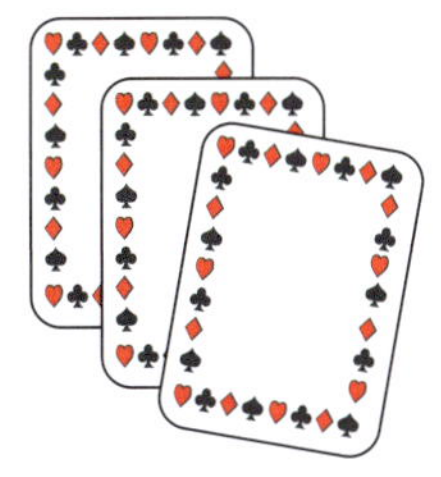

Looking for patterns

Using only the numbers **2** and **3** make 4, 5, 6, 7, etc.
Can you make all the numbers from 2 to 20?

2 + 2 = 4

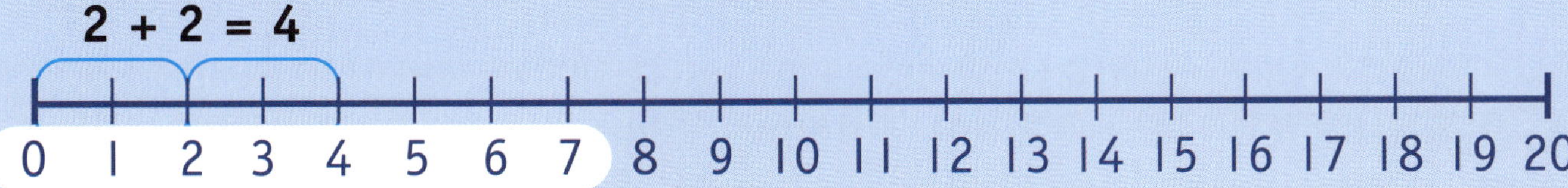

Doubles and near doubles

1 Write the doubles.

a

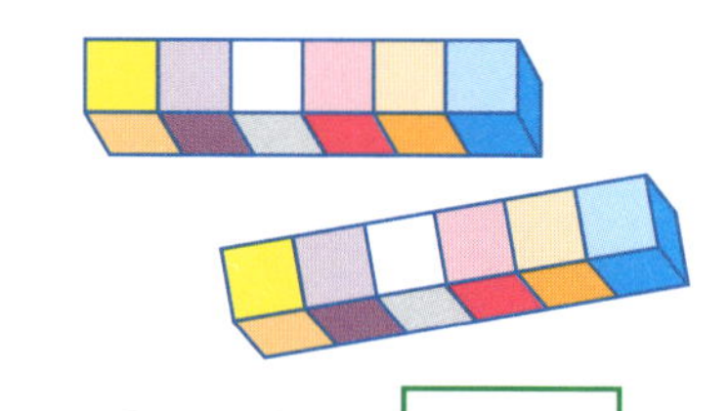

6 + 6 = ☐

b

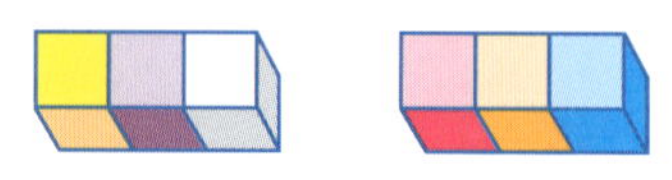

3 + 3 = ☐

c

7 + 7 = ☐

d

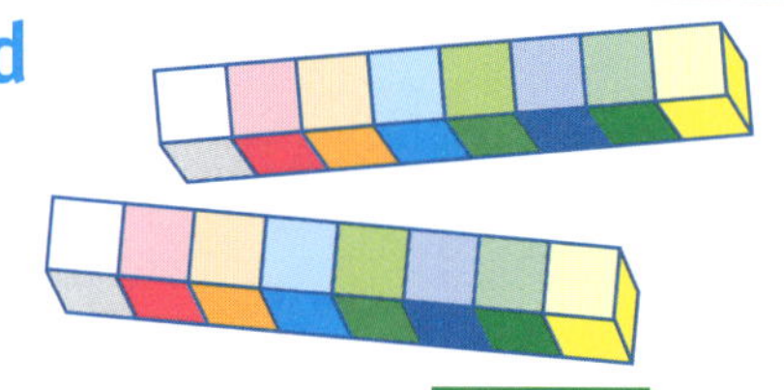

8 + 8 = ☐

e

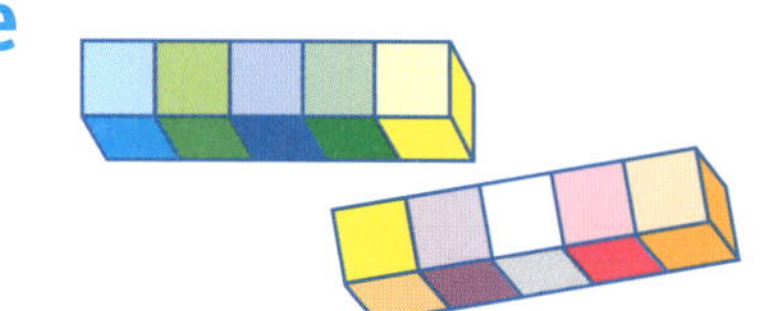

5 + 5 = ☐

f

9 + 9 = ☐

2 How much to buy 2 of each?

a

$11

$11 + $11 = $ ☐

b

$15

$15 + $15 = $ ☐

c

$12

$12 + $12 = $ ☐

d

$14

$14 + $14 = $ ☐

e

$22

$22 + $22 = $ ☐

f

$13

$13 + $13 = $ ☐

3 Some numbers are near doubles. For 7 + 8, think 7 + 7 + 1.

a 5 + 6 = ______ **b** 9 + 8 = ______ **c** 4 + 5 = ______

d 11 + 12 = ______ **e** 6 + 7 = ______ **f** 9 + 10 = ______

g 8 + 7 = ______ **h** 14 + 13 = ______ **i** 20 + 21 = ______

Challenge! In questions 1 and 2, what is double the answer?

Making 20

How many more to make 20? Draw dots.

1  $11 + \square = 20$

2 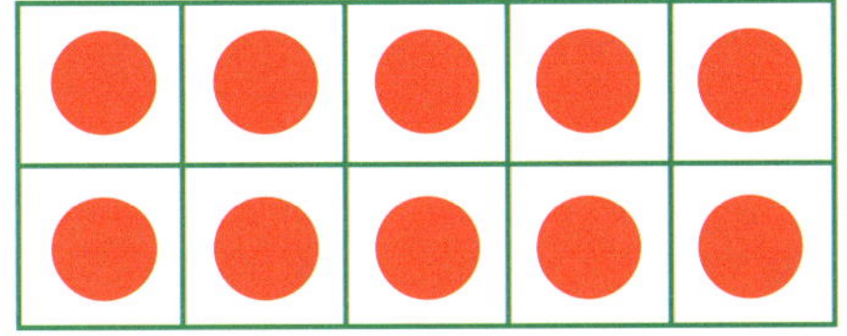 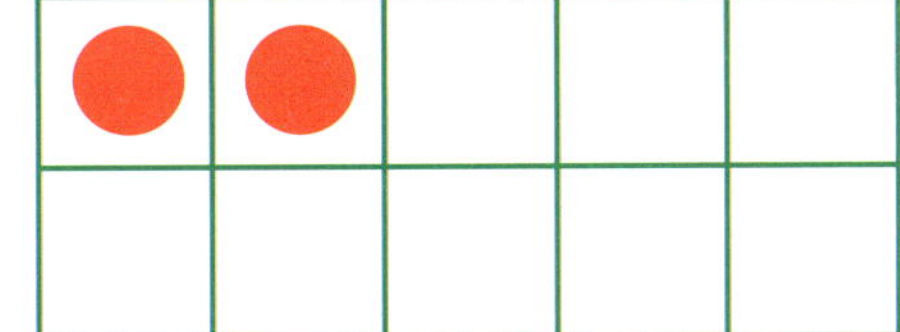 $12 + \square = 20$

3  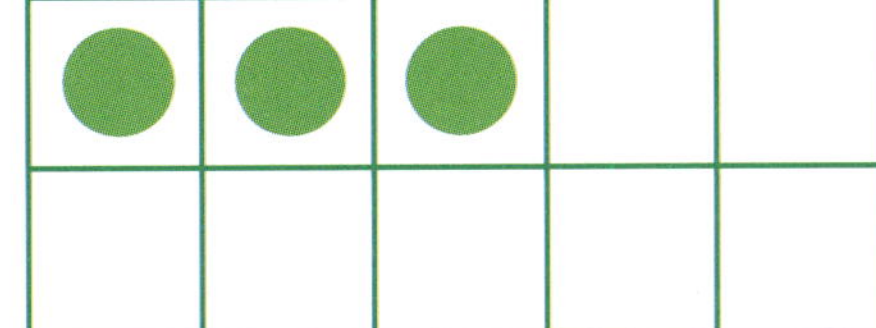 $13 + \square = 20$

4 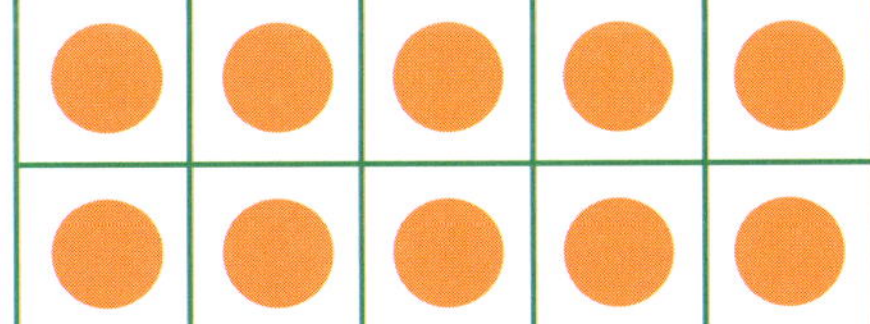 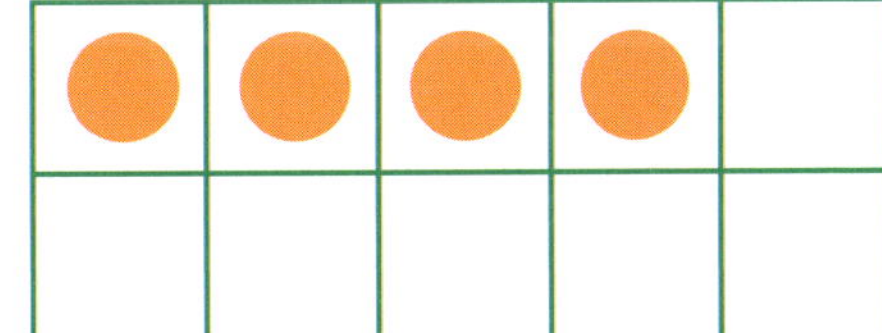 $14 + \square = 20$

5 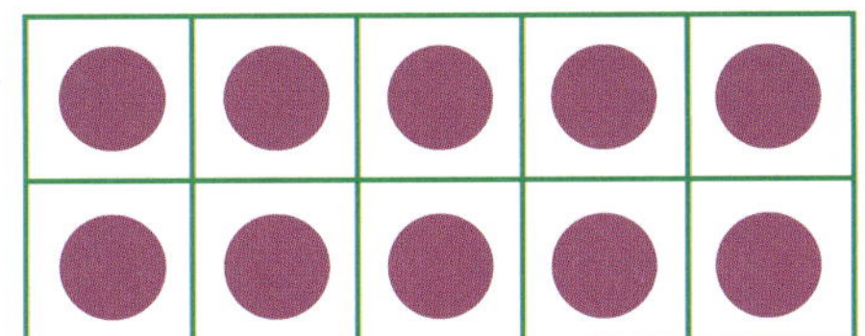 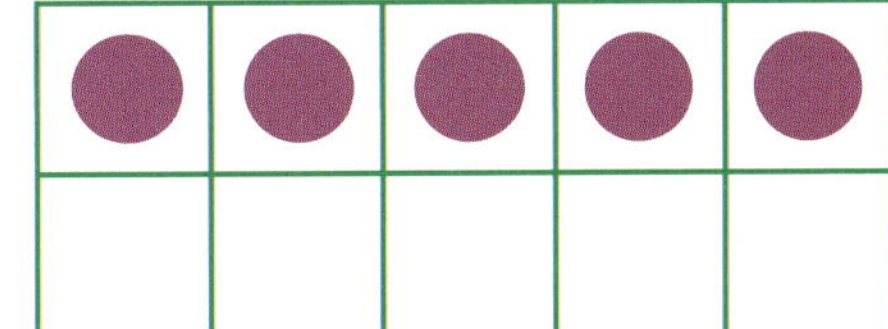 $15 + \square = 20$

6 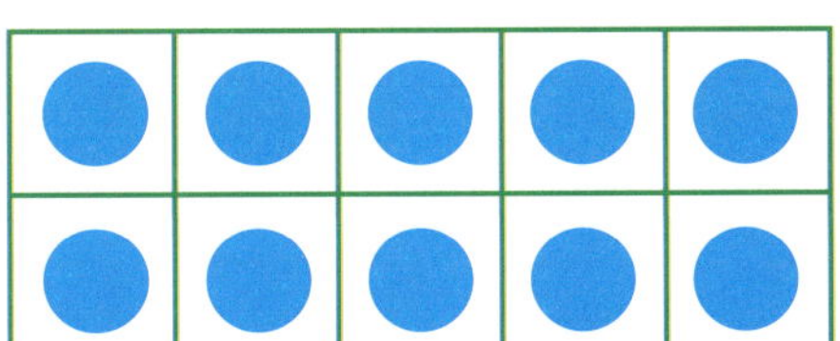 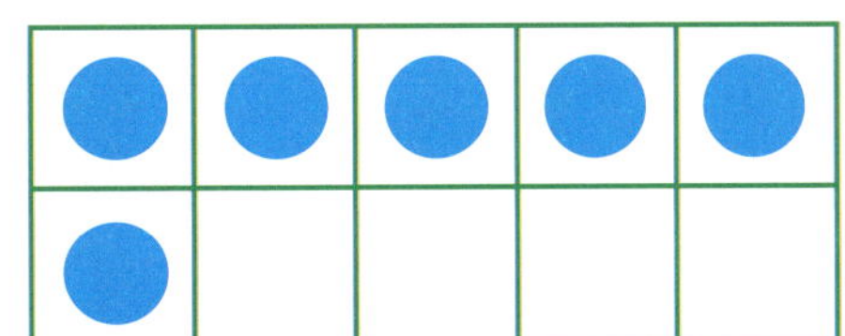 $16 + \square = 20$

7 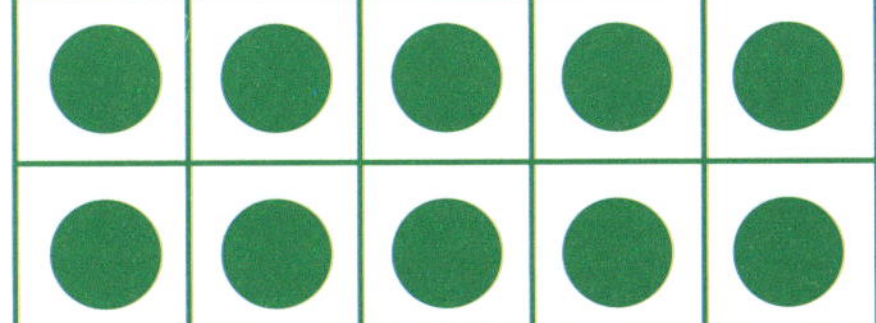 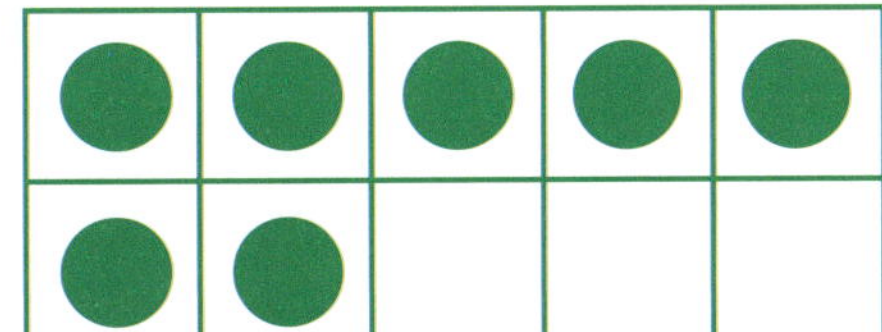 $17 + \square = 20$

8 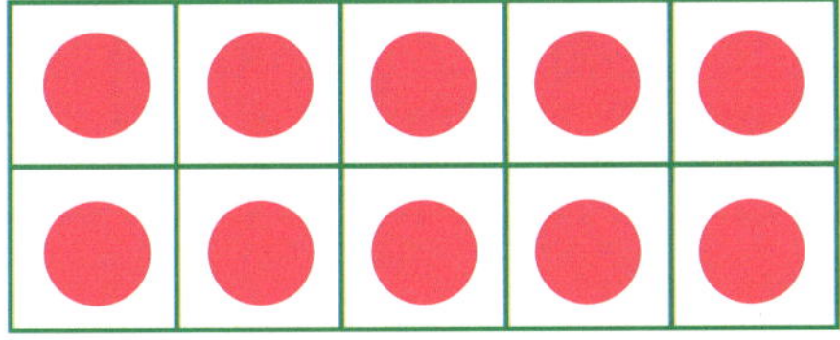 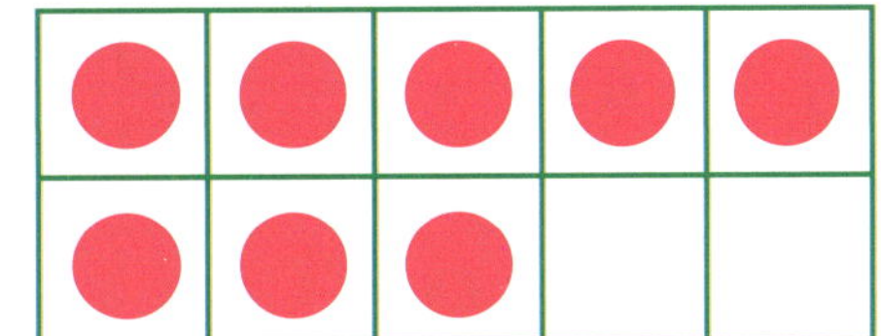 $18 + \square = 20$

9 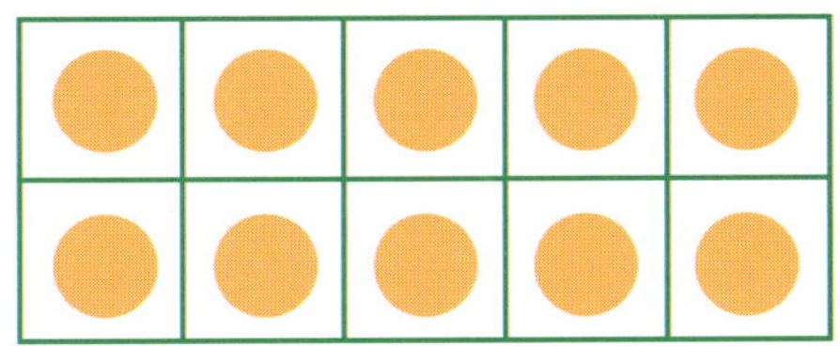 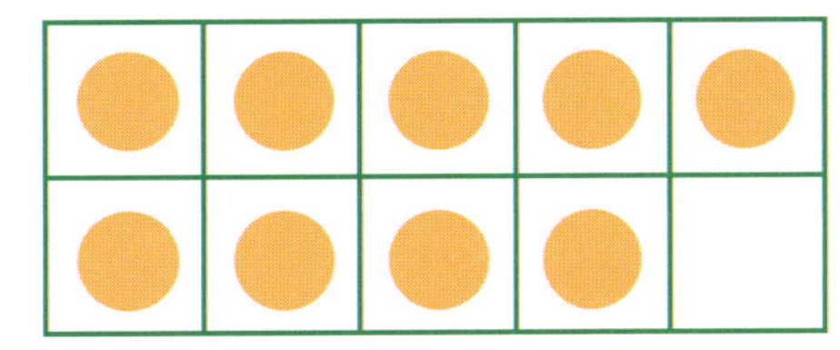 $19 + \square = 20$

Number facts – equivalence

1 Make the dominoes equal.

a

=

2 + 4 = 3 + ☐

b

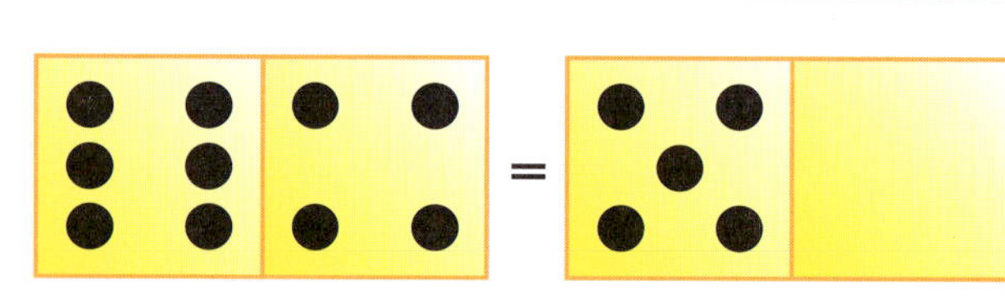

4 + 1 = ☐ + ☐

c

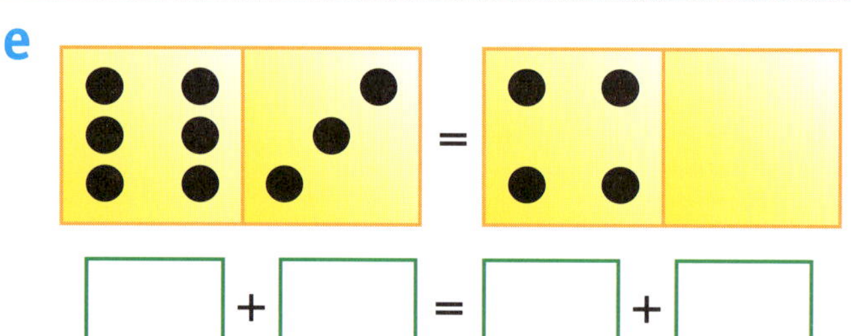

☐ + ☐ = ☐ + ☐

d

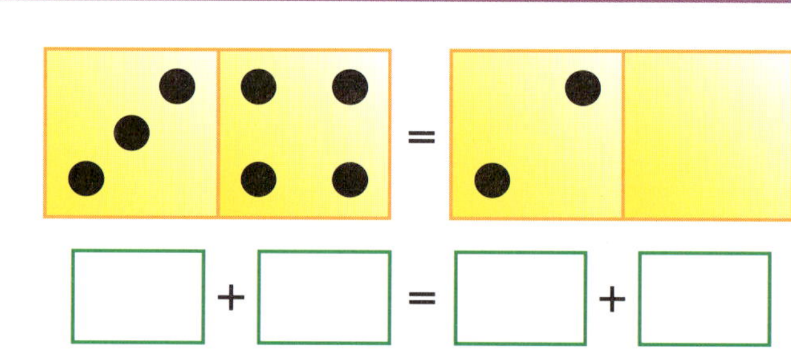

☐ + ☐ = ☐ + ☐

e

=

☐ + ☐ = ☐ + ☐

f

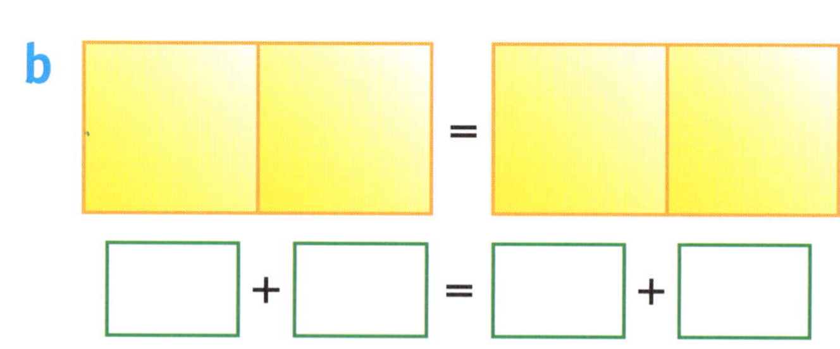

☐ + ☐ = ☐ + ☐

2 Draw your own.

a

=

☐ + ☐ = ☐ + ☐

b

=

☐ + ☐ = ☐ + ☐

3 Complete.

a 7 + 3 = 2 + ☐

b 6 + 6 = 8 + ☐

c 9 + 3 = 5 + ☐

d 10 + 5 = 7 + ☐

e 8 + 8 = 3 + ☐

f 12 + 8 = 9 + ☐

Challenge!

a 10 + 30 = 20 + ☐

b 60 + 40 = 30 + ☐

Mastery Checklist

I can:

- ☐ make 10 to add.
- ☐ use a number line to add.
- ☐ use doubles and near doubles to add.
- ☐ find equal additions.

Problem solving

Domino squares

1 Make each side of the domino square add to 8. Use these dominoes.

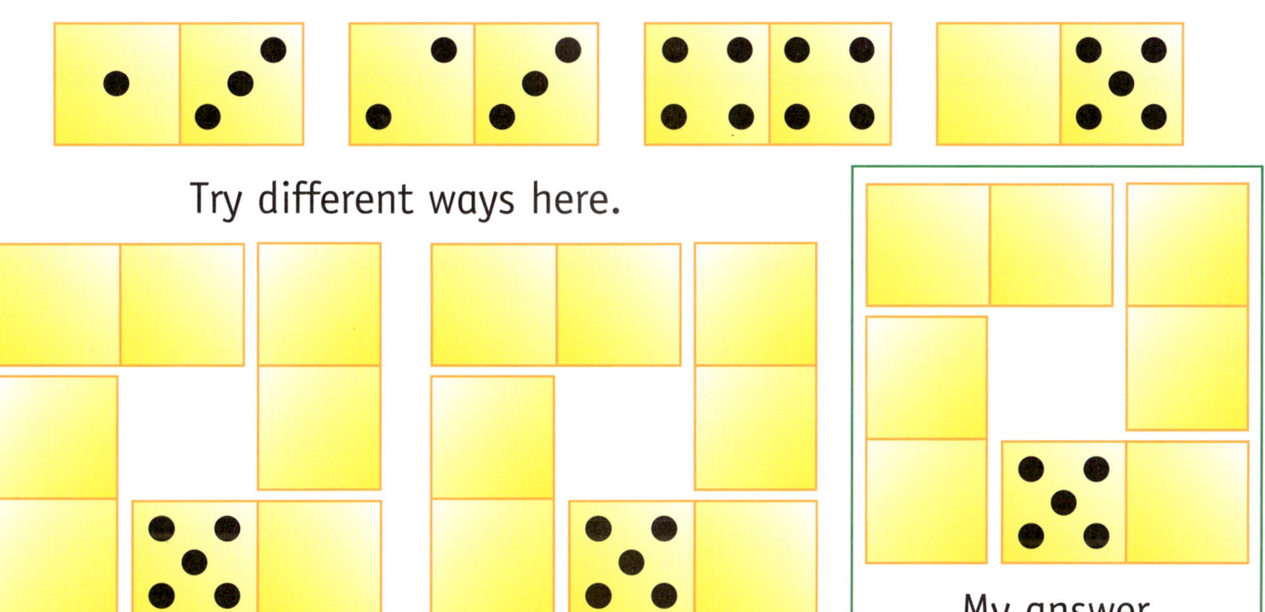

2 This time each side adds to 12. Use these dominoes.

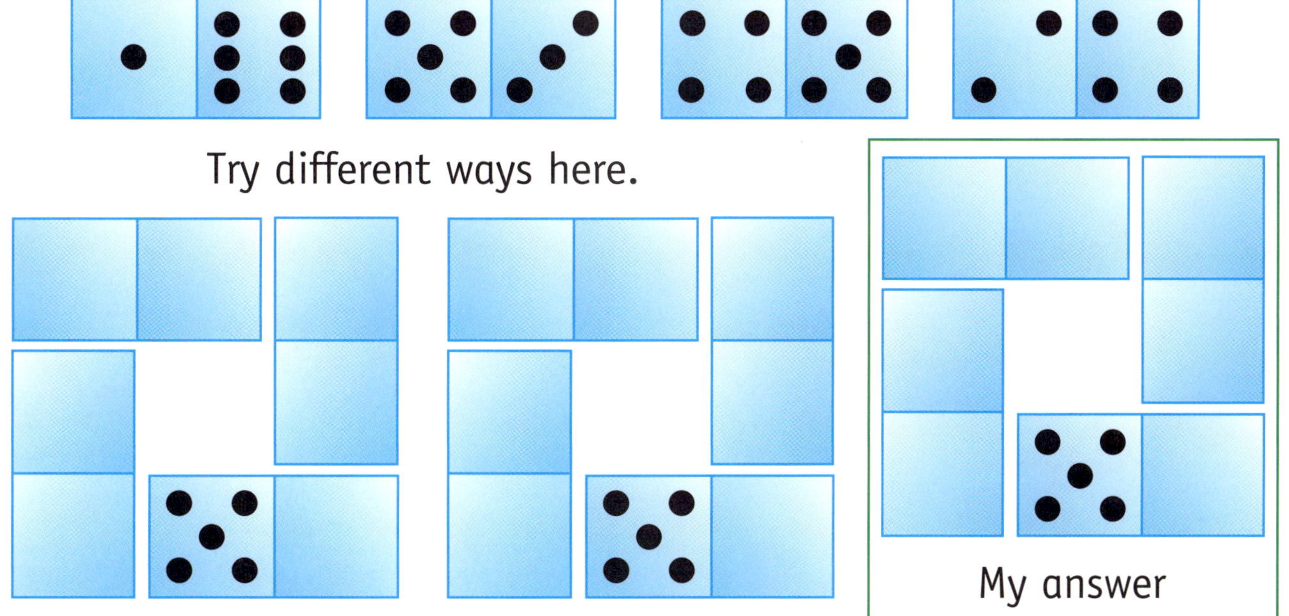

Is there more than one way to make the square? ____________

I can solve a problem by:

☐ using number bonds to find equal additions. ☐ using guess and check.

Counting the room

Investigation 1

1 Estimate how many pages altogether. ______________
How many pages in all the Best Stories? ______________
How many pages in all the Top Tales? ______________
How many pages altogether? ______________
Was your estimate close? ______________

2 Estimate how many pencils altogether. ______________
How many red pencils? ________ How many green pencils? ________
How many pencils altogether? ______________
Was your estimate close? ______________

Hint! Make and count smaller groups first!

3 Estimate how many children. ______________
Now count them. ____________ Was your estimate close? ____________

AC9M2N01 Number **MA1-WM-01** Working mathematically • Apply mathematical techniques to solve problems • Communicate their thinking and reasoning coherently and clearly
MAE-RWN-02 Representing whole numbers A • Use counting sequences of ones with two-digit numbers and beyond • Represent the structure of groups of ten in whole numbers

Counting the room

Investigation 1

Do we have enough rulers, books and pencils for everyone in the class? How many are there? How can you count large groups? Estimate first. Use pictures, numbers and words to help you count.

estimate and count items in the room

Rulers

____

____

Show/tell how you worked out the total.

____

____

____

To solve these problems I need to know how to:

- ☐ count forwards and backwards to 100.
- ☐ make estimates of numbers up to 100.
- ☐ count by 2s.
- ☐ count by 5s.
- ☐ count by 10s.

I enjoyed this task!

☆☆☆☆☆

Revision

Shade one bubble.

1 Which one is a rectangle?

2 What does this number line show?

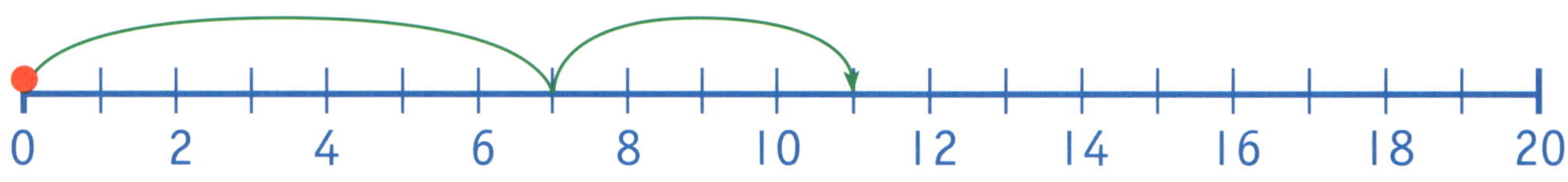

8 + 4 = 11   11 − 7 = 4   7 + 4 = 11   11 + 4 = 7

3 What is ten more than 46?

10   56   65   106

4 Which number is between 35 and 60?

24   61   56   80

5 How many triangles?

Write your answer in the box.

Revision

6 A circle has ______ corners?

Shade one bubble.

4 ◯ 6 ◯ 0 ◯ 1 ◯

7 Max has 12 cards. Amy has 7. How many altogether?

20 ◯ 21 ◯ 127 ◯ 19 ◯

8 69, 70, 71, ______ , ______ , 74, 75, 76

The missing numbers are:

71, 72 ◯ 73, 74, ◯ 70, 72, ◯ 72, 73 ◯

9

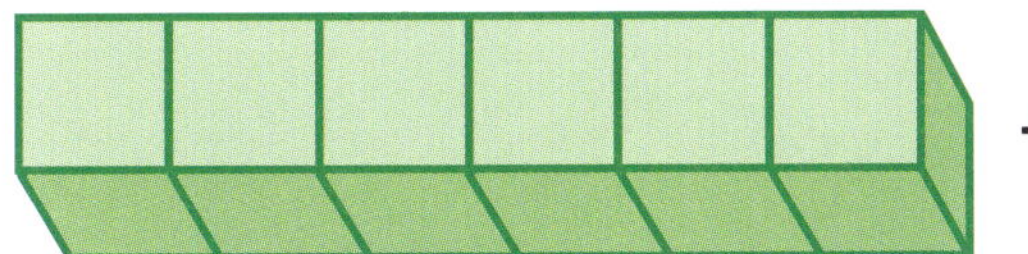

+

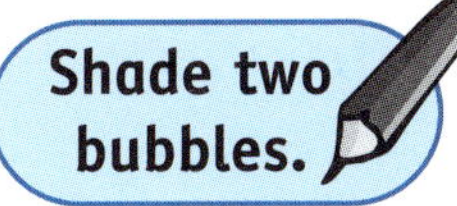

Which of these equals the above picture?

8 + 1 ◯ 9 + 2 ◯ 2 + 8 ◯ 3 + 7 ◯

10 Which shapes have parallel lines?

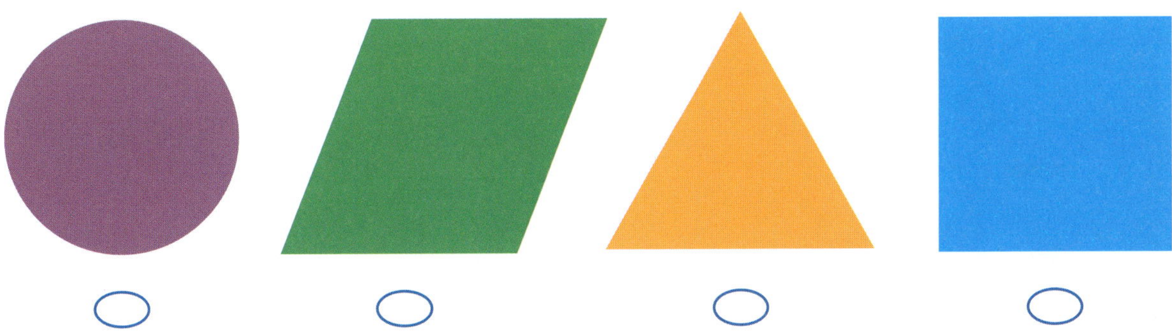

◯ ◯ ◯ ◯

O'clock and half-past

1 What time is it?

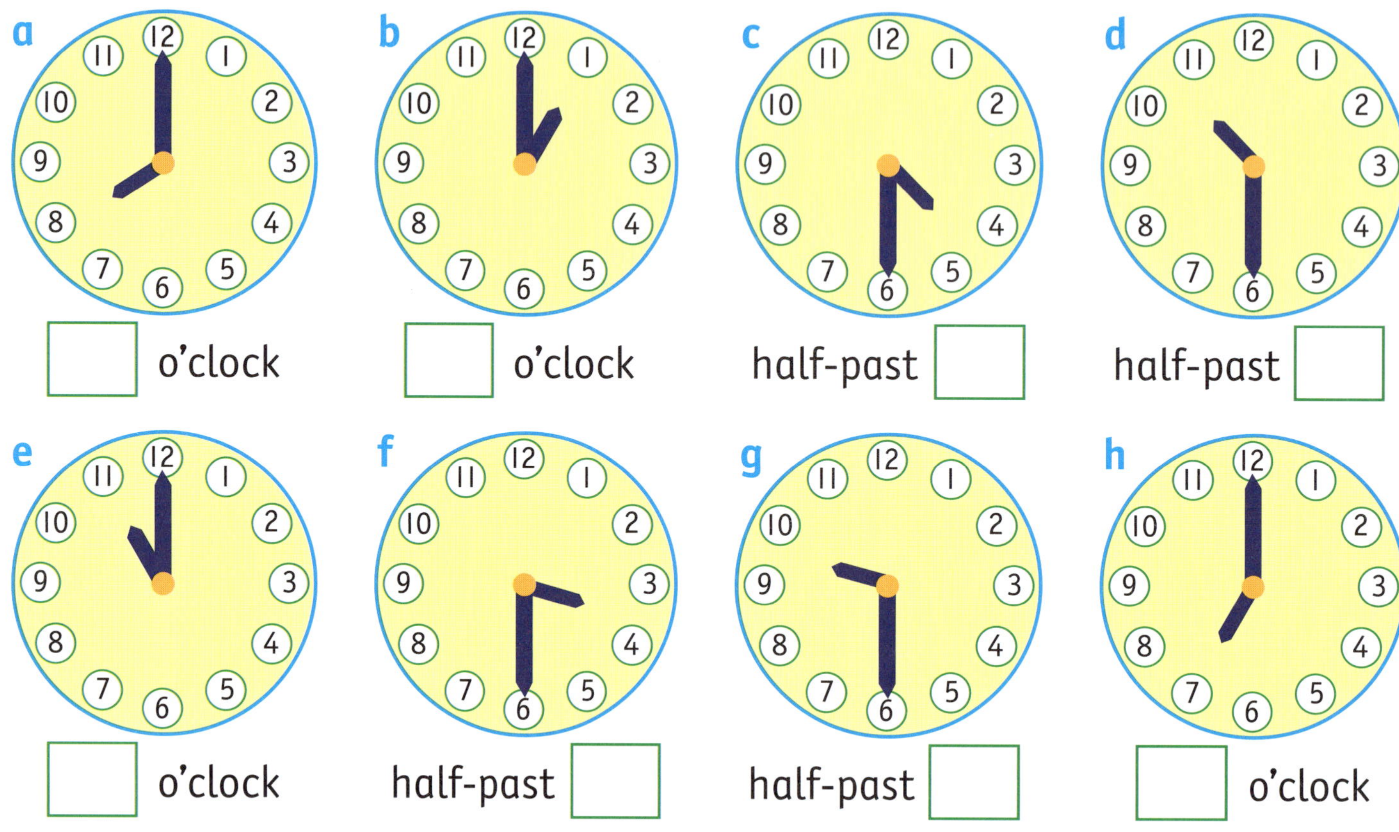

2 Draw hands on the clocks.

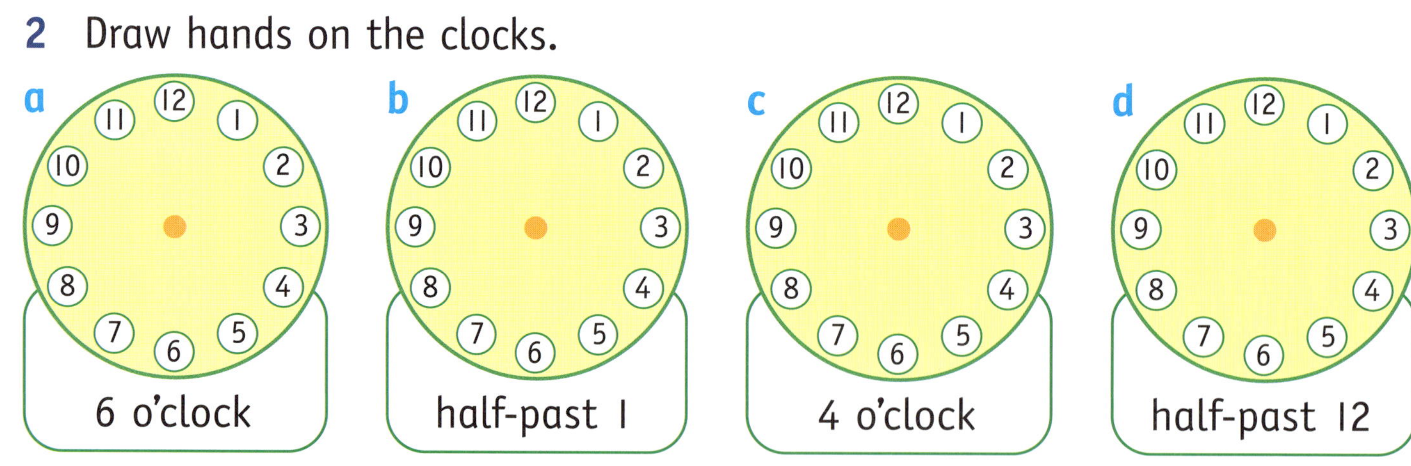

Challenge! The minute hands are missing. What is the time?

Digital time

o'clock
big hand on 12
half-past
big hand on 6

1 What time is it?

2 Write the digital time.

The calendar

Calendar 2023

JANUARY

S	M	T	W	T	F	S
1	2	3	4	5	6	7
8	9	10	11	12	13	14
15	16	17	18	19	20	21
22	23	24	25	26	27	28
29	30	31				

FEBRUARY

S	M	T	W	T	F	S
			1	2	3	4
5	6	7	8	9	10	11
12	13	14	15	16	17	18
19	20	21	22	23	24	25
26	27	28				

MARCH

S	M	T	W	T	F	S
			1	2	3	4
5	6	7	8	9	10	11
12	13	14	15	16	17	18
19	20	21	22	23	24	25
26	27	28	29	30	31	

APRIL

S	M	T	W	T	F	S
						1
2	3	4	5	6	7	8
9	10	11	12	13	14	15
16	17	18	19	20	21	22
23	24	25	26	27	28	29
30						

MAY

S	M	T	W	T	F	S
	1	2	3	4	5	6
7	8	9	10	11	12	13
14	15	16	17	18	19	20
21	22	23	24	25	26	27
28	29	30	31			

JUNE

S	M	T	W	T	F	S
				1	2	3
4	5	6	7	8	9	10
11	12	13	14	15	16	17
18	19	20	21	22	23	24
25	26	27	28	29	30	

JULY

S	M	T	W	T	F	S
						1
2	3	4	5	6	7	8
9	10	11	12	13	14	15
16	17	18	19	20	21	22
23	24	25	26	27	28	29
30	31					

AUGUST

S	M	T	W	T	F	S
		1	2	3	4	5
6	7	8	9	10	11	12
13	14	15	16	17	18	19
20	21	22	23	24	25	26
27	28	29	30	31		

SEPTEMBER

S	M	T	W	T	F	S
					1	2
3	4	5	6	7	8	9
10	11	12	13	14	15	16
17	18	19	20	21	22	23
24	25	26	27	28	29	30

OCTOBER

S	M	T	W	T	F	S
1	2	3	4	5	6	7
8	9	10	11	12	13	14
15	16	17	18	19	20	21
22	23	24	25	26	27	28
29	30	31				

NOVEMBER

S	M	T	W	T	F	S
			1	2	3	4
5	6	7	8	9	10	11
12	13	14	15	16	17	18
19	20	21	22	23	24	25
26	27	28	29	30		

DECEMBER

S	M	T	W	T	F	S
					1	2
3	4	5	6	7	8	9
10	11	12	13	14	15	16
17	18	19	20	21	22	23
24	25	26	27	28	29	30
31						

1 How many days?

January		February		March		April	
May		June		July		August	
September		October		November		December	

2 **a** Tick the months with 30 days. **b** Circle the months with 31 days.

3 Circle these dates on the calendar.

a today
b your birthday
c New Year's Day
d 6th of August
e 15th of January
f 1st of June
g 28th of February
h Anzac Day
i 18th of October

The calendar

1 If today is the 5th of June, what date will it be:

a tomorrow? ______

b in 1 week? ______

c in 3 weeks? ______

d in 1 month? ______

30 days has September, April, June and November. All the rest have 31 except for February which has 28 or 29.

2 Choose your favourite month of the year. ______

Number the days. Colour any special days.

Sun	Mon	Tues	Wed	Thur	Fri	Sat

3 Write the months for each season.

Summer ______ ______

Autumn ______ ______

Winter ______ ______

Spring ______ ______

Challenge! How many days until New Year's Day? ☐

Graphing our birthdays

collect data from your class

In which month is your birthday?

1 Draw a ☺ for every child in your class.

January								
February								
March								
April								
May								
June								
July								
August								
September								
October								
November								
December								

2 Colour one box for each child's birthday.

Subtraction to ten

– means take away.

1 How many toys? ☐

a 8 – 3 = ☐ b 8 – 6 = ☐ c 8 – 4 = ☐

d 8 – 7 = ☐ e 8 – 2 = ☐ f 8 – 5 = ☐

2 Colour match the answers in the grid.

4 – 2 6 – 3

5 – 4 8 – 1 7 – 3

7 – 2 10 – 1 10 – 2

8 – 8 9 – 3

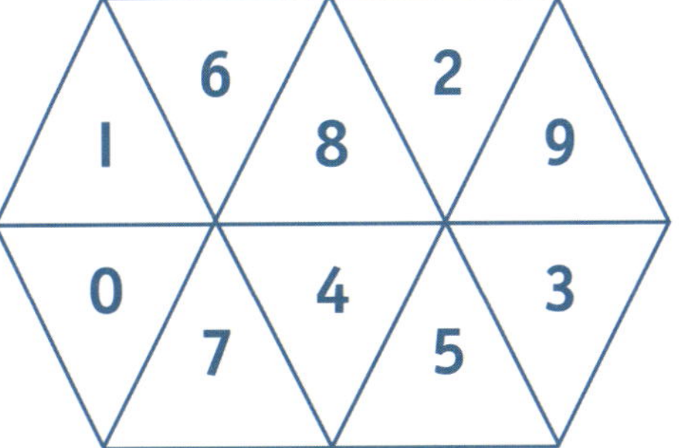

3 a 

5 birds.
3 fly away.
How many left? ☐

b 

9 kangaroos.
3 hop away.
How many left? ☐

c 

8 puppies.
5 get sold.
How many left? ☐

d 

7 bugs.
4 get eaten.
How many left? ☐

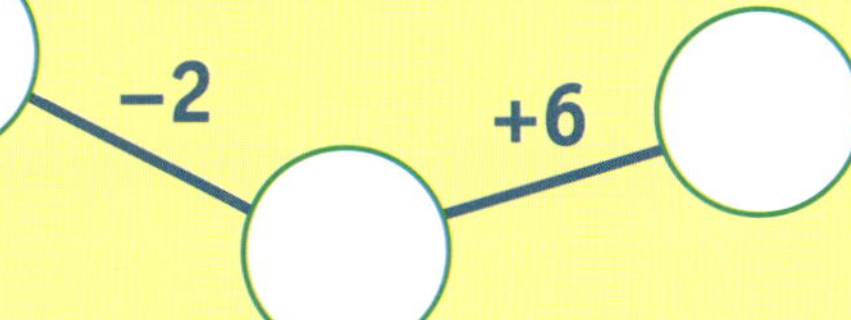

Subtraction to ten

1

a 2 fly away.
How many left?

6 - 2 =

b 4 are lost.
How many left?

10 - 4 =

c 3 swim away.
How many left?

d 4 run away.
How many left?

e 2 are eaten.
How many left?

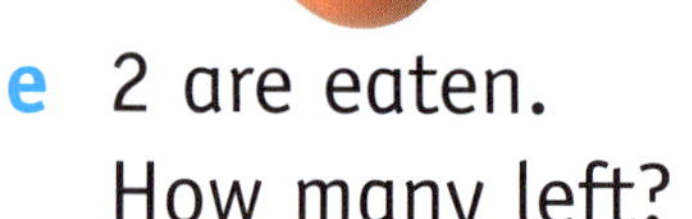

f 6 fall down.
How many left?

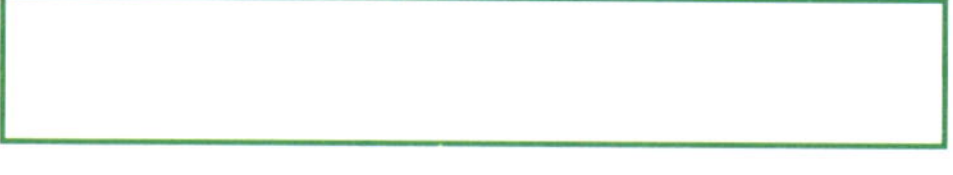

2

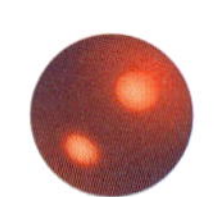          

a 10 – 2 = ☐　b 10 – 0 = ☐　c 10 – 5 = ☐

d 10 – 4 = ☐　e 10 – 7 = ☐　f 10 – 9 = ☐

Mastery Checklist

I can:
- ☐ tell the time to half hours on analog and digital clocks.
- ☐ use a calendar.
- ☐ subtract within 10.

Counting back

1 Count back 3 spaces from each sign.

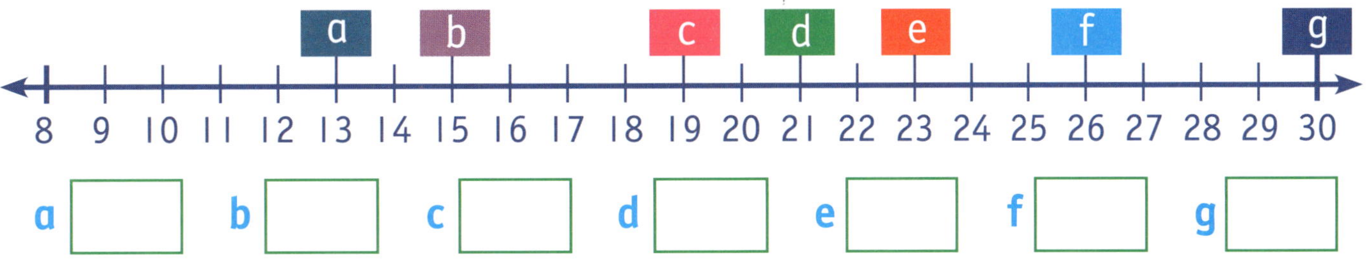

2 Now, count back another 2 spaces.

3 How much change from $20?

Difference

Difference means to subtract.

1 Count on to find the difference.

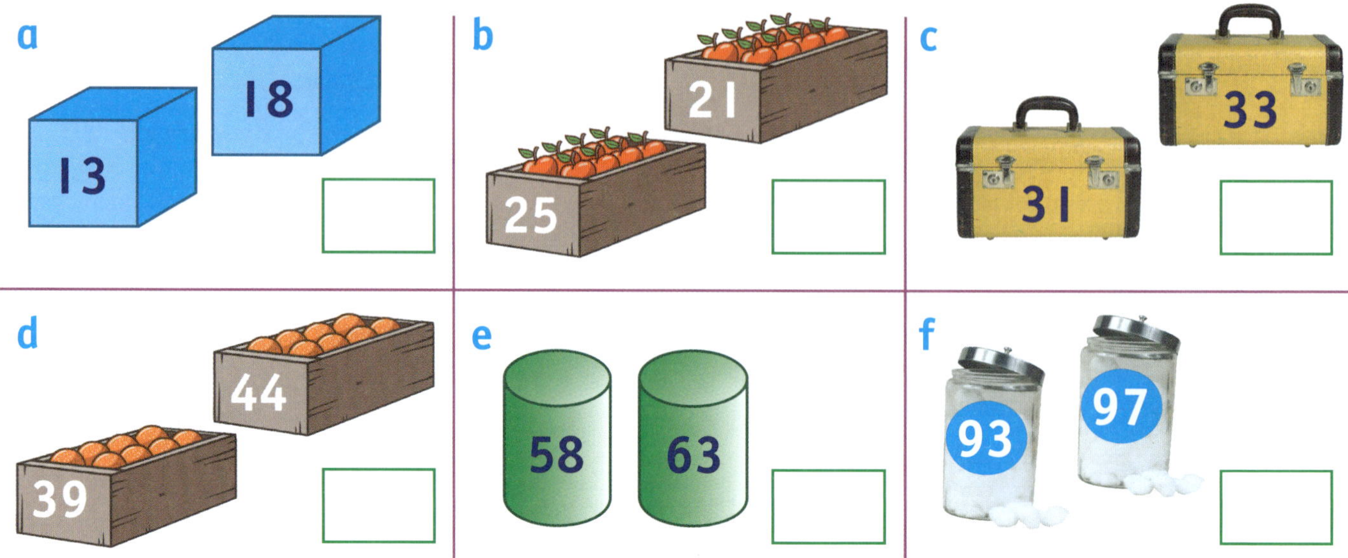

2 Write the difference as a number sentence.

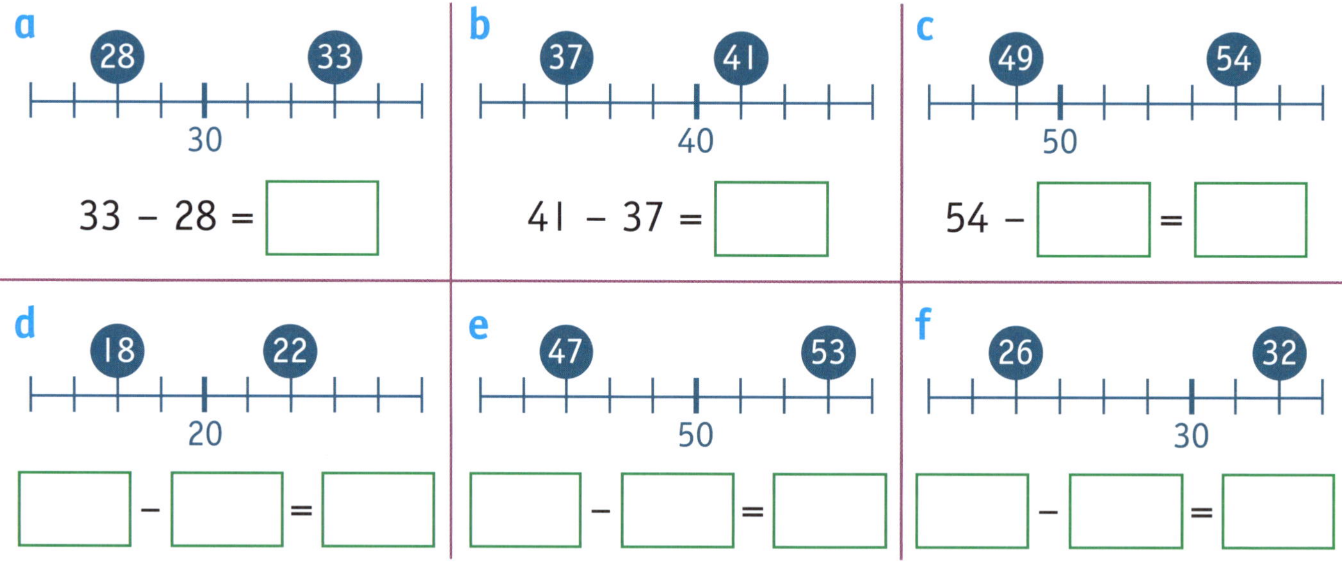

3 Write your own.

Looking for patterns

Find pairs of numbers with a difference of 6.

6

Problem solving

Game Zone

Alice and Zac went to Game Zone.
They spent all their money.
Show how they spent their money.

Alice	Zac

How would you spend $12 at Game Zone?

I can solve a problem by:

☐ subtracting money. ☐ writing equations or drawing a diagram.

Lighter and heavier

1 Circle the:

2 Circle the heavier one. Check by hefting or use a [balance].

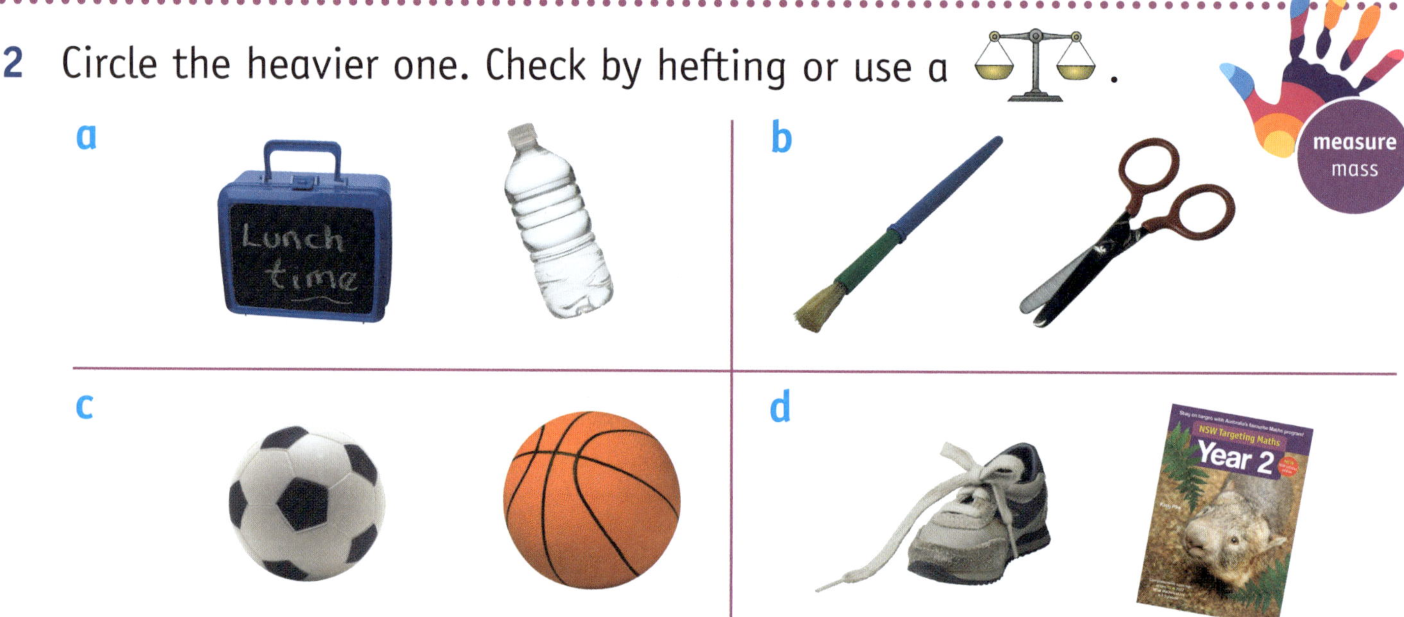

3 Circle the lighter one.

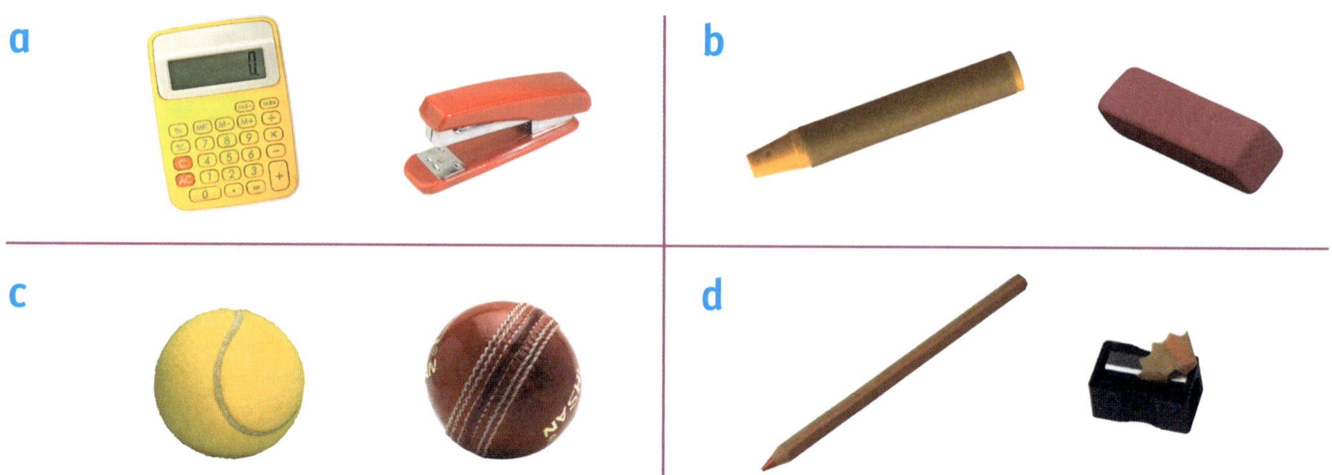

Challenge! Number the objects in question 3 from numbers 1–8, 1 being lightest and 8 heaviest.

Measuring mass

measure mass with a balance scale

1 Use a balance scale and blocks to measure.

a The brush weighs ☐ blocks.

b The scissors weigh ☐ blocks.

c The glue weighs ☐ blocks.

d The stapler weighs ☐ blocks.

e 

The sharpener weighs ☐ blocks.

f Five pencils weigh ☐ blocks.

g 

The key weighs ☐ blocks.

h 

Three crayons weigh ☐ blocks.

i The ruler weighs ☐ blocks.

j ✓ Tick the heaviest. Circle the lightest.

2 Circle the one that weighs more.

a 

How much more? ☐ blocks

b  

How much more? ☐ blocks

3 Finish the sentence by writing 'more' or 'less'. Write the difference.

a The brush weighs ______________ than the sharpener.
The difference is ☐ blocks.

b The crayons weigh ______________ than the stapler.
The difference is ☐ blocks.

Mastery Checklist

I can:

- ☐ subtract using a number line.
- ☐ find the difference between two numbers.
- ☐ measure and compare mass using an equal-arm balance.

Halves and quarters

Fraction notation

$\frac{1}{2}$ = one half
$\frac{1}{4}$ = one quarter

1 Colour to match the label.

a
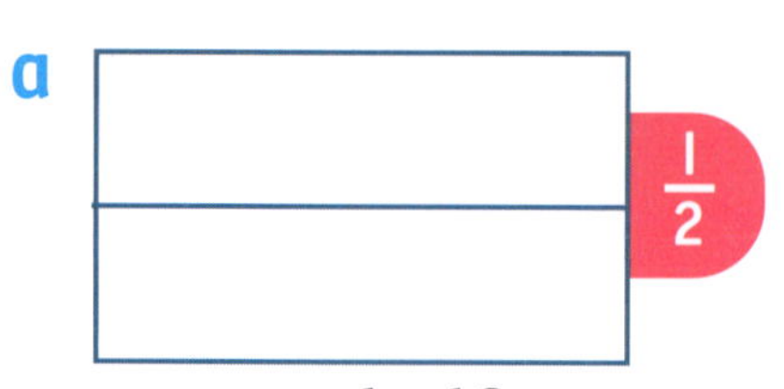

one half

b

one quarter

c

one half

d
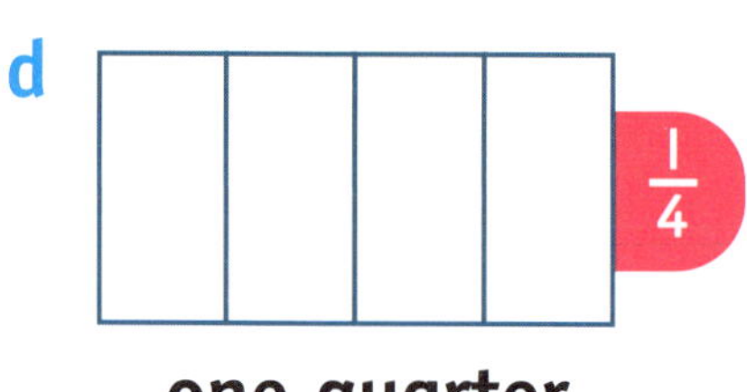

one quarter

e

one quarter

f
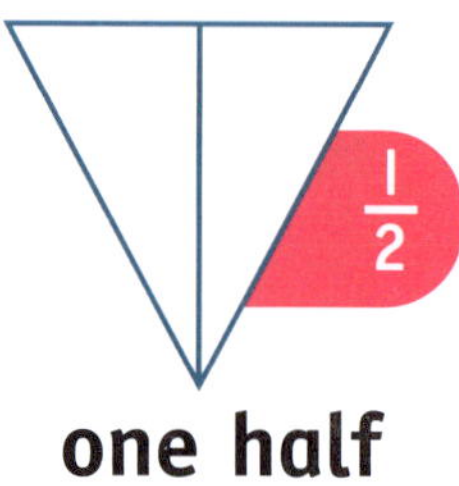

one half

2 Colour one half ($\frac{1}{2}$).

a
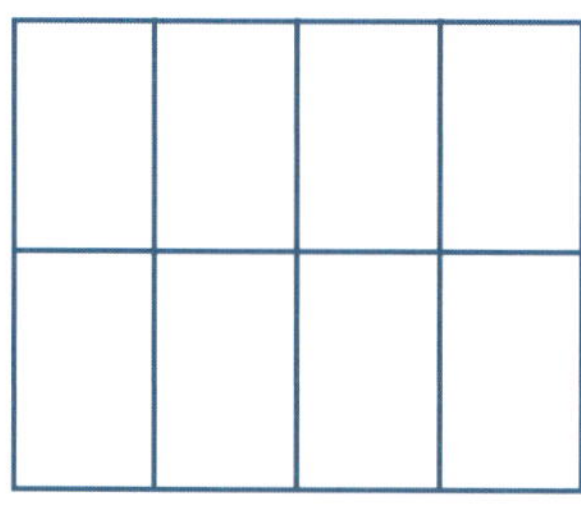

b
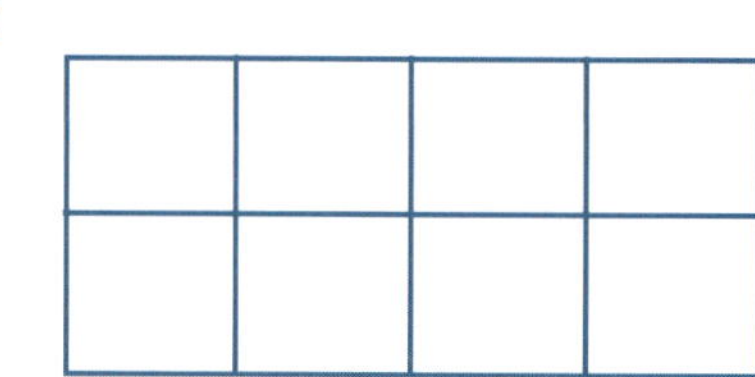

c
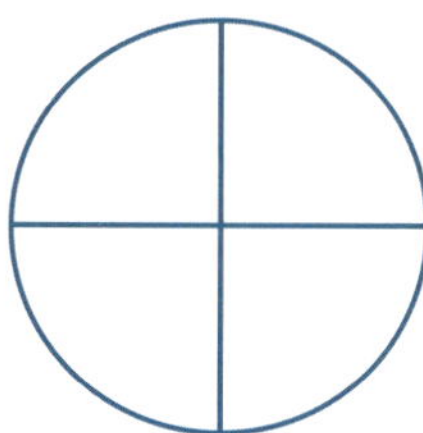

d
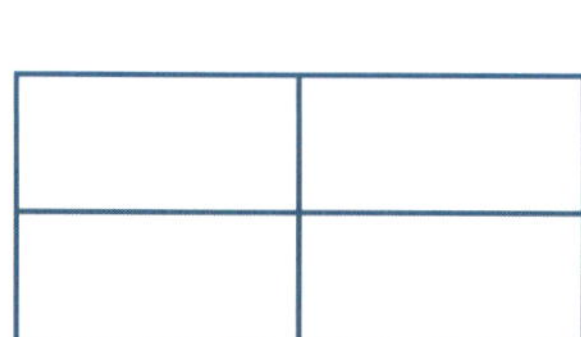

e
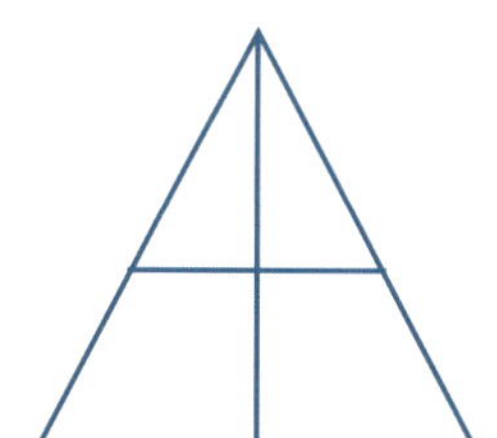

f
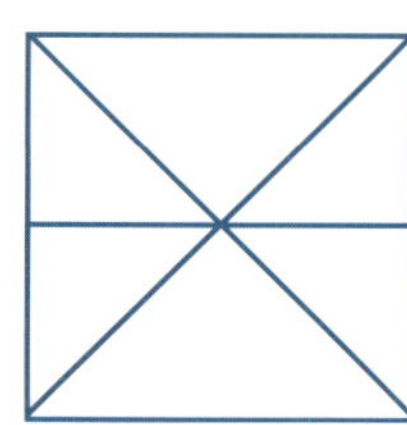

3 Colour one quarter ($\frac{1}{4}$).

a
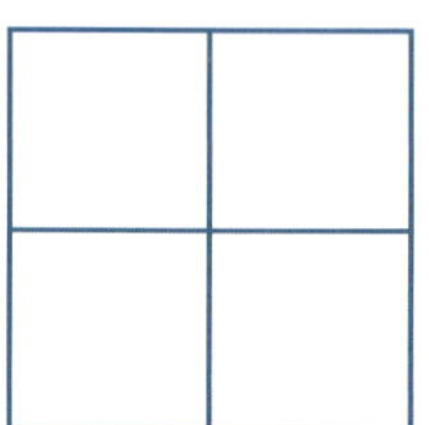

b
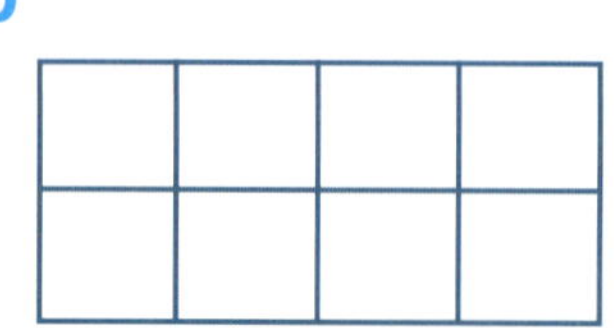

c
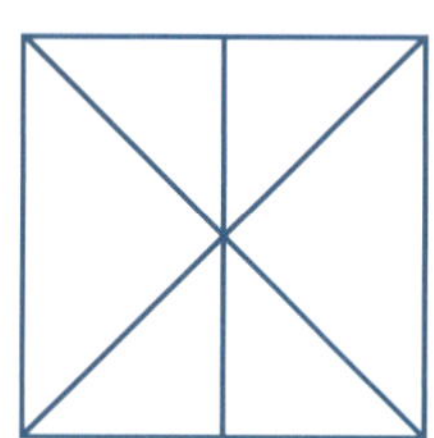

d
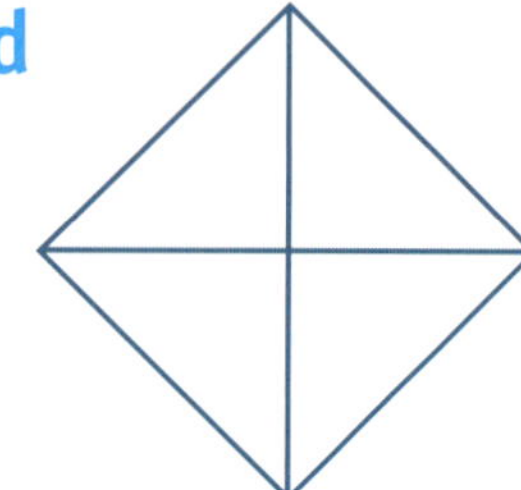

e

f
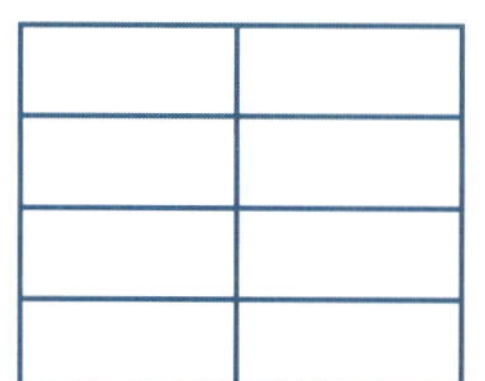

g

Fractions

1 What fraction is blue, one half ($\frac{1}{2}$) or one quarter ($\frac{1}{4}$)?

a
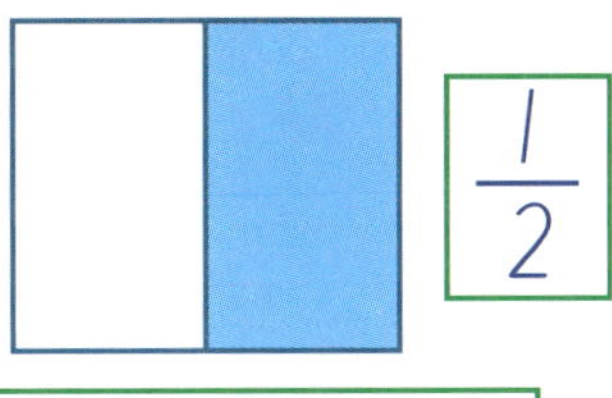
$\frac{1}{2}$

b
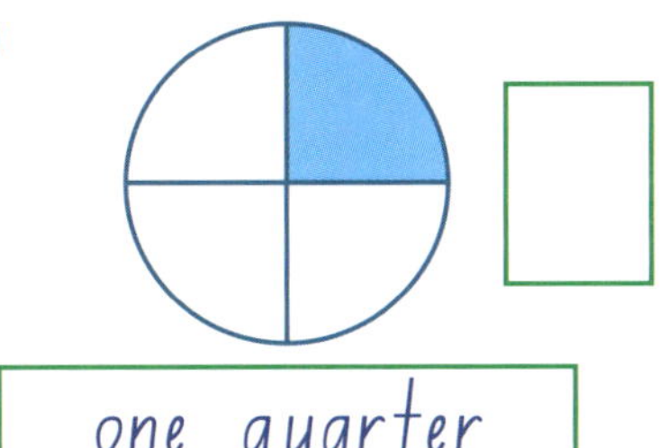
one quarter

c
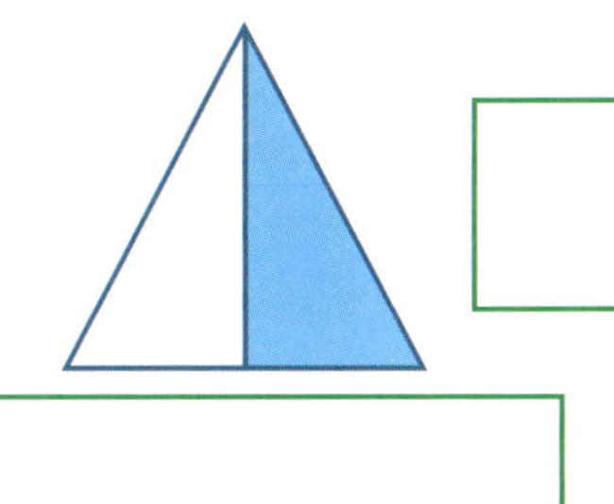

d
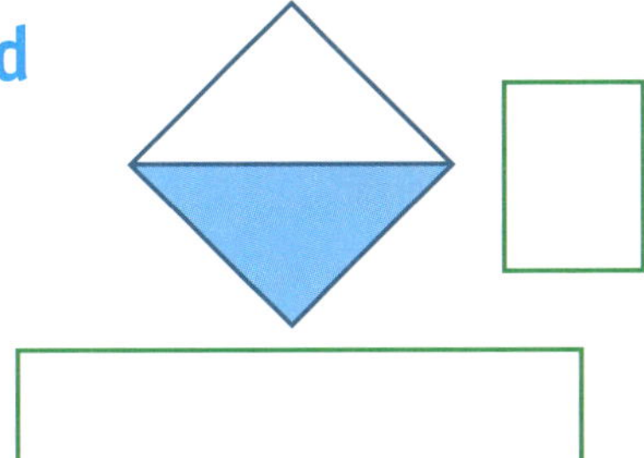

e
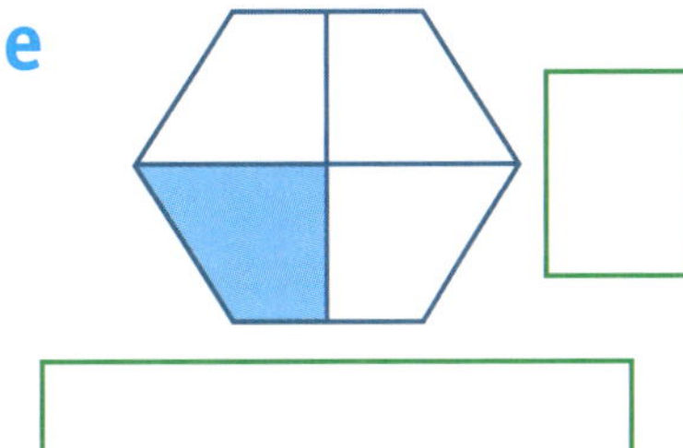

f
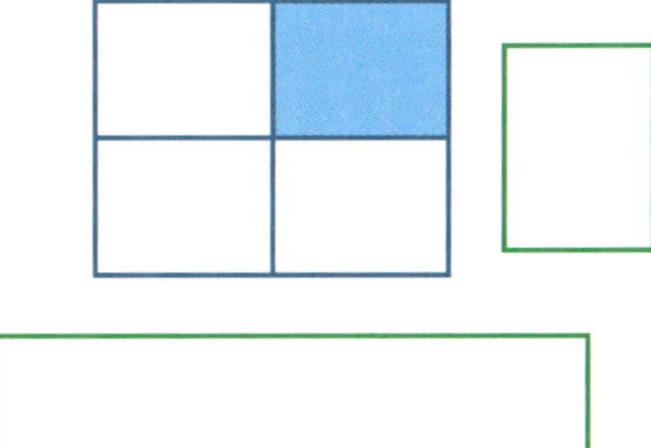

2 Write 'more' or 'less'.

a
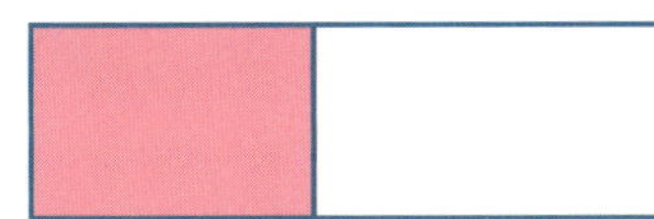
than a half

b
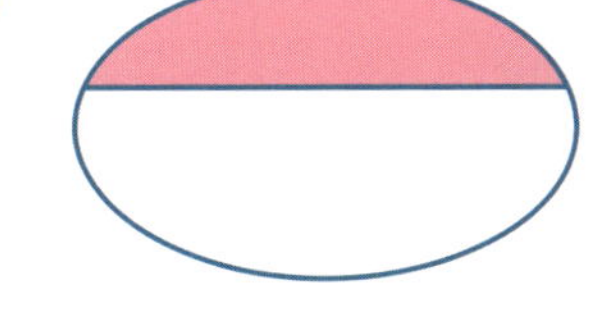
than a half

c
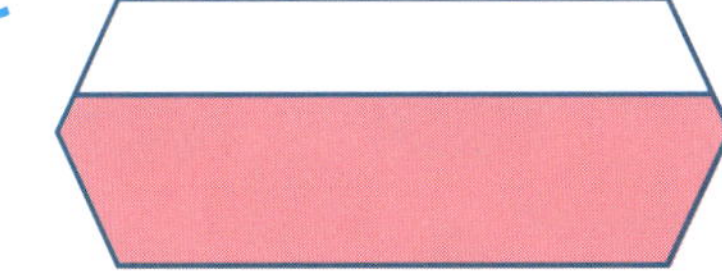
than a half

d
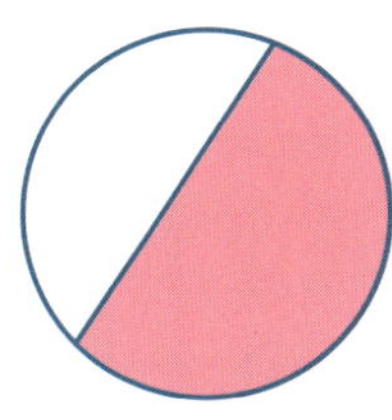
than a half

e
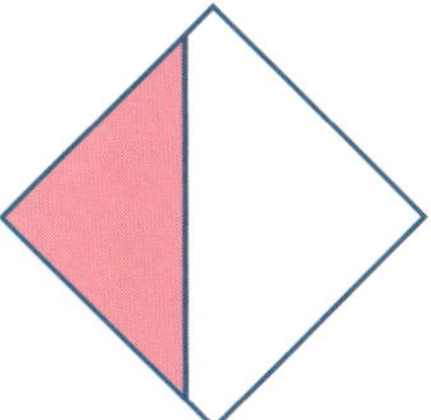
than a half

f
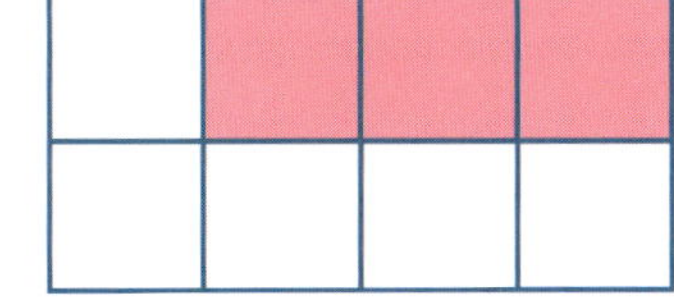
than a half

Challenge!

Paul buys one half of each pizza. How many pieces in each half?

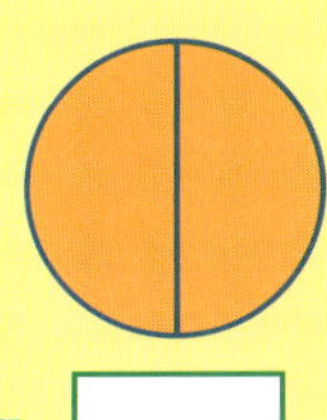
a

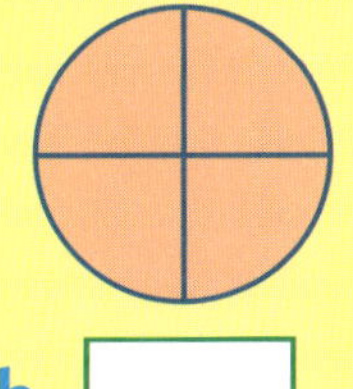
b

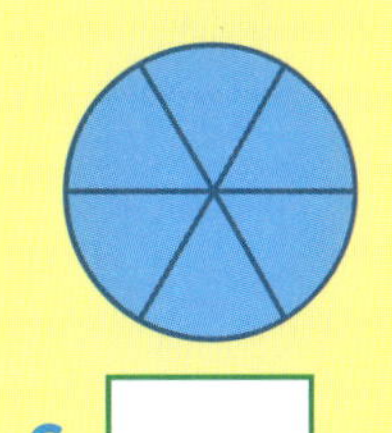
c

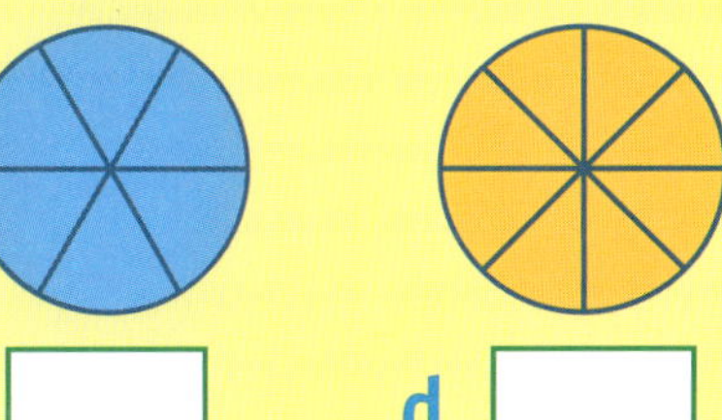
d

Half a collection

Halves are two equal parts.

1 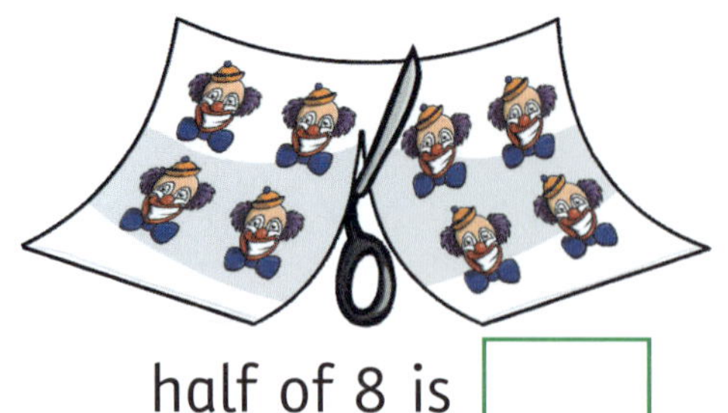

half of 8 is ☐

2 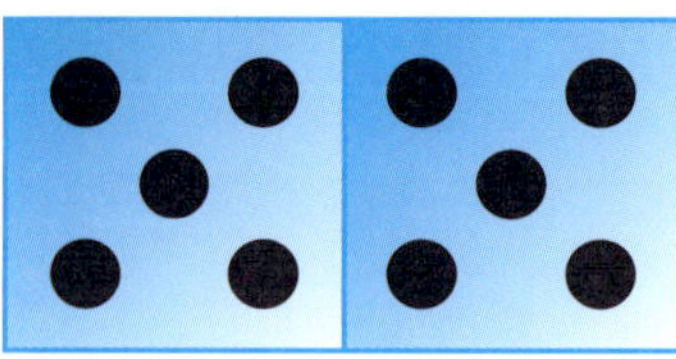

half of 10 is ☐

3 

half of ☐ is ☐

4 

half of ☐ is ☐

Divide into equal halves.

5 

half of ☐ is ☐

6 

half of ☐ is ☐

7 Ned had 12 cards.
He gave half of them away.
How many left? ☐

8 Maria ate half of the biscuits.
There are 10 left.
How many were there? ☐

Draw a diagram

18 animals.
Half are cats.
How many cats?

☐

Sharing a collection

1 Share food equally. Each child will get:

☐ bananas

☐ cakes

☐ strawberries

☐ lollies

☐ orange

2 Give half to each child. Circle the two halves.

a

$\frac{1}{2}$ of 6 is ☐

b

$\frac{1}{2}$ of 10 is ☐

c

$\frac{1}{2}$ of 8 is ☐

d

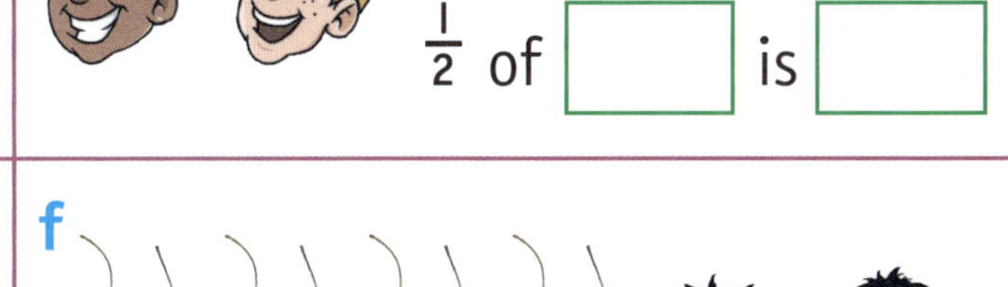

$\frac{1}{2}$ of ☐ is ☐

e

$\frac{1}{2}$ of ☐ is ☐

f

$\frac{1}{2}$ of ☐ is ☐

Challenge!

What is: **a** $\frac{1}{2}$ of 8? ☐ **b** $\frac{1}{4}$ of 8? ☐

c one half of 20? ☐ **d** one quarter of 20? ☐

e $\frac{1}{2}$ of 40? ☐ **f** $\frac{1}{4}$ of 40? ☐ Can you see a pattern?

Fractions of length

Whole **Halves** **Quarters**

1 Draw a line to cut this length in half.

2 Draw a line to cut each half in half.

3 What fraction did you cut this length into? ______________________

4 Draw lines to cut these lengths into quarters.

a
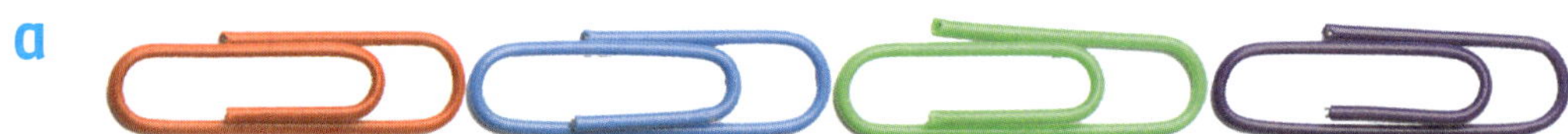

b

c

d

e

Measuring capacity

Capacity is how much it will hold.

measure capacity

1 How much water does it hold?

Choose a , or to measure.

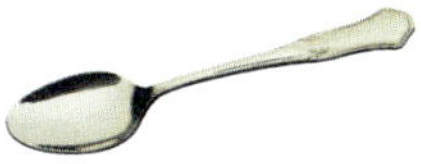

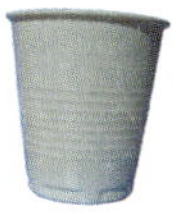

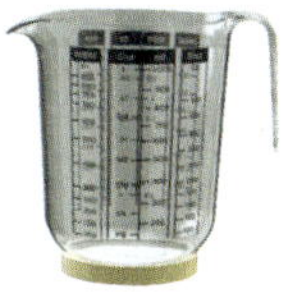

a

☐ jugs

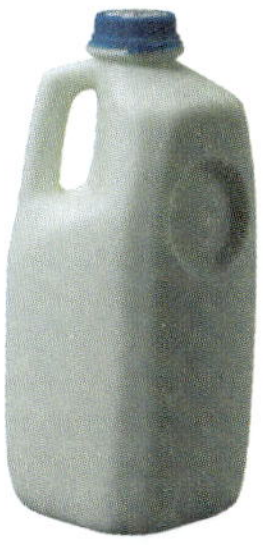

b

☐ ______

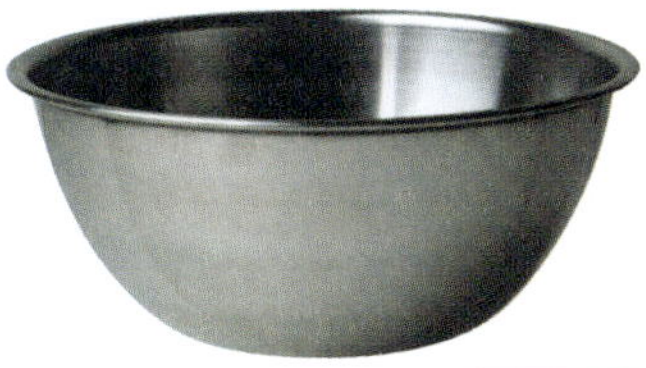

c

☐ ______

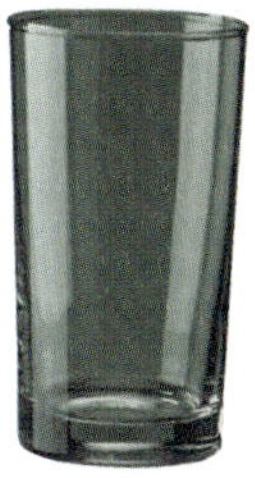

d

☐ ______

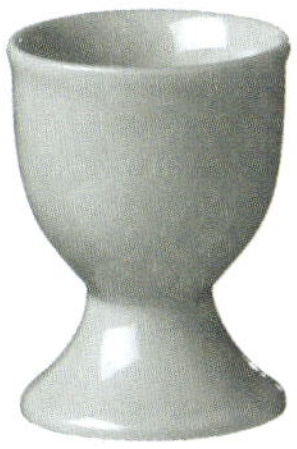

e

☐ ______

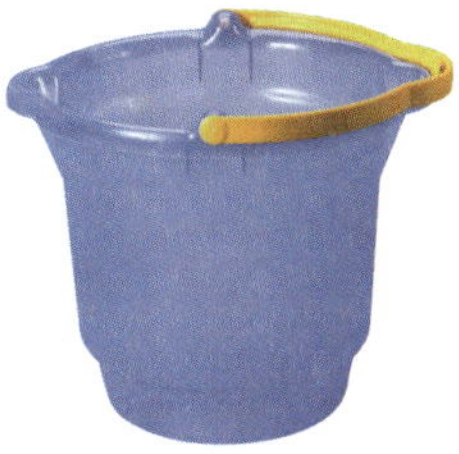

f

☐ ______

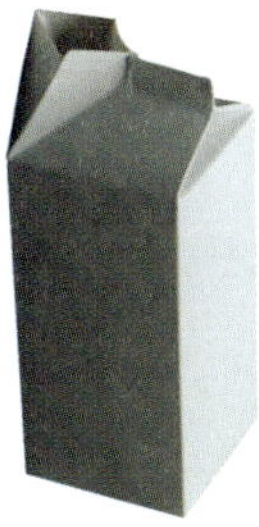

2 Draw in order from holds least to holds most.

3 How many cups does each bottle hold? Estimate using elastic bands. Measure to check.

Bottle 1

Estimate ☐ cups

Measure ☐ cups

Bottle 2

Estimate ☐ cups

Measure ☐ cups

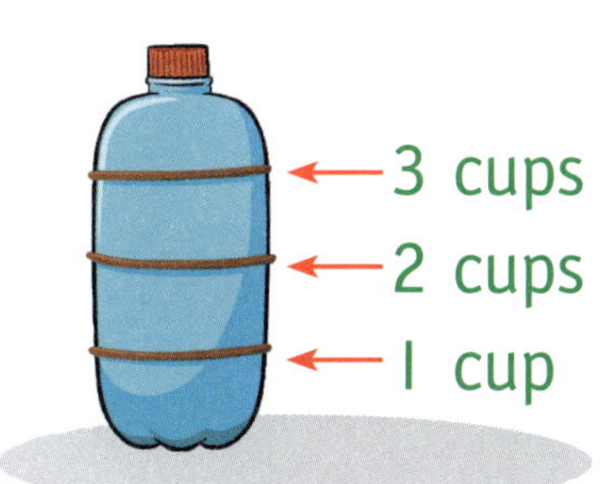

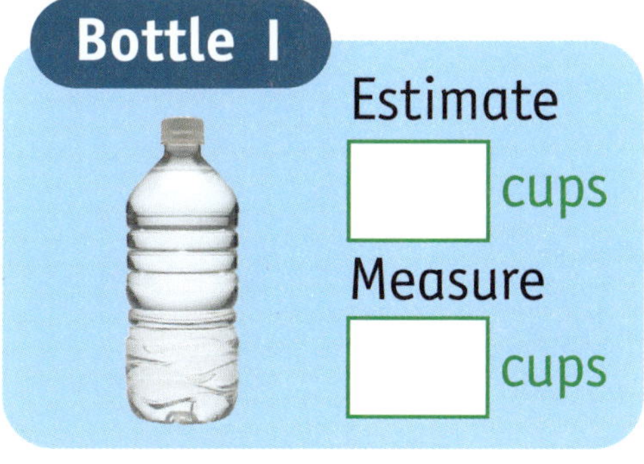

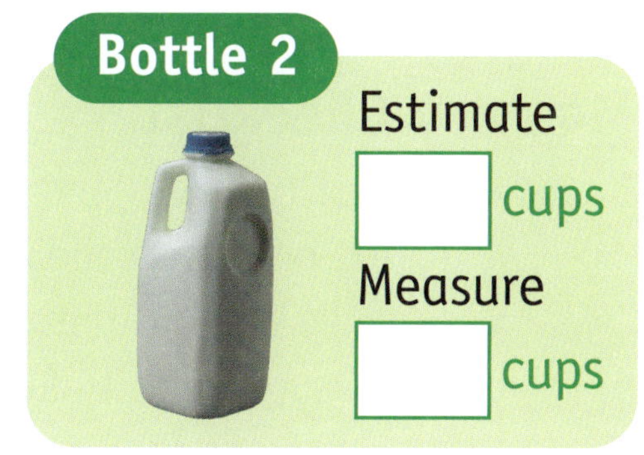

Volume

Volume is the amount of space it takes up.

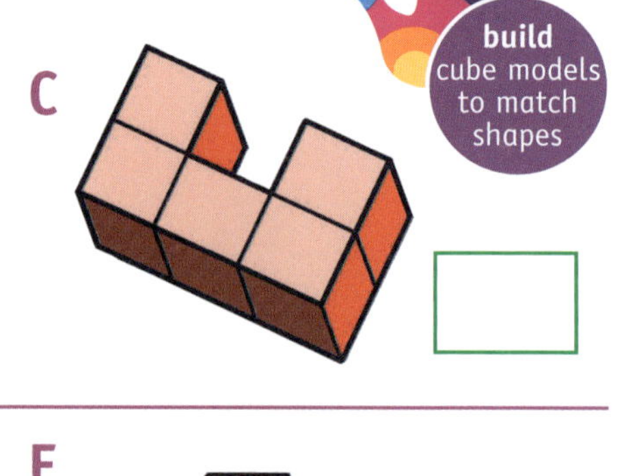

Use cubes to build these shapes.

1 How many cubes in each shape?

A

☐

B

☐

C

☐

D ☐

E ☐

F ☐

2 Which shape uses:

a the most cubes? ________ b the least cubes? ________

Which shape has:

c the largest volume? ________ d the smallest volume? ________

e Order the shapes from smallest to largest volume.

smallest ☐ ☐ ☐ ☐ ☐ ☐ **largest**

3 Join shapes with the same volume.

Mastery Checklist

I can:
- ☐ identify halves and quarters in shapes.
- ☐ find half of a collection.
- ☐ divide a length into halves and quarters.
- ☐ measure capacity in cups and volume in cubes.

Problem solving

Cube volume

How many different shapes can you make with a volume of 8 cubes? Make models using blocks. Draw them below.

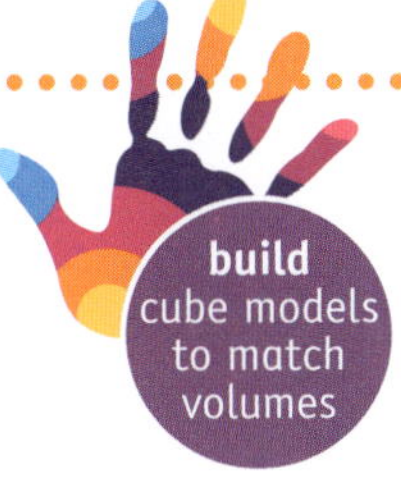

I can solve a problem by:

☐ counting volume in cubes. ☐ building a model and drawing a diagram.

Revision • Term 1

1 Count forwards:

a by ones.

87, 88, ☐ ☐ ☐

b by tens.

12, 22, ☐ ☐ ☐

2 Count backwards:

a by ones.

62, 61, ☐ ☐ ☐

b by tens.

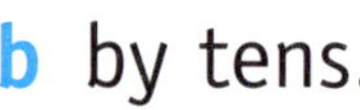

100, 90, ☐ ☐ ☐

3

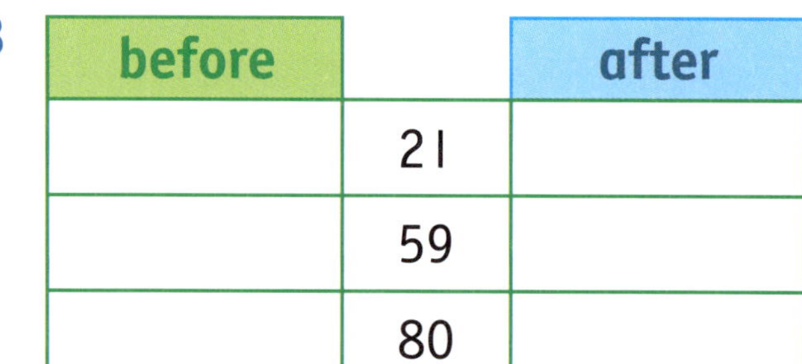

before		after
	21	
	59	
	80	

4 Order from smallest to largest.

77, 14, 90, 21, 39

5 a

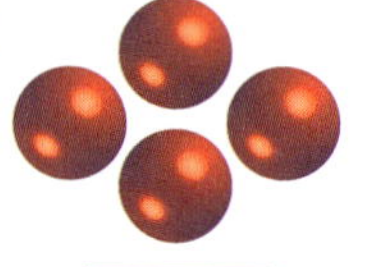
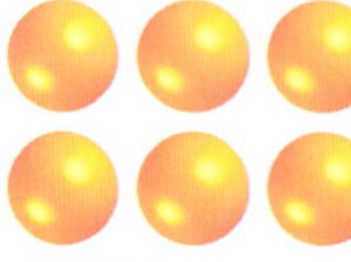

☐ + ☐ = ☐

b Colour the ones that match.

6 | 3 + 3 | 6 + 1 | 2 + 5 | 4 + 2

6 a 4 fly away.

How many left?

b 3 are eaten.

How many left?

7

	Number of sides	Number of corners
a		
b		
c		

8 a 6 − 2 = ☐

b 10 − 5 = ☐

c 9 − 3 = ☐

9 Does it show a flip, slide or turn?

a

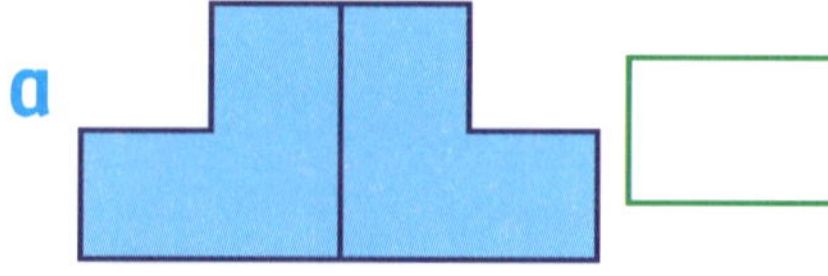

b

10 Draw the lines of symmetry.

11 What time is it?

a

b

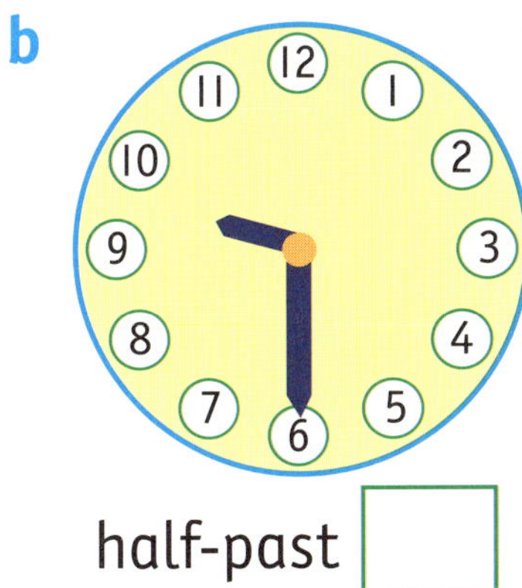

half-past

12 Circle the heavier one.

a

b

13 How many cubes?

a

b

c Tick the shape with the smallest volume.

14 How many days in September?

15 Colour one half.

a b

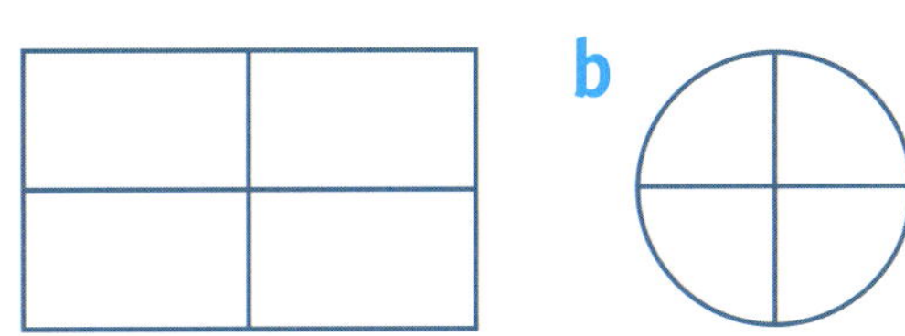

16 Colour one quarter.

a b

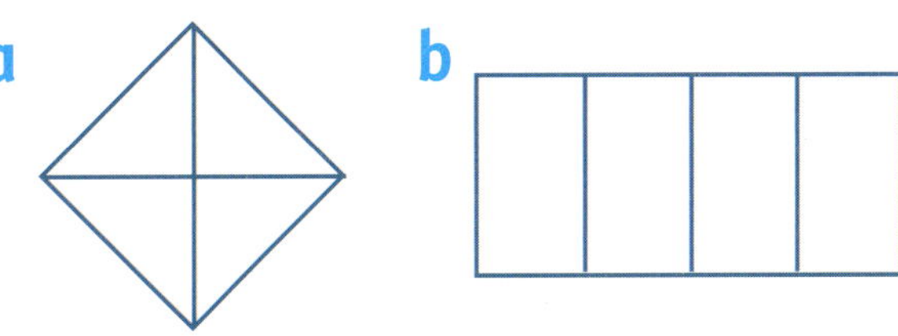

17 2A's favourite fruits

Colour the graph.

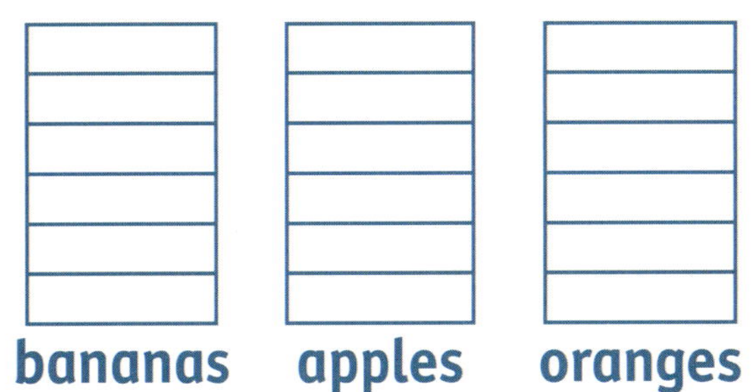

Making twenty

0 1 2 3 4 5 6 7 8 9 10 11 12 13 14 15 16 17 18 19 20

1 How many more to make 20? Draw and write how many.

a 14 + ☐ = 20

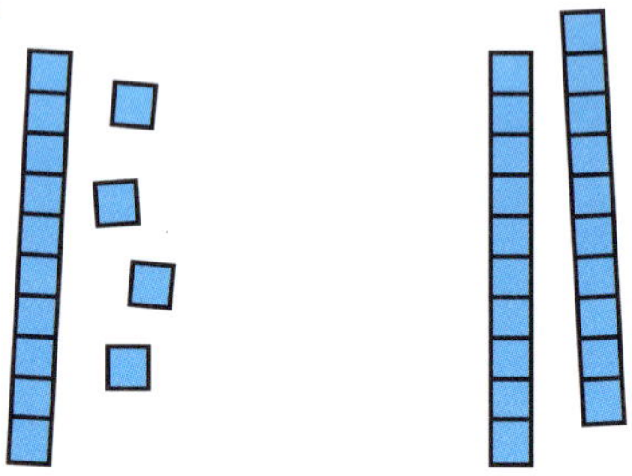

b ☐ + ☐ = ☐

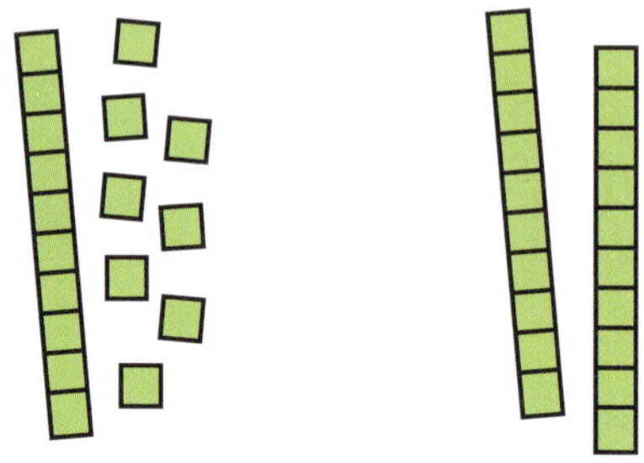

c ☐ + ☐ = ☐

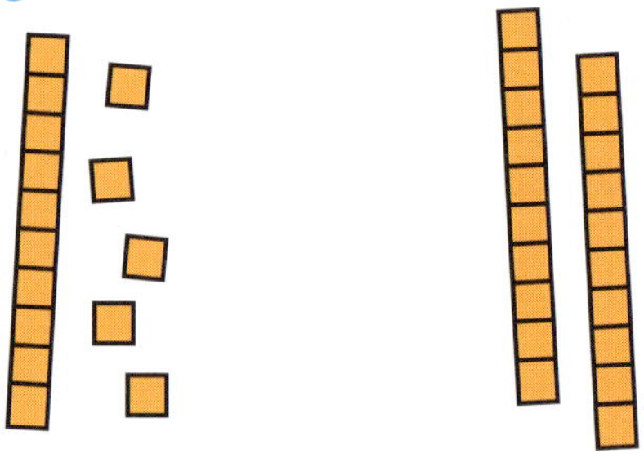

d ☐ + ☐ = ☐

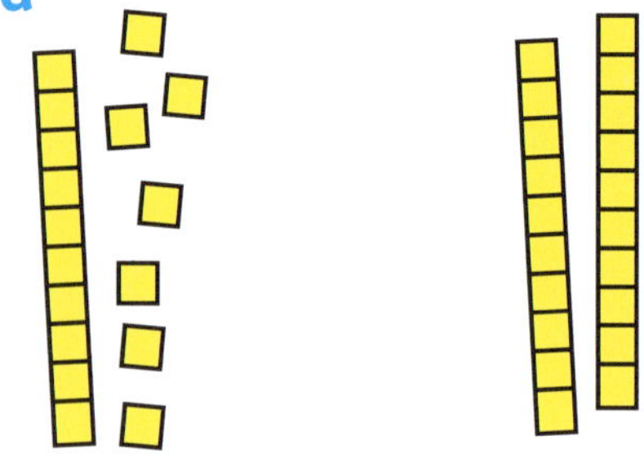

e ☐ + ☐ = ☐

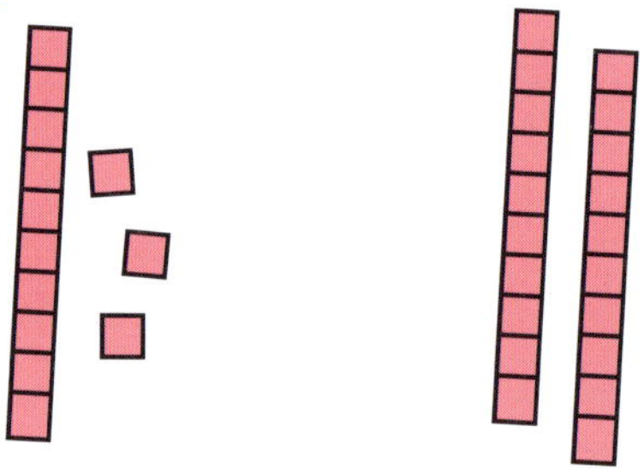

f ☐ + ☐ = ☐

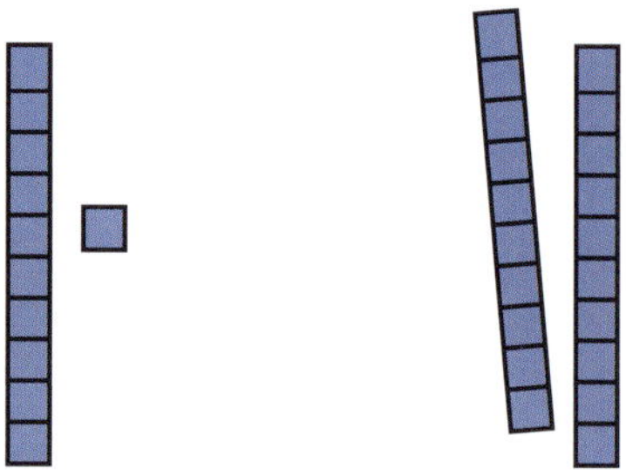

2 How many more to make 20? Write the number.

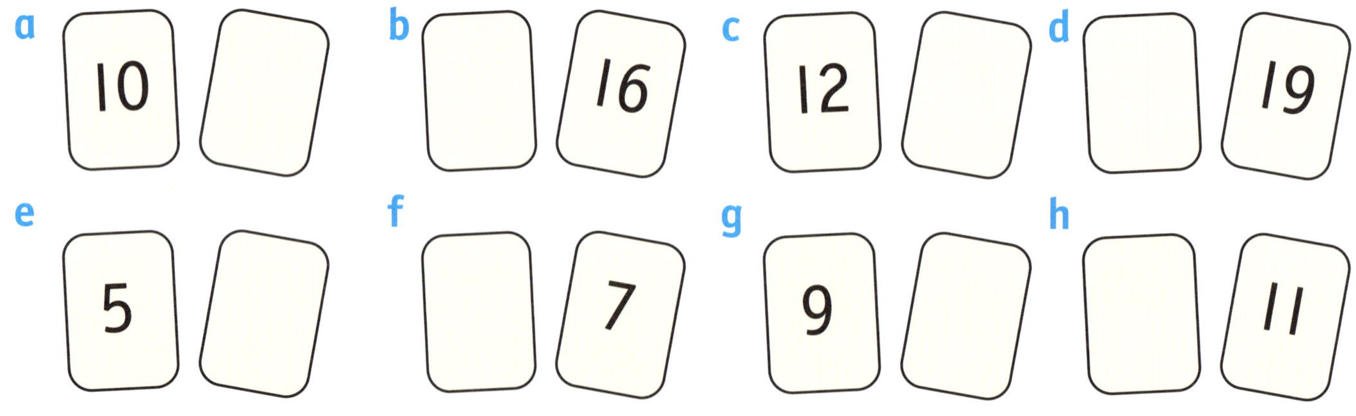

Challenge! Find 3 numbers that add to 20.
How many answers can you find?

Adding three or more numbers

Look for two numbers that add to ten.

6 + 8 + 4
= 10 + 8
= 18

= 10
1 + 9
2 + 8
3 + 7
4 + 6
5 + 5

1 a 6 + 5 + 4 = ______ b 7 + 3 + 5 = ______ c 2 + 6 + 8 = ______
d 5 + 9 + 5 = ______ e 9 + 7 + 1 = ______ f 3 + 10 + 7 = ______
g 2 + 9 + 8 = ______ h 5 + 7 + 5 = ______ i 1 + 8 + 9 = ______
j 4 + 8 + 6 = ______ k 7 + 6 + 3 = ______ l 6 + 6 + 4 = ______
m 8 + 5 + 2 = ______ n 9 + 7 + 3 = ______ o 2 + 8 + 10 = ______

2 Make each pair add to 20.

1	2	3	4	5	6	7	8	9	10

3 Now look for two numbers that add to 20.

a 9 + 18 + 2 = ______ b 15 + 8 + 5 = ______
c 9 + 7 + 11 = ______ d 8 + 14 + 6 = ______
e 6 + 17 + 3 = ______ f 4 + 3 + 16 = ______
g 12 + 3 + 8 = ______ h 17 + 9 + 3 = ______
i 1 + 6 + 19 = ______ j 7 + 10 + 10 = ______
k 6 + 14 + 9 = ______ l 8 + 9 + 12 = ______

Challenge!

a 7 + 8 + 3 + 2 = ☐ b 9 + 6 + 2 + 4 = ☐
c 14 + 2 + 6 + 18 = ☐ d 12 + 3 + 8 + 17 = ☐

Shopping with money

1 How much more money do you need? Draw it.

a $20

b  $20

c  $30

d  $30

e  $40

f  $50

Challenge! How many ways can you make $20?
Draw some here using

AC9M2N06 Number MA1-CSQ-01 Combining and separating quantities B • Form multiples of ten when adding and subtracting two-digit numbers

Equivalence with coins

1 Draw one coin to match.

a =

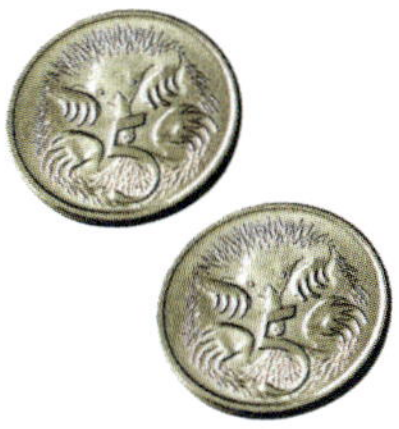

b =

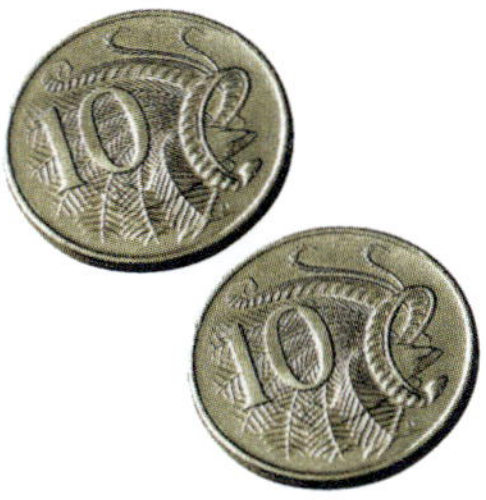

c =

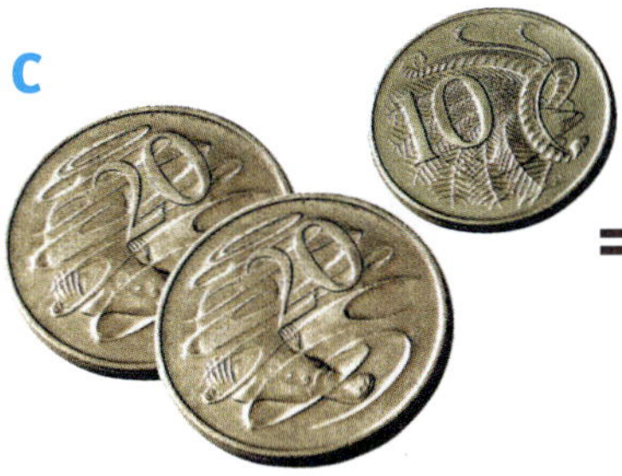

d =

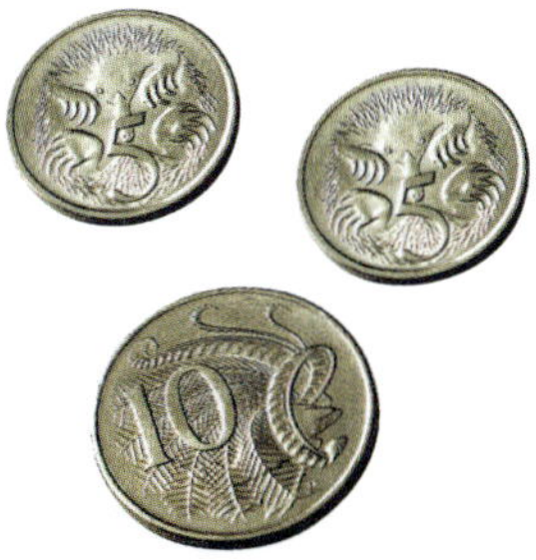

e =

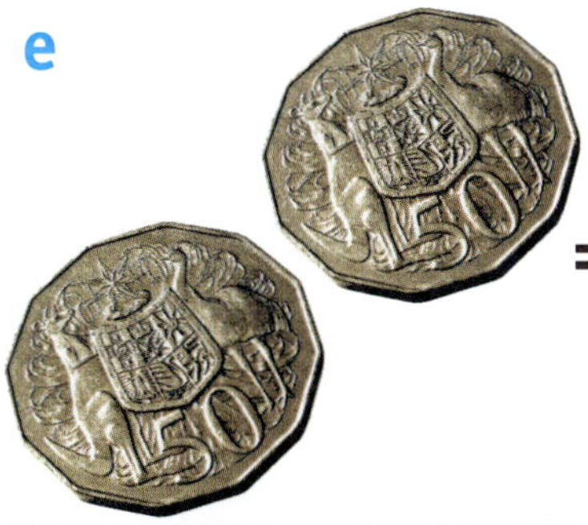

f =

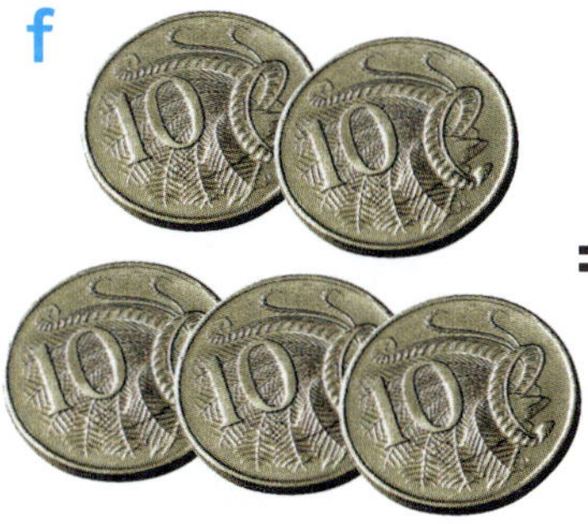

g =

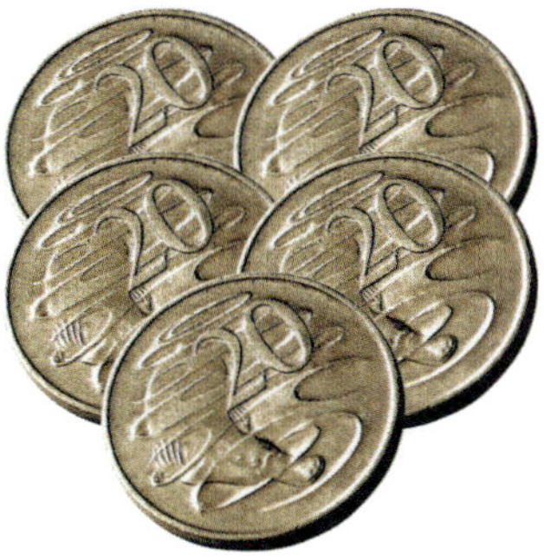

h =

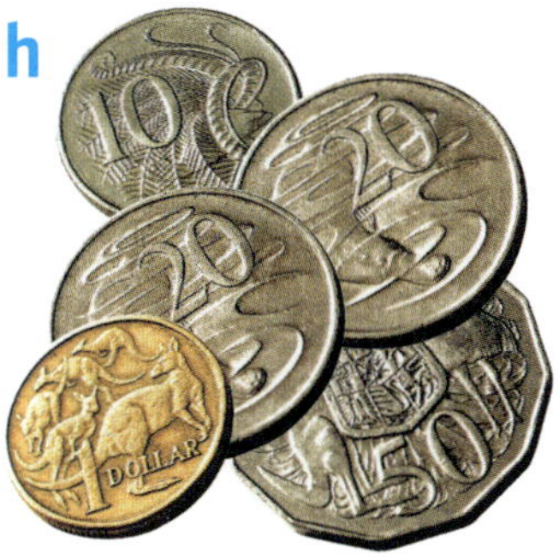

Challenge!

Make $2 in different ways. Draw two ways here.

= 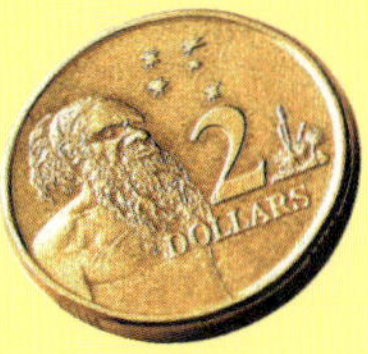 =

Addition – bridging ten

1

a 7 + 5 = ______

add 3 add 2

5 6 7 8 9 **10** 11 12 13 14 15

7 and 3 make 10. And 2 more makes 12.

b 9 + 3 = ______

5 6 7 8 9 **10** 11 12 13 14 15 16 17 18 19 **20**

c 8 + 7 = ______

5 6 7 8 9 **10** 11 12 13 14 15 16 17 18 19 **20**

d 9 + 8 = ______

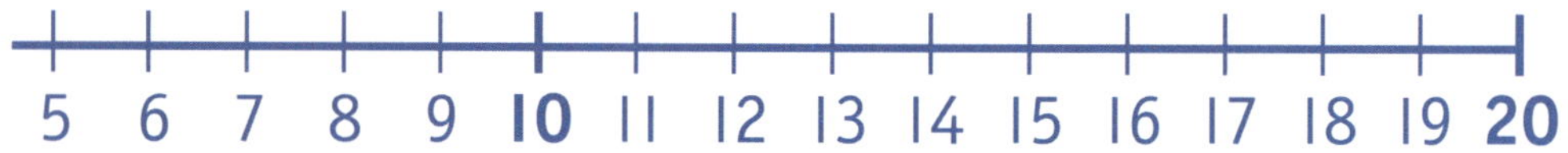

5 6 7 8 9 **10** 11 12 13 14 15 16 17 18 19 **20**

2 How much for both?

a **$9** **$5**

$9 + $5 = ☐

b **$6** **$7**

☐ + ☐ = ☐

c **$3** **$5**

☐ + ☐ = ☐

d **$7** **$5**

☐ + ☐ = ☐

3 17 + 5 = ______

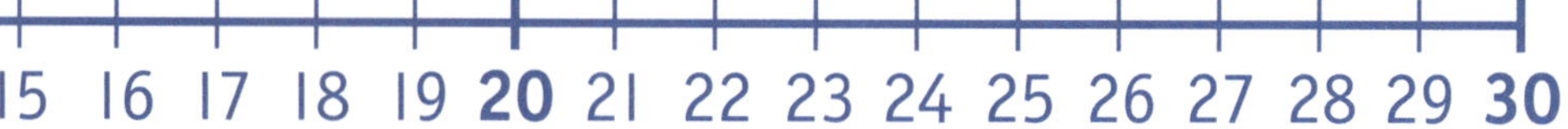

15 16 17 18 19 **20** 21 22 23 24 25 26 27 28 29 **30**

Mastery Checklist

I can:
- ☐ add to make 20.
- ☐ add dollars and cents amounts.
- ☐ add 3 or more numbers.
- ☐ make a 10 to add on a number line.

Problem solving

Zoo Count

Penny went to the zoo. She counted legs.

How many animals did she see altogether? ___________

elephants
16 legs

camels
12 legs

kangaroos
16 legs

penguins
20 legs

lions
12 legs

giraffes
24 legs

I can solve a problem by:

☐ counting by 2s and 4s. ☐ drawing a picture..

Length

measure length in informal units

1 Make a measuring cat this long or use a MAB ten block.

2 Use it to measure these things.

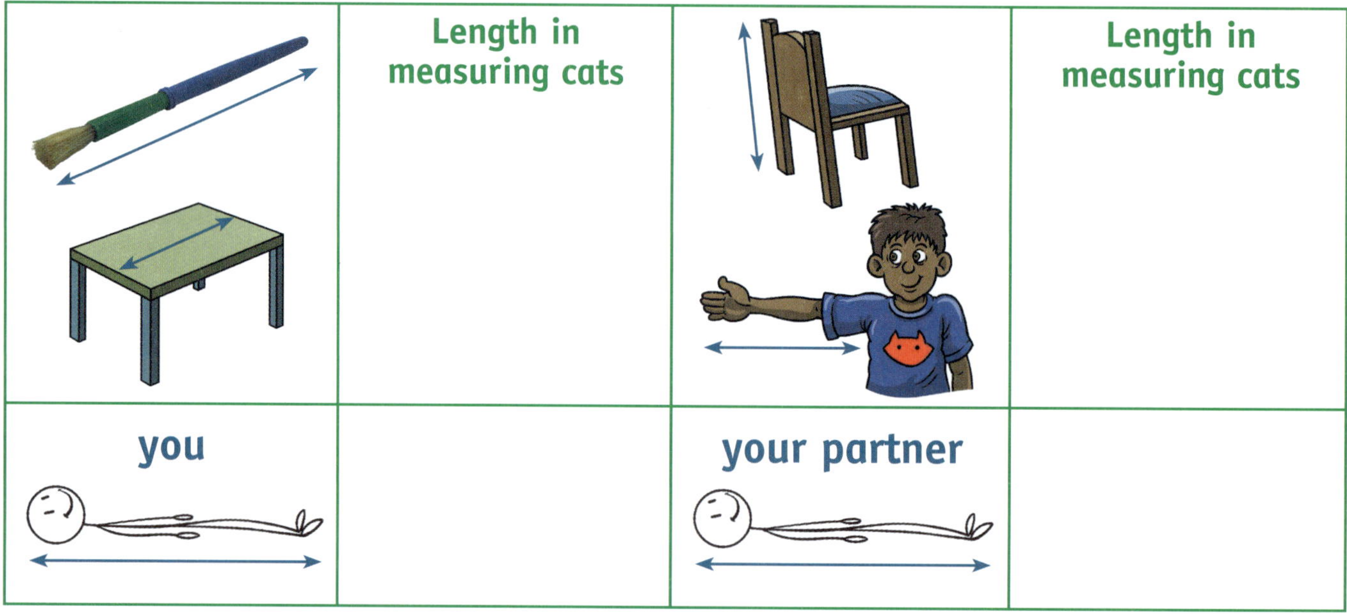

	Length in measuring cats		Length in measuring cats
you		your partner	

3 How many beads long is each object?

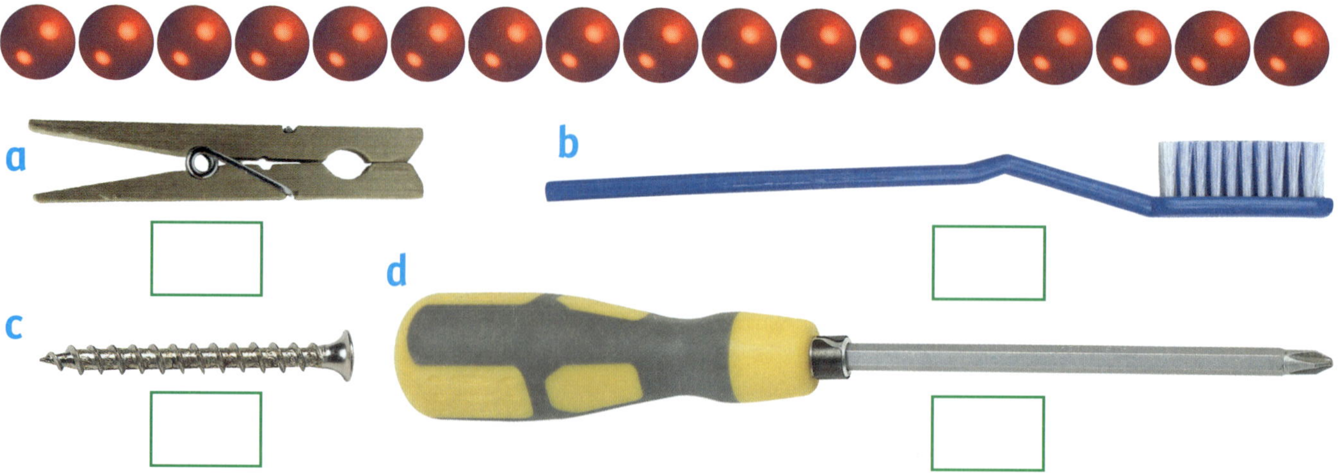

Challenge! Cut a piece of string as long as your body. Find things that match. Write a list.

Length

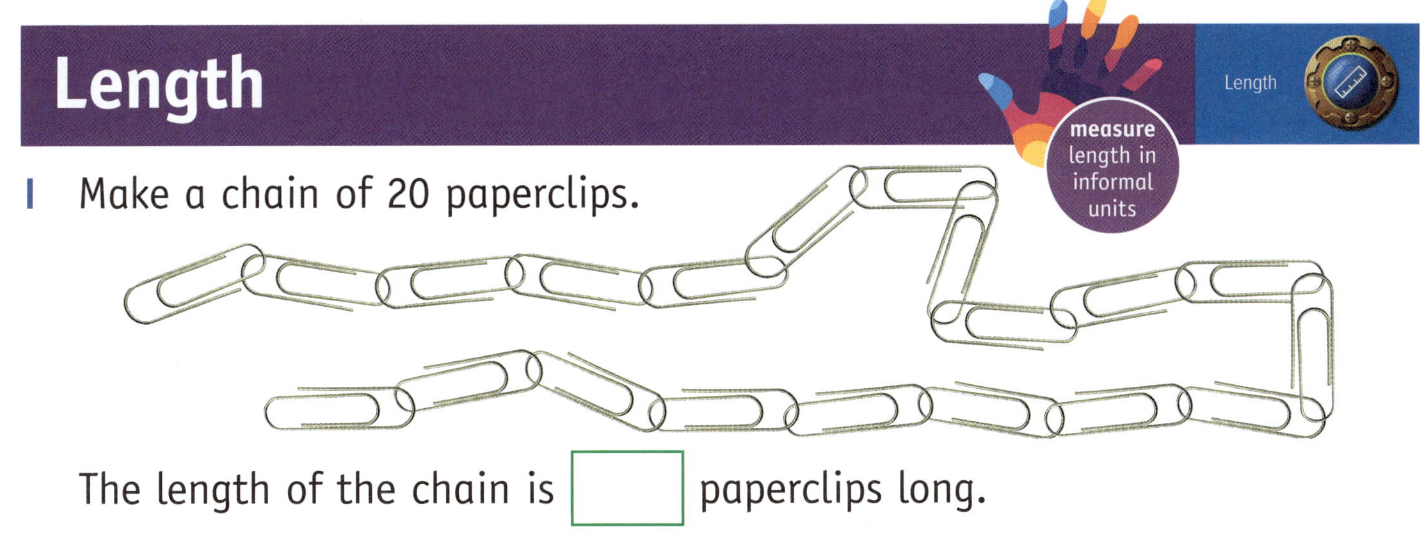

1 Make a chain of 20 paperclips.

The length of the chain is ☐ paperclips long.

2 Measure these things using your chain. Work with a partner.

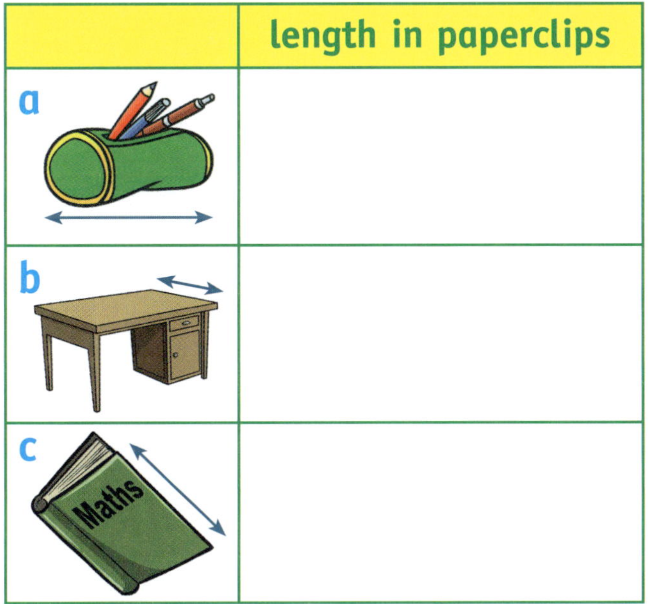

	length in paperclips
a	
b	
c	

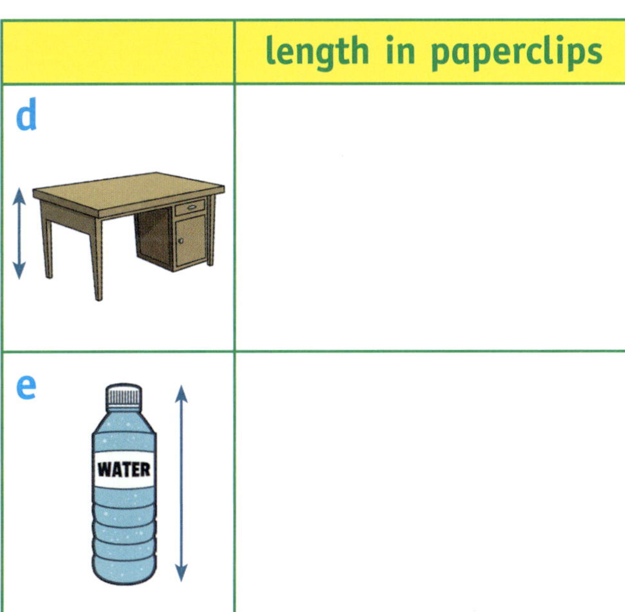

	length in paperclips
d	
e	

3 a Which is longer, the book or the pencil case? ____________

b Which is taller, the desk or the drink bottle ? ____________

c Place the things in question 2 in order, from shortest to longest.

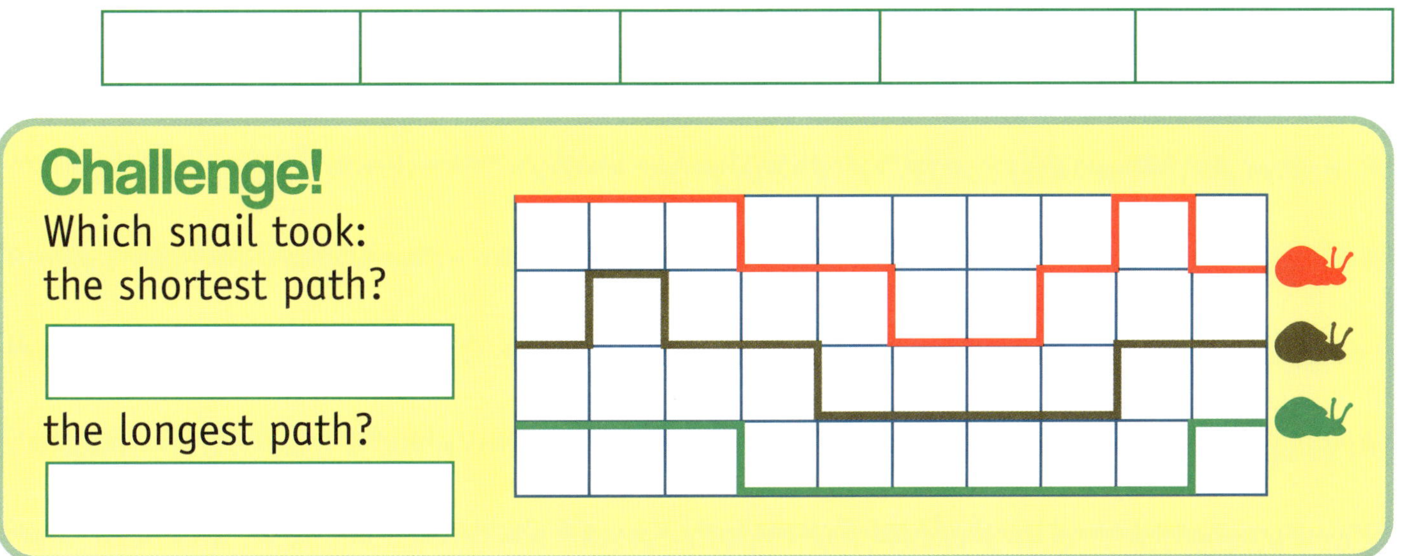

Challenge!

Which snail took:

the shortest path?

☐

the longest path?

☐

The metre

measure length in metres

1 Make a metre long measure.

Use or or

2 Use it to measure the following. Match each to a label.

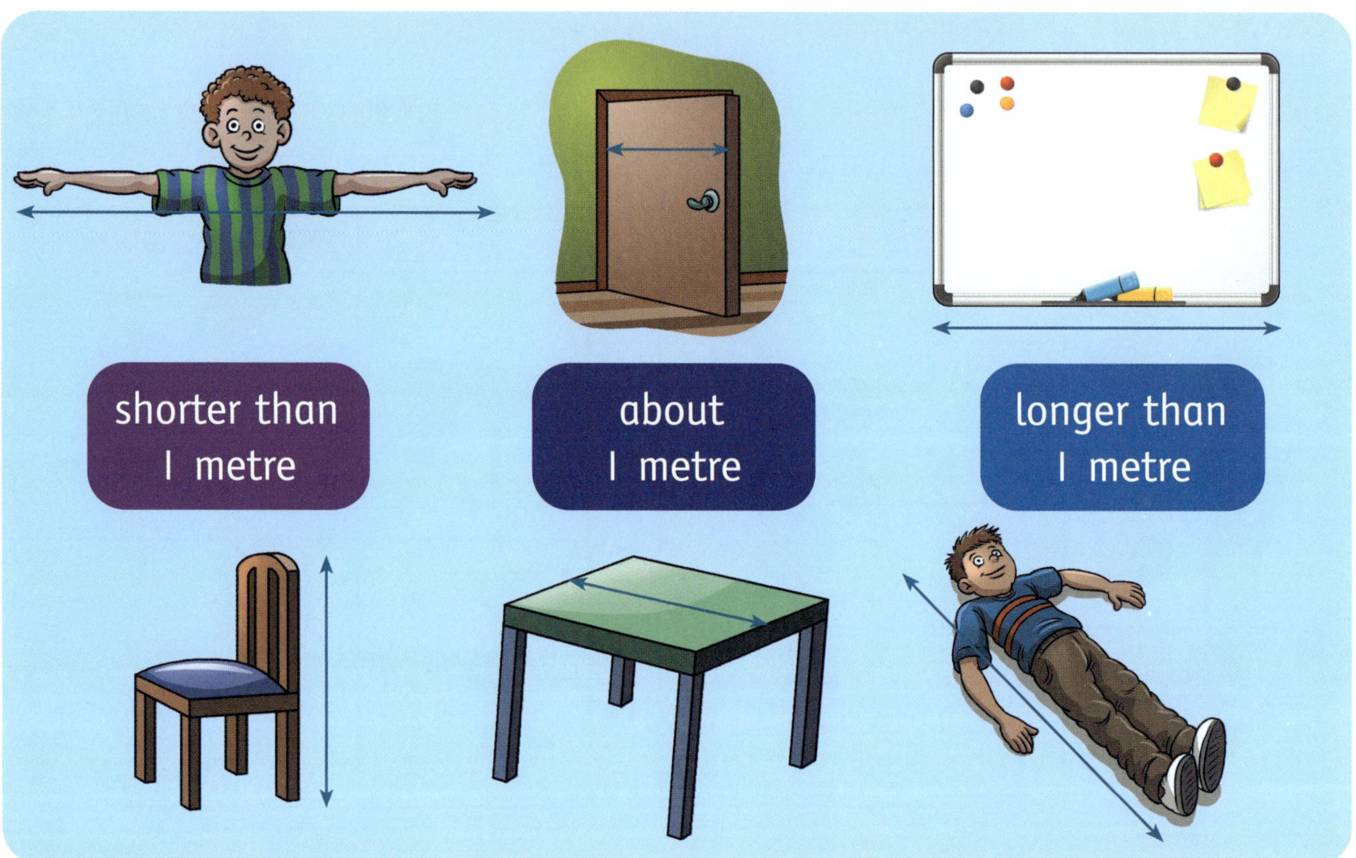

3 Measure other things.

shorter than 1 metre	about 1 metre	longer than 1 metre

Challenge! Find something that is half a metre long.

Measuring in metres

The tiger is about **3 metres** long.

1 metre | **1 metre** | **1 metre**

measure length in metres

1 Estimate each length in metres. Then measure each length.

a about ☐ metres
☐ metres

b about ☐ metres
☐ metres

c about ☐ metres
☐ metres

d about ☐ metres
☐ metres

e about ☐ metres ☐ metres

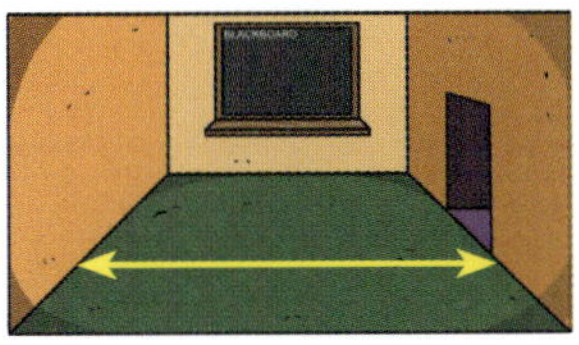

Challenge!

Estimate how far it is from your classroom to:

the canteen ☐ the office ☐ playground ☐.

How could you measure these lengths?

Mastery Checklist

I can: ☐ measure length using informal units. ☐ compare lengths.
☐ compare items to 1 metre. ☐ measure in metres.

Subtraction on a number line

Jump backwards along the number line to take away.

1

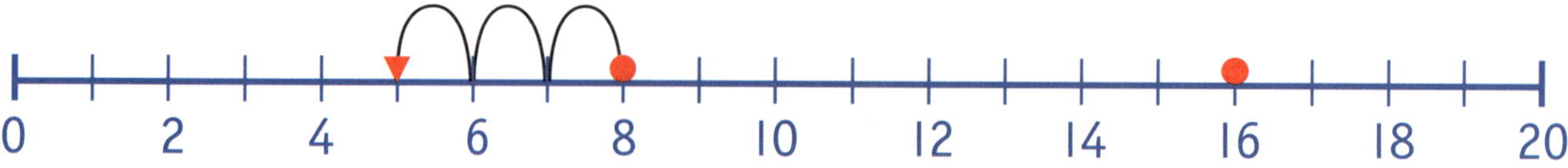

a 8 − 3 = ☐ **b** 16 − 2 = ☐ **c** 20 − 4 = ☐

2

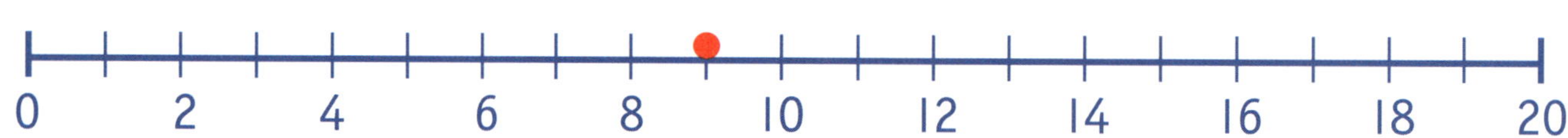

a 9 − 5 = ☐ **b** 18 − 3 = ☐ **c** 15 − 6 = ☐

3

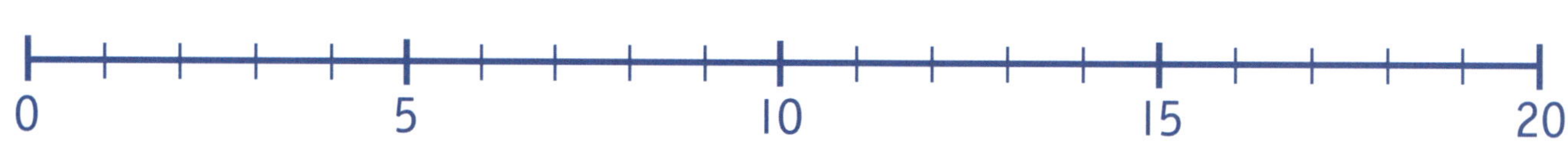

a 11 − 3 = ☐ **b** 19 − 4 = ☐ **c** 13 − 5 = ☐

4

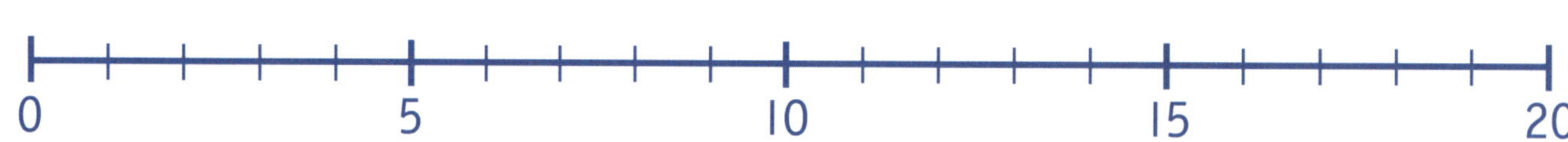

a 13 − 5 = ☐ **b** 12 − 3 = ☐ **c** 19 − 6 = ☐

d 11 − 4 = ☐ **e** 14 − 2 = ☐ **f** 15 − 8 = ☐

Challenge!

A frog makes 4 equal jumps from 12 m to 0.

How long is each jump?

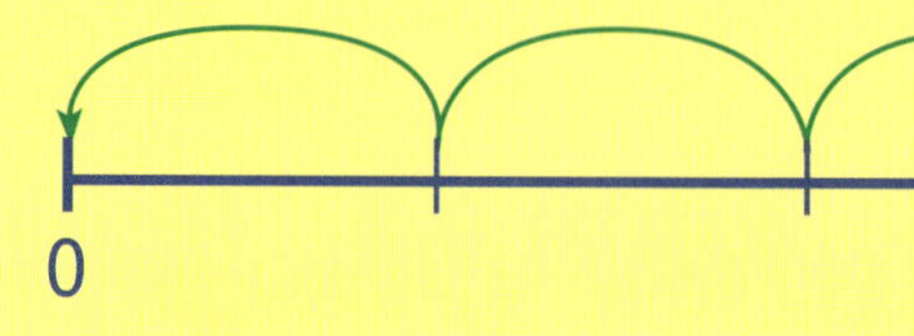

AC9M2N04 Number **MA1-CSQ-01** Combining and separating quantities B • Represent and reason about additive relations

Subtraction to twenty

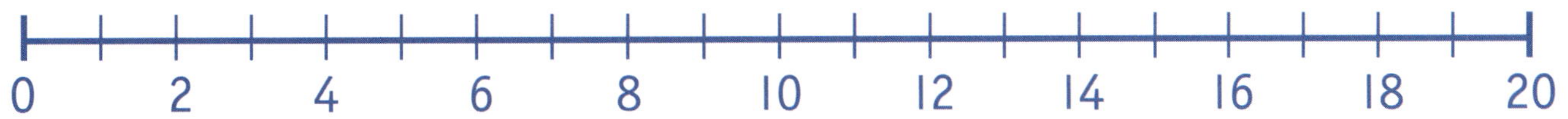

1 Write a number sentence. Find the change.

a

$ [ ] – $ [ ] = $ [ ]

b

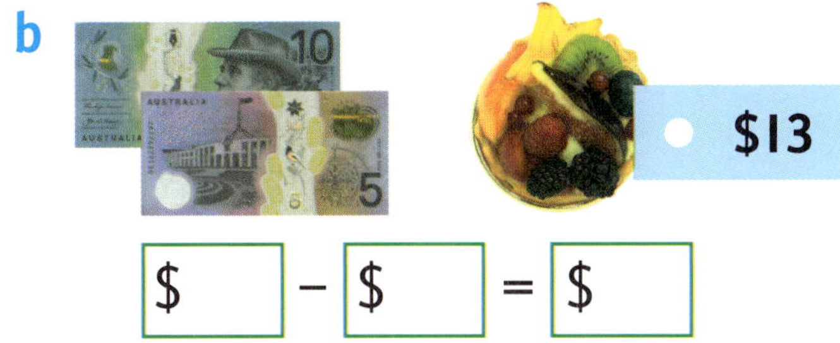

$ [ ] – $ [ ] = $ [ ]

c

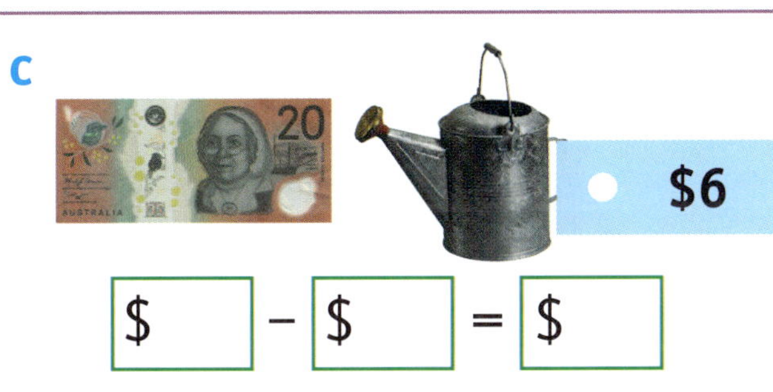

$ [ ] – $ [ ] = $ [ ]

d

$ [ ] – $ [ ] = $ [ ]

2 Take away the ten first, then the ones.

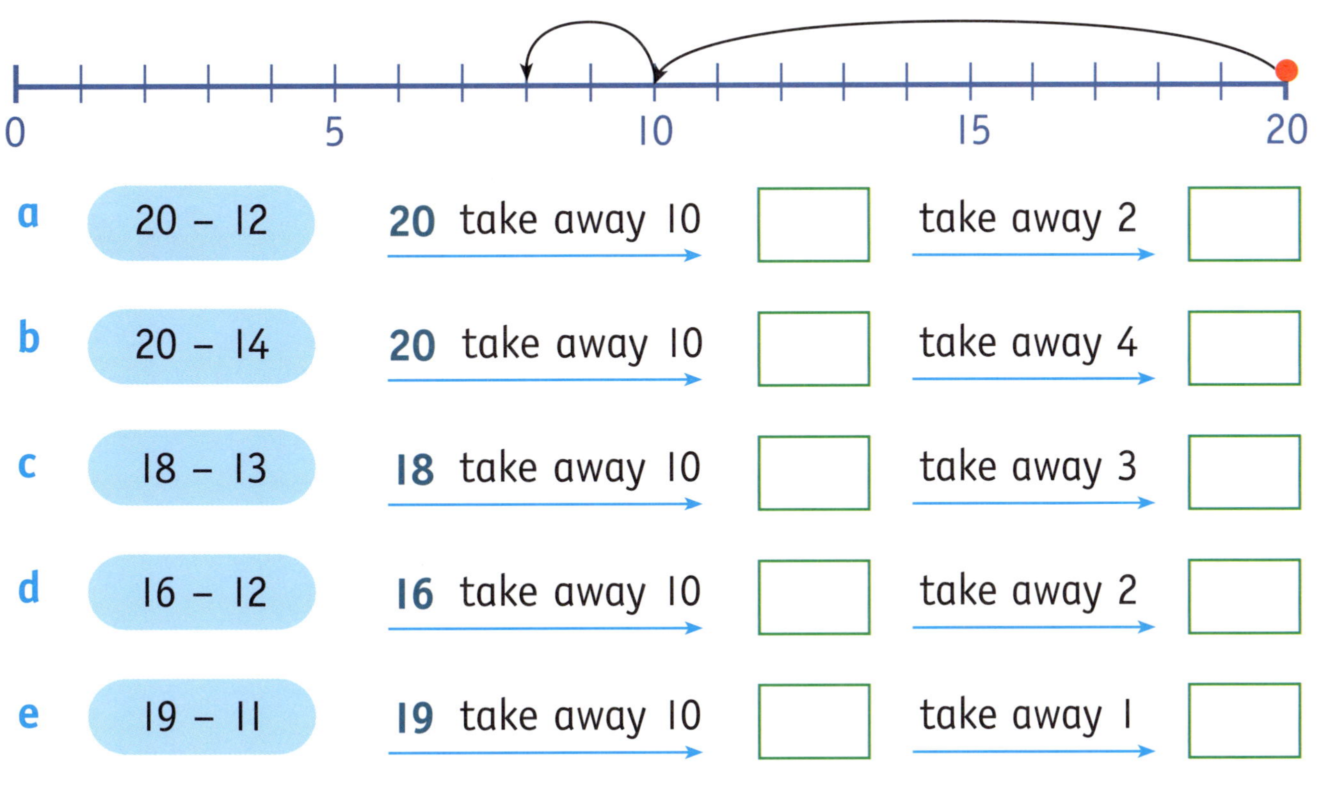

a	20 – 12	**20** take away 10	[ ]	take away 2	[ ]
b	20 – 14	**20** take away 10	[ ]	take away 4	[ ]
c	18 – 13	**18** take away 10	[ ]	take away 3	[ ]
d	16 – 12	**16** take away 10	[ ]	take away 2	[ ]
e	19 – 11	**19** take away 10	[ ]	take away 1	[ ]
f	17 – 14	**17** take away 10	[ ]	take away 4	[ ]

Adding and subtracting

Related facts

1 Complete.

a

2 + 4 = ☐　6 − 2 = ☐

4 + 2 = ☐　6 − 4 = ☐

b

5 + 3 = ☐　8 − 5 = ☐

3 + 5 = ☐　8 − 3 = ☐

c

10 + 5 = ☐

5 + ☐ = ☐

15 − 5 = ☐

15 − 10 = ☐

d

7 + 6 = ☐　13 − 6 = ☐

6 + 7 = ☐　13 − 7 = ☐

e

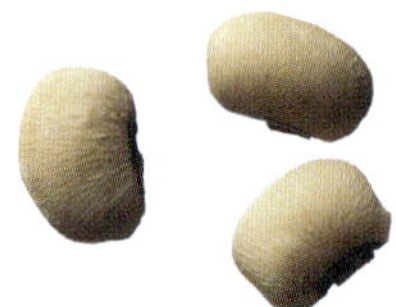

12 + 3 = ☐　15 − 3 = ☐

3 + 12 = ☐　15 − 12 = ☐

f

15 + 4 = ☐　19 − 4 = ☐

4 + 15 = ☐　19 − 15 = ☐

Draw a diagram

James has 6 birds.
Each bird is either red, green or blue. How many green birds could James have? ☐

Linking addition and subtraction

1 Write 2 additions and 2 subtractions for each picture.

a

☐ + ☐ = ☐ ☐ − ☐ = ☐

☐ + ☐ = ☐ ☐ − ☐ = ☐

b

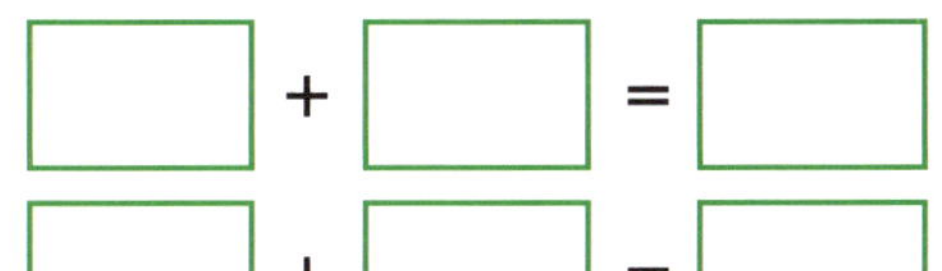

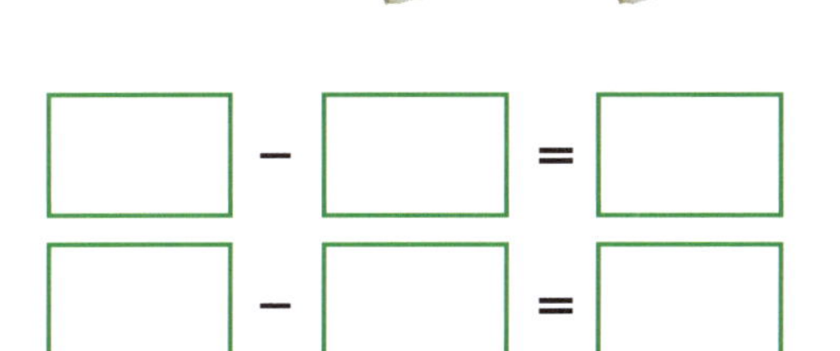

☐ + ☐ = ☐ ☐ − ☐ = ☐

☐ + ☐ = ☐ ☐ − ☐ = ☐

c

☐ + ☐ = ☐ ☐ − ☐ = ☐

☐ + ☐ = ☐ ☐ − ☐ = ☐

Looking for patterns

Write additions for 12. How many are there?
Can you see a pattern?

☐ + ☐ = 12

Number mountains

1 Complete the number sentences.

a

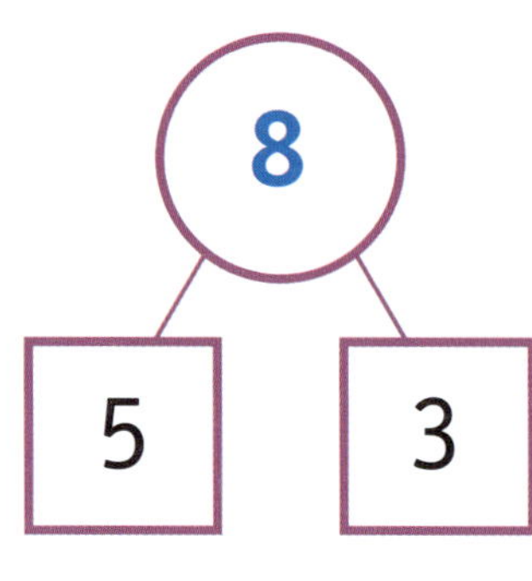

☐ + 3 = 8

8 − 3 = ☐

b

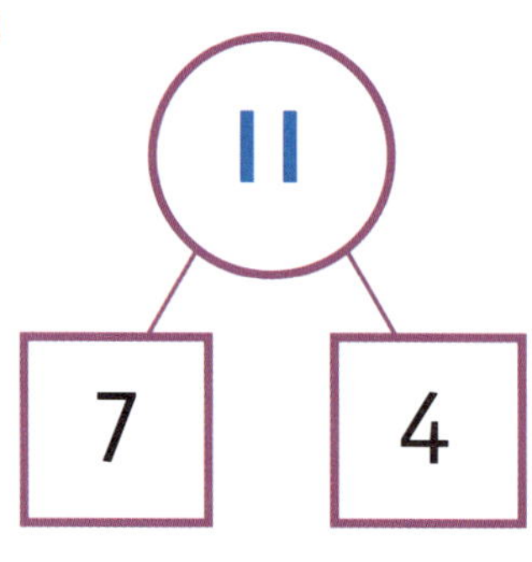

7 + ☐ = 11

11 − ☐ = 7

c

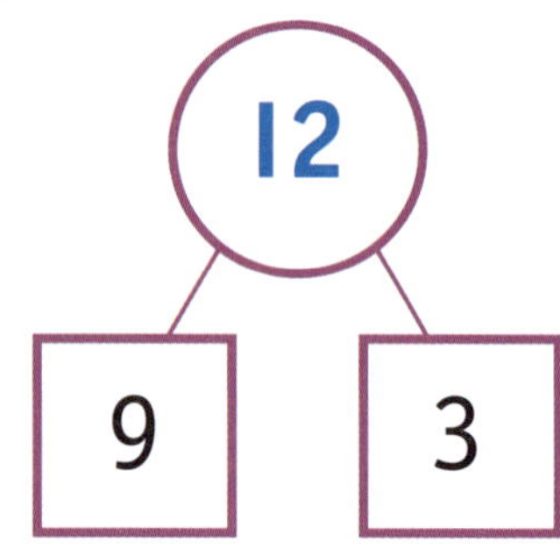

9 + 3 = ☐

☐ − 3 = 9

2 Complete the number mountains.

a

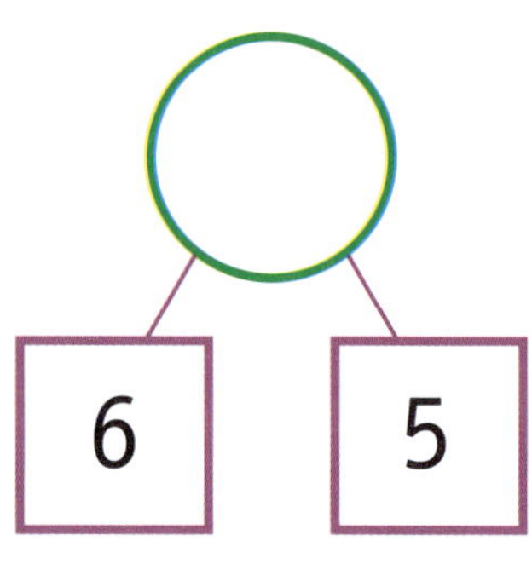

6 + 5 = 11

11 − 5 = 6

b

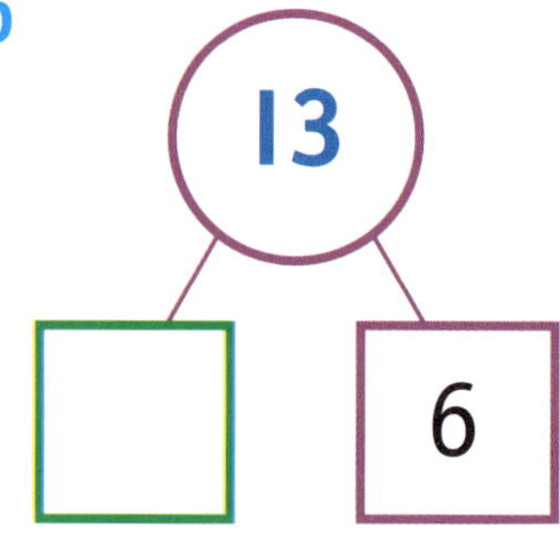

7 + 6 = 13

13 − 6 = 7

c

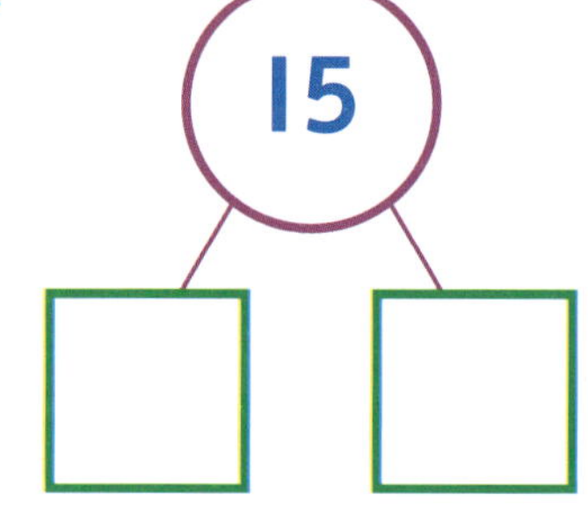

9 + 6 = 15

15 − 6 = 9

d

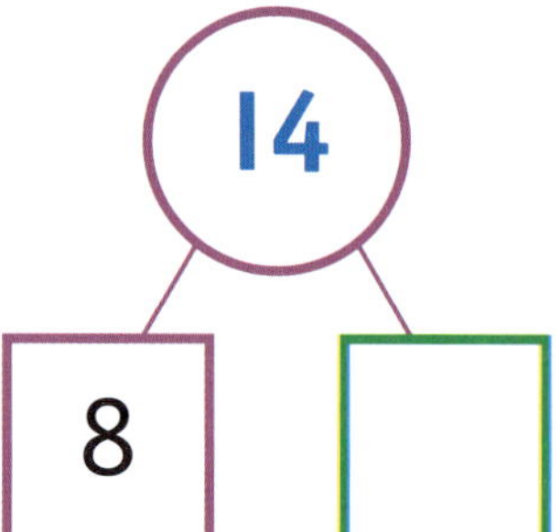

8 + ☐ = 14

14 − ☐ = 8

e

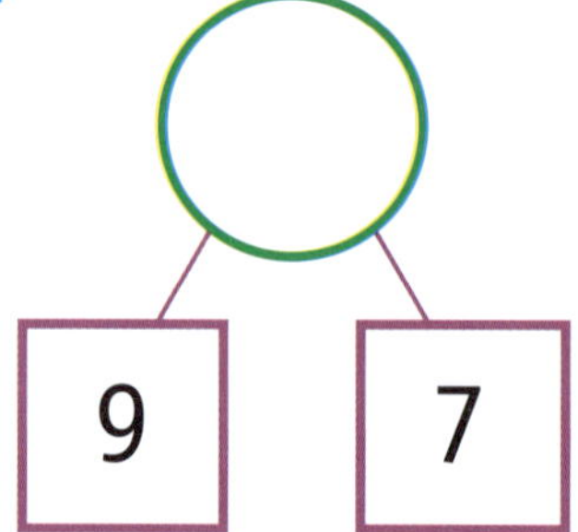

9 + 7 = ☐

☐ − 7 = 9

f

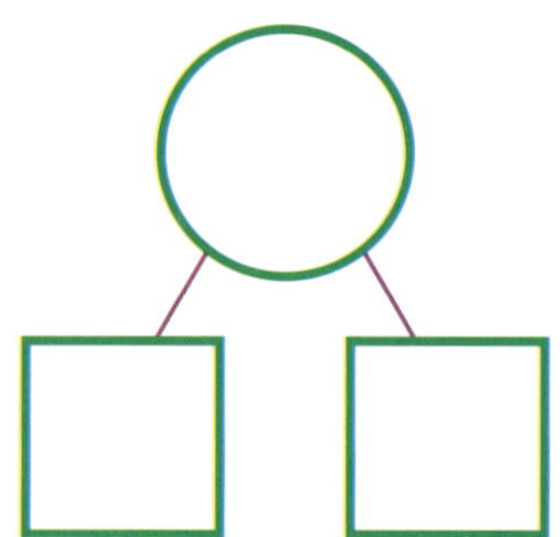

8 + 5 = 13

13 − 5 = 8

Related number sentences

Complete the related number sentences and diagrams.

1 Mei has 12 pencils. 7 are green. The rest are purple. How many are purple?

a 12 − 7 = ☐

b 7 + ☐ = 12

c

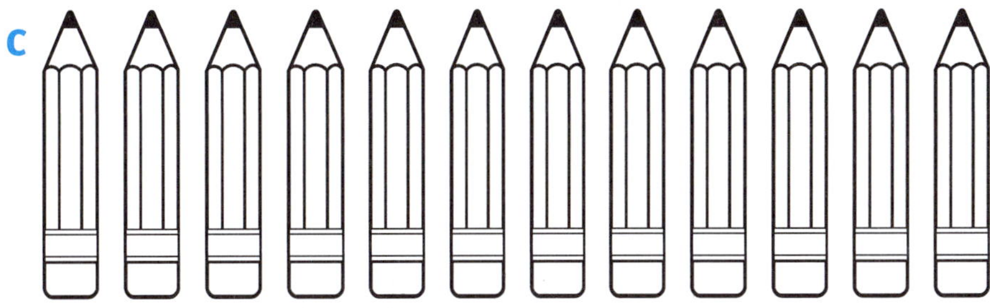

2 Tim made 15 cakes. 8 are strawberry. How many are chocolate?

a 15 − 8 = ☐

b 8 + ☐ = 15

c

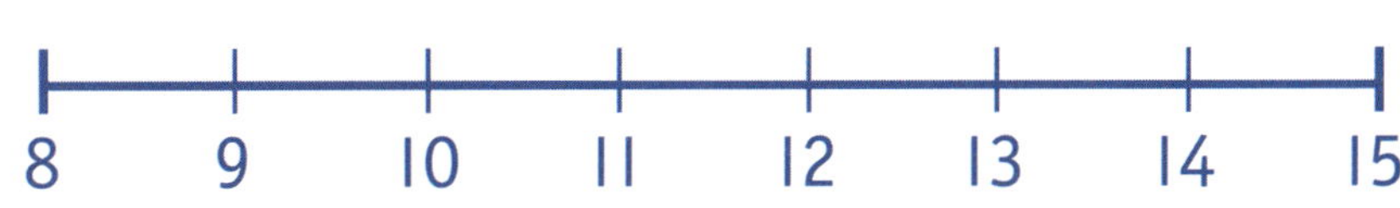

3 Raj owns 14 hats. 9 are caps. How many are beanies?

a 14 − 9 = ☐

b 9 + ☐ = 14

c

4 Maria has $13. She spent $9. How much is left?

a 13 − 9 = ☐

b 9 + ☐ = 13

c Draw a diagram.

Calculator patterns

1 Press 2 + + = Now keep pressing = . Write each number.

2									

2 Press 3 + + = Now keep pressing = . Write each number.

3									

3 Press 10 + + = Now keep pressing = . Write each number.

10									

4 Press 20 + + 5 = Now keep pressing = . Write each number.

20									

5 Press 60 – – 3 = Now keep pressing = . Write each number.

60									

6 Press 100 – – 2 = Now keep pressing = . Write each number.

100									

Mastery Checklist

I can:
- ☐ subtract on a number line.
- ☐ find related addition and subtraction equations.
- ☐ use inverse equations to solve problems.

Problem solving

Mothers' Day Stall

You have $20 to spend. How could you spend all your money?

Check your work by adding.

Challenge! What presents would you like to see at the Mothers' Day Stall? Draw them and write some prices.

I can solve a problem by:

☐ subtracting from 20. ☐ adding to check my answer.

Measuring me

Investigation 2

Clever Dr Watt has discovered that some body lengths are the same. She measured height, arm-span, hand-span, foot length, around her fist and more! But Dr Watt's findings are a secret.

Your challenge: find out which body measurements match.

Do this with a partner. Measure and compare lengths.

measure body lengths

Measure and label

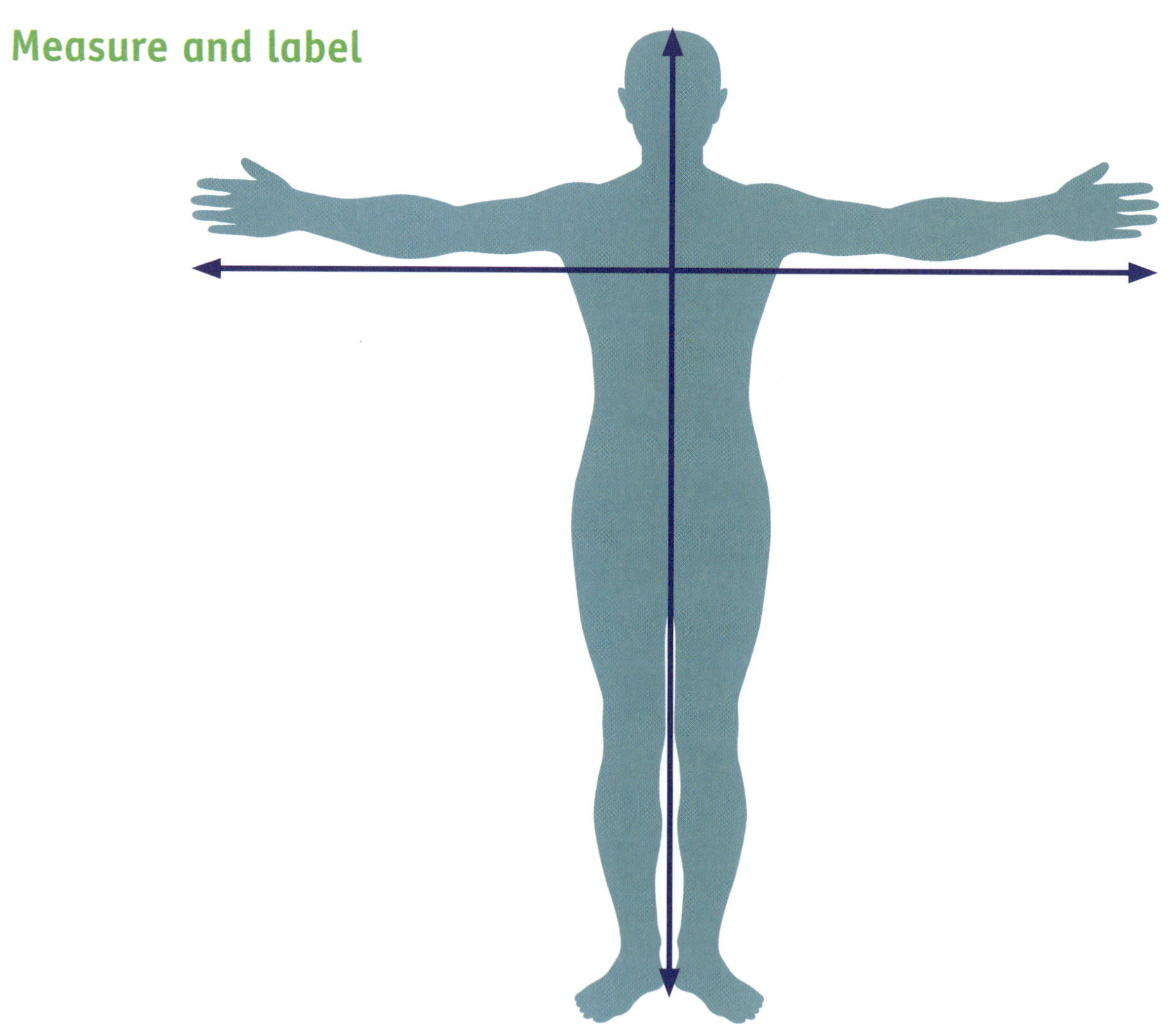

What did you find out?

Measuring me

Investigation 2

Measure and label:

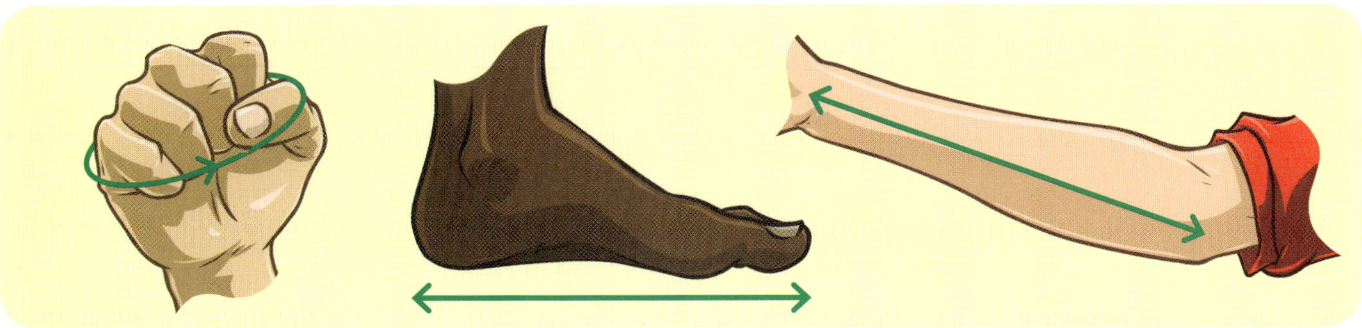

What did you find? ______________________________

How will this help when you buy shoes and socks?

____

Measure and label:

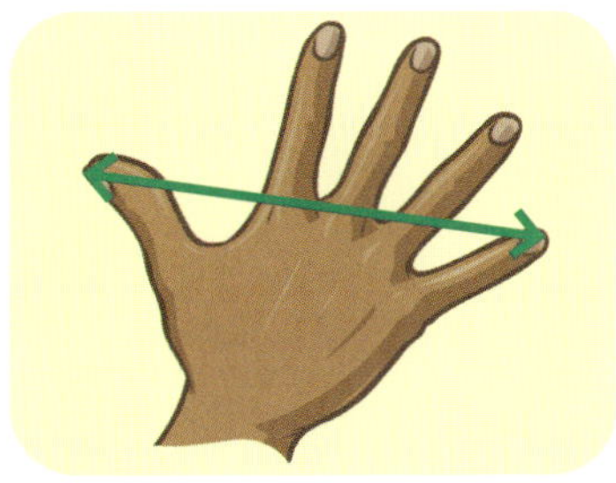

Measure things in your classroom using your hand-span. List them.
Give two ticks to the ones that are easy to measure with a hand-span.

____

____

____

____

To carry out these tasks I need to:

- [ ] measure lengths.
- [ ] measure curved lengths.
- [ ] compare measurements.
- [ ] measure with a hand-span.
- [ ] use the words measure, long, short, longer, shorter, more than, less than.

I enjoyed this task!

☆☆☆☆☆

Revision

1 How long is this python?

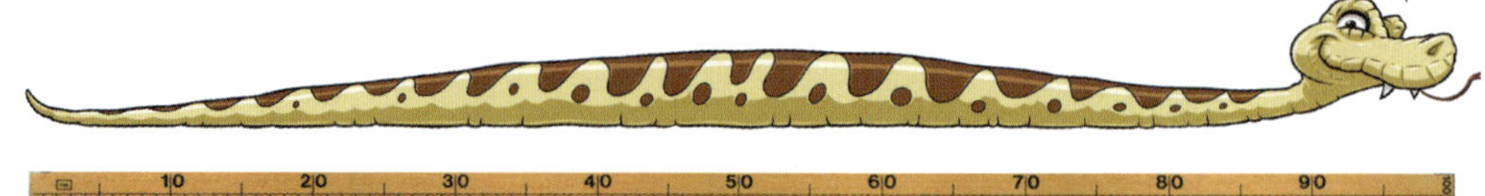

I metre

More than I metre | Less than I metre | About I metre

2 What number sentence did Jodi enter to make this answer?

7 + 12 | 9 + 9 | 11 + 9 | 12 + 6

3 George, Yuen and Will are talking about summer. Which one is correct?

January, February and March are summer months!

George

December, January and February are best because they are summer months.

Yuen

We have summer in October, November and December!

Will

Revision

4 Which one has the largest volume?

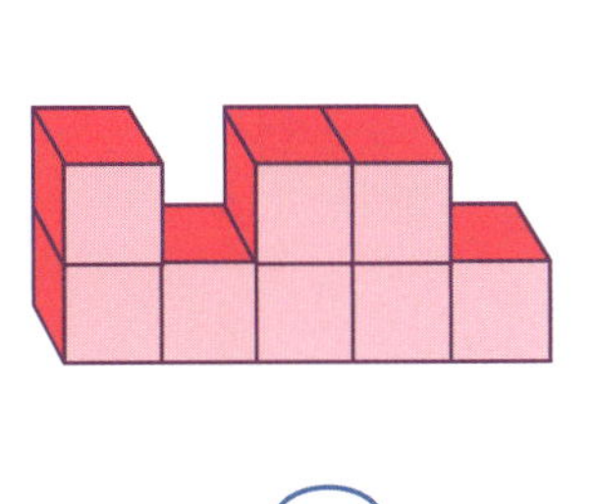
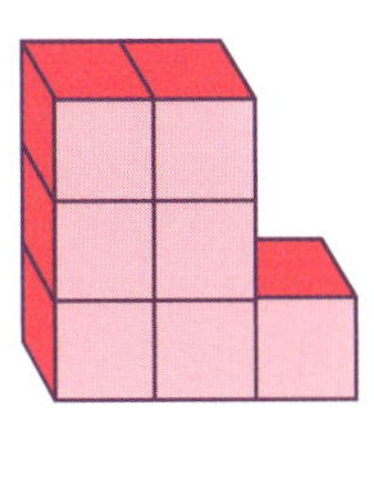
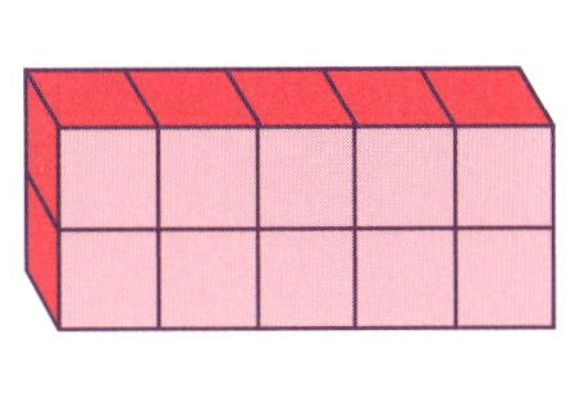
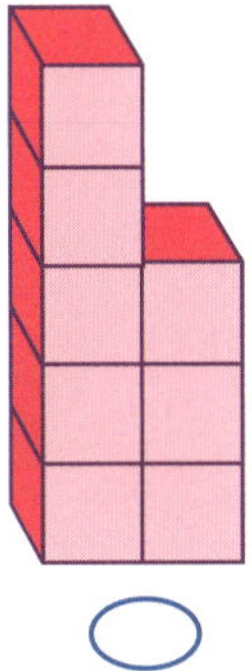

5 Write 4 related number sentences.

Write equations.

☐ + ☐ = ☐ ☐ + ☐ = ☐

☐ − ☐ = ☐ ☐ − ☐ = ☐

6 My pencil case is longer than the book.
The calculator is shorter than the book.
Which is longest?

7 If I subtract 7 from this pile, how many are left?

Write an equation.

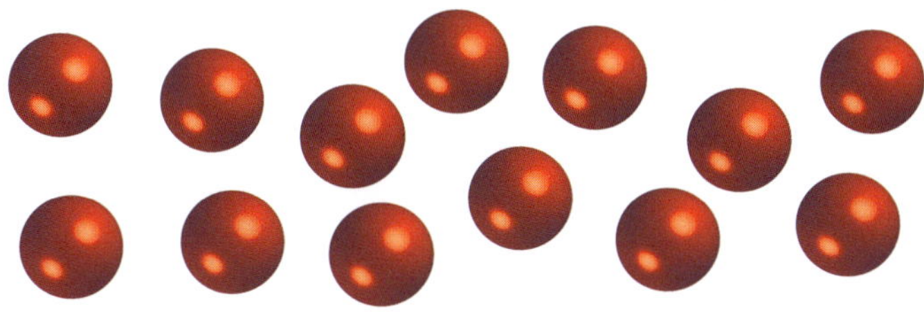

Naming 3D objects

1 Match.

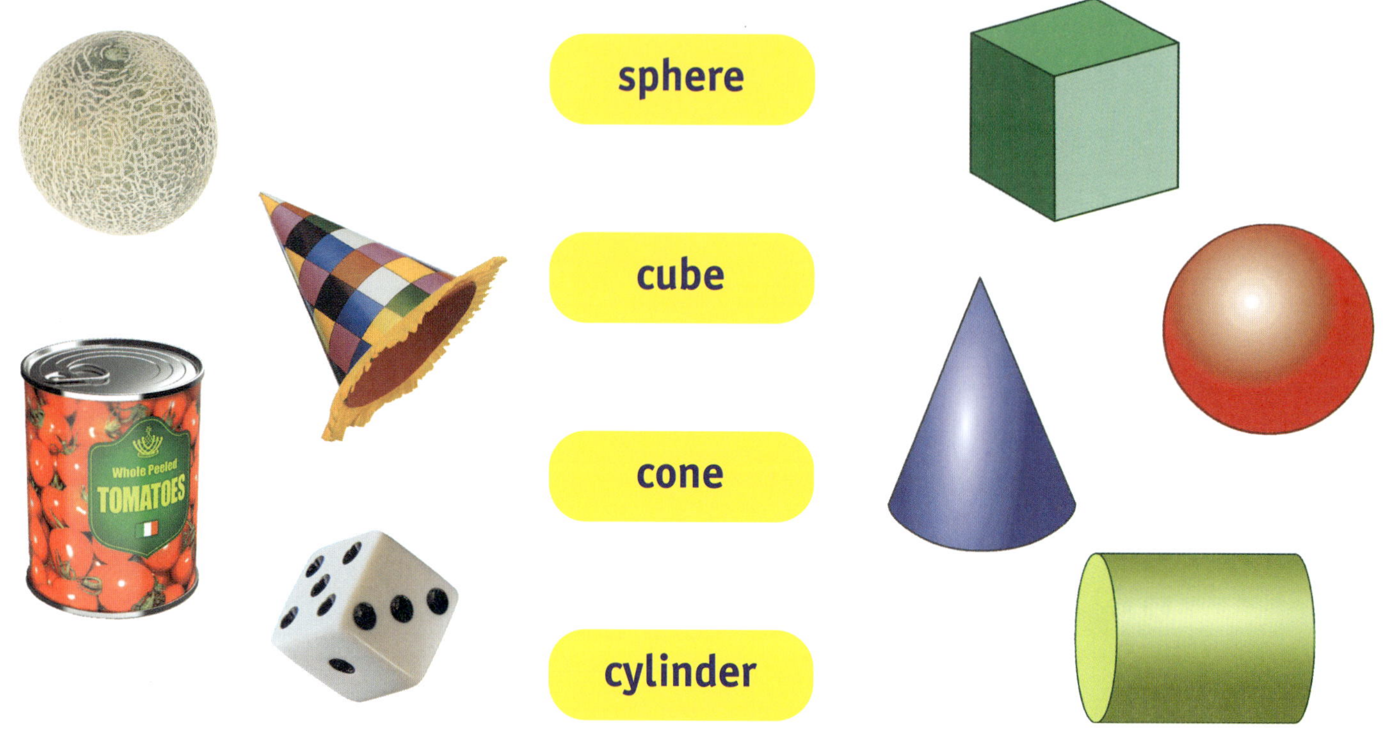

2 How many?

a

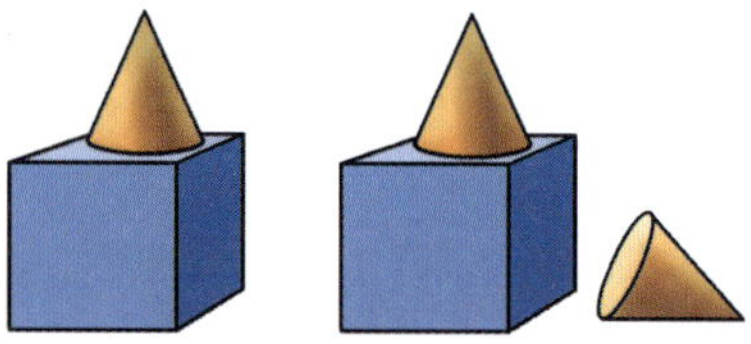

☐ cubes

☐ cones

b

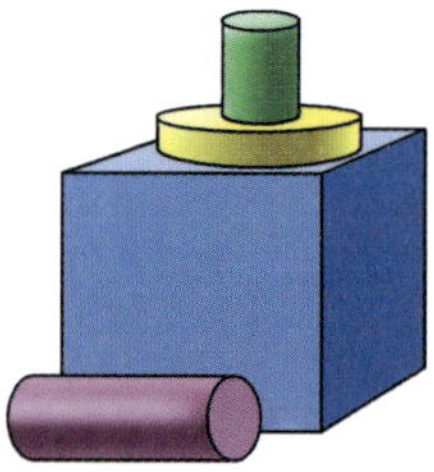

☐ cubes

☐ cylinders

c

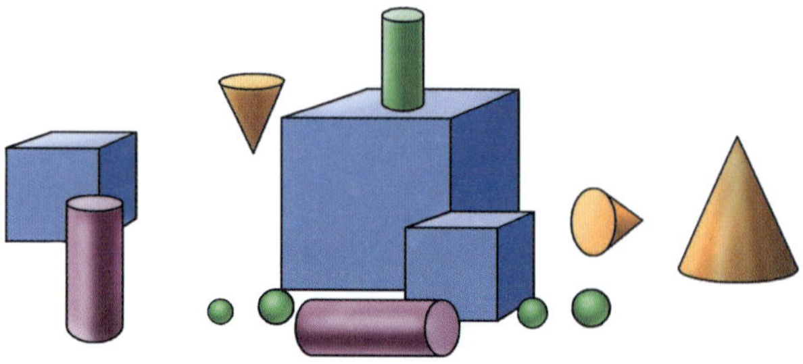

☐ cubes

☐ cylinders

☐ cones

☐ spheres

Challenge!

How many?

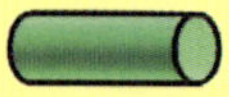

☐

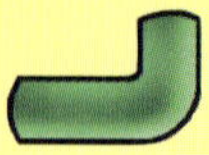

☐

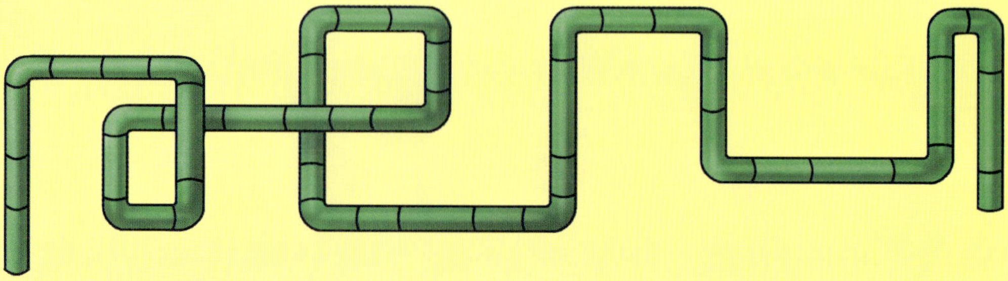

Faces, edges and corners

1 Shapes can have flat faces or curved surfaces. Count the faces.

a

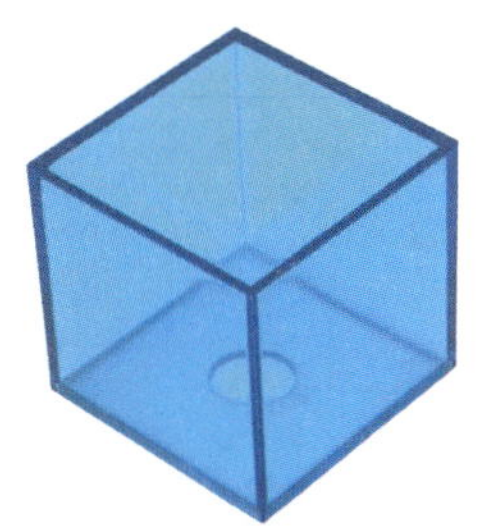

cubes have ☐ faces

b

cones have ☐ faces

c

cylinders have ☐ faces

d

spheres have ☐ faces

2 Vertices are corners. Count the vertices and the edges.

a

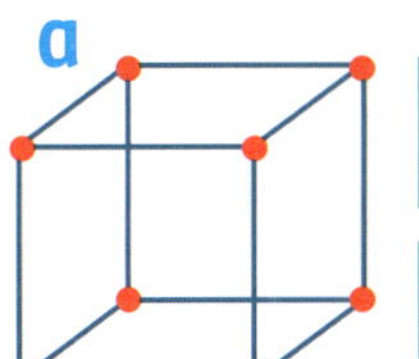

☐ vertices

☐ edges

b

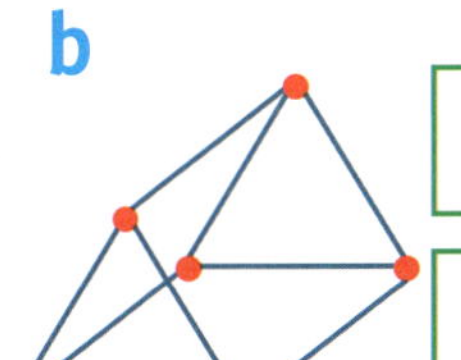

☐ vertices

☐ edges

c

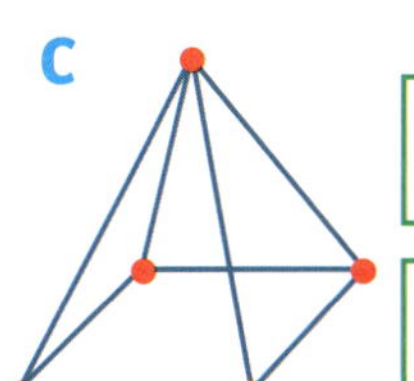

☐ vertices

☐ edges

3 Circle the objects with 6 faces.

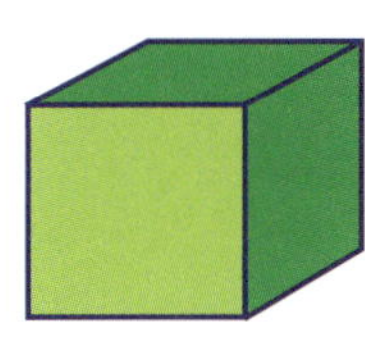

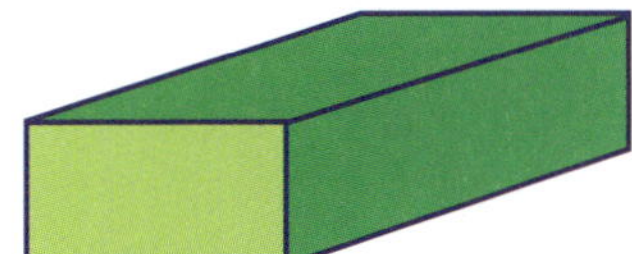

4 What am I? Match.

I have 1 face that is a circle and 1 curved surface.	**cylinder**	**I have 2 faces that are circles and 1 curved surface.**
	cone	
I have 1 curved surface.	**cube**	**I have 6 square faces and 8 vertices.**
	sphere	

Faces of 3D objects

A **face** is a flat surface.

1 Name the shape of the face.

square
circle
rectangle
triangle
hexagon

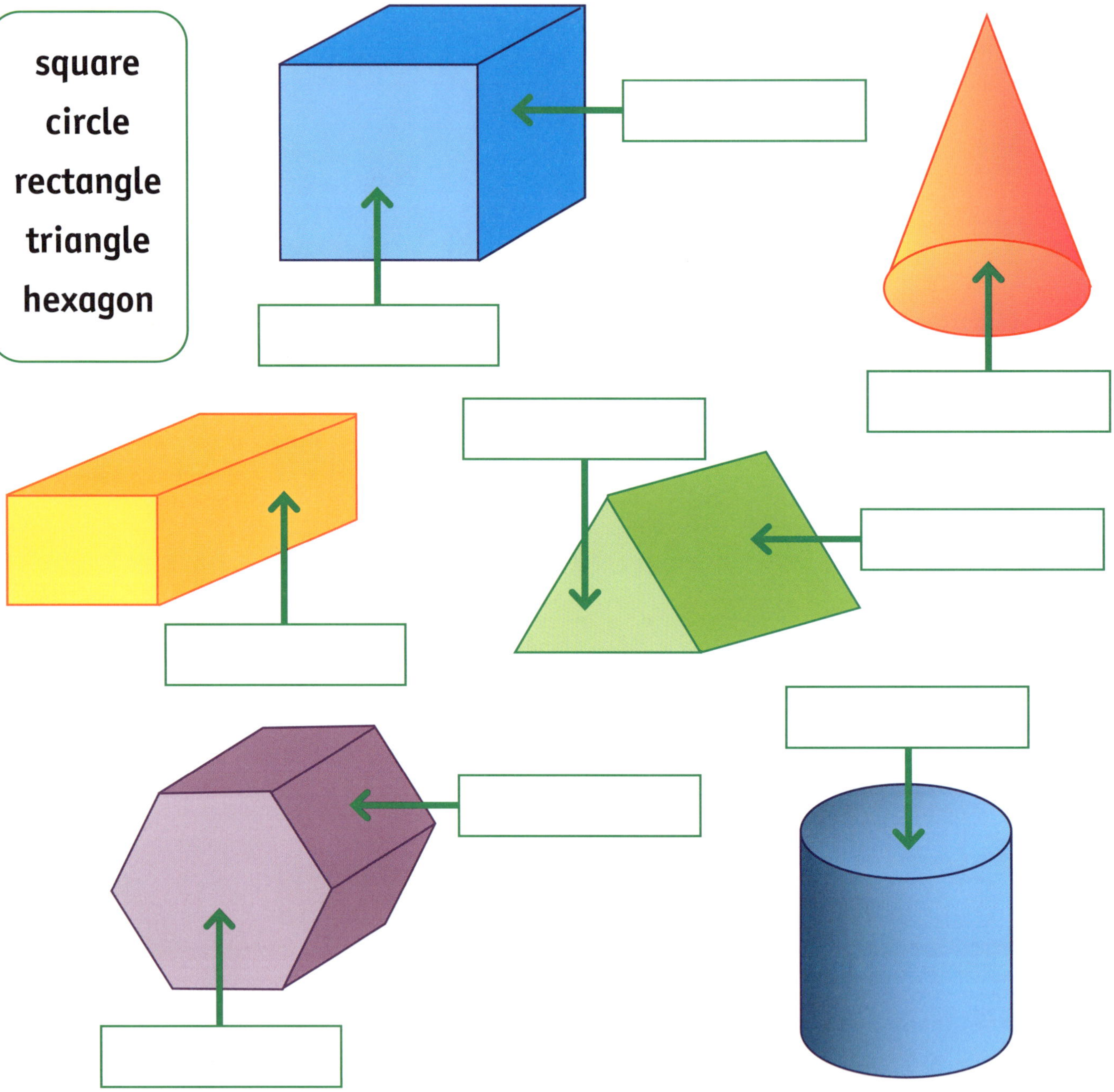

Challenge!

What object could you make out of these faces?

a 6 squares

b 2 triangles and 3 rectangles

Looking at 3D objects

1 Colour the different views.

front → front  side 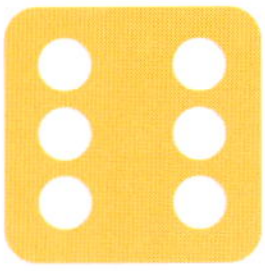 top

a

b

c

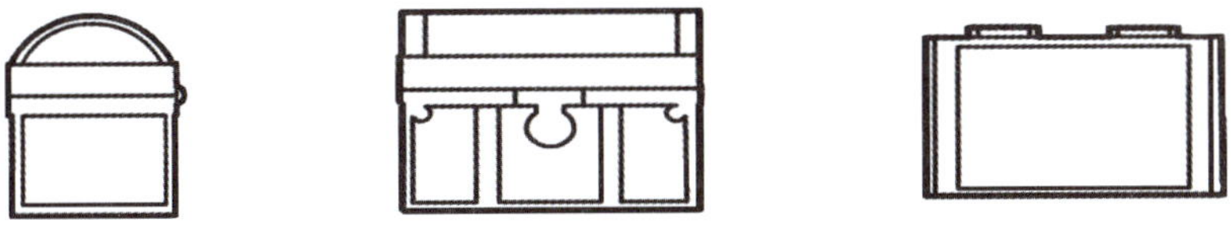

d

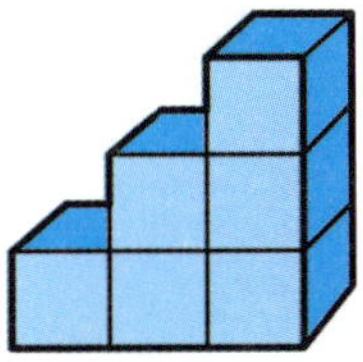

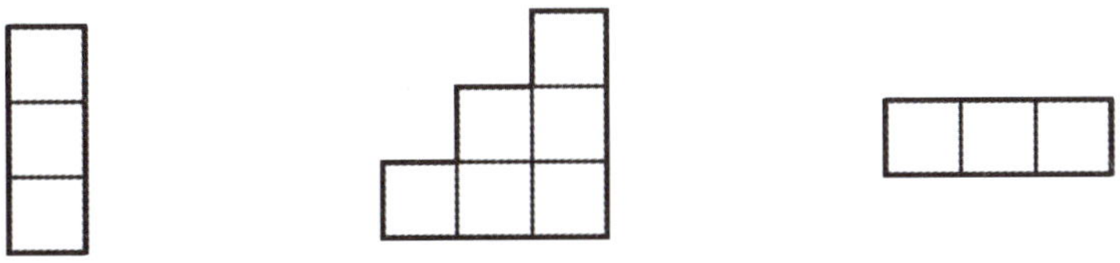

Challenge! Make as many different shapes as you can using 5 cubes. How many are there? ☐

Mastery Checklist

I can: ☐ identify 3D objects.
☐ count and name features of 3D objects.
☐ name flat surfaces of 3D objects as 2D shapes.
☐ identify different views of 3D objects.

Problem solving

3D models

1 Can you make a skeleton model of these 3D objects using just matchsticks and plasticine?

a cube b cylinder c square pyramid
d cone e triangular prism f rectangular prism

build 3D models

2 Draw the models you can make.

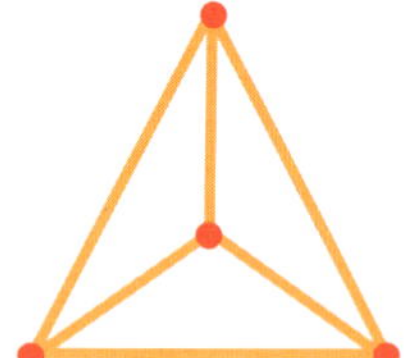

3 Which 3D objects **cannot** be made with matchsticks and plasticine?

____

4 Why? ____

____

____

I can solve problems by:

☐ knowing the features of 3D objects. ☐ building a model.

AC9M2SP01 Space **MA1-WM-01** Working mathematically • Apply mathematical techniques to solve problems • Communicate their thinking and reasoning coherently and clearly
MA1-3DS-01 Three-dimensional spatial structure B • 3D objects: Describe the features of three-dimensional objects

Counting by fives

1 Count in fives.

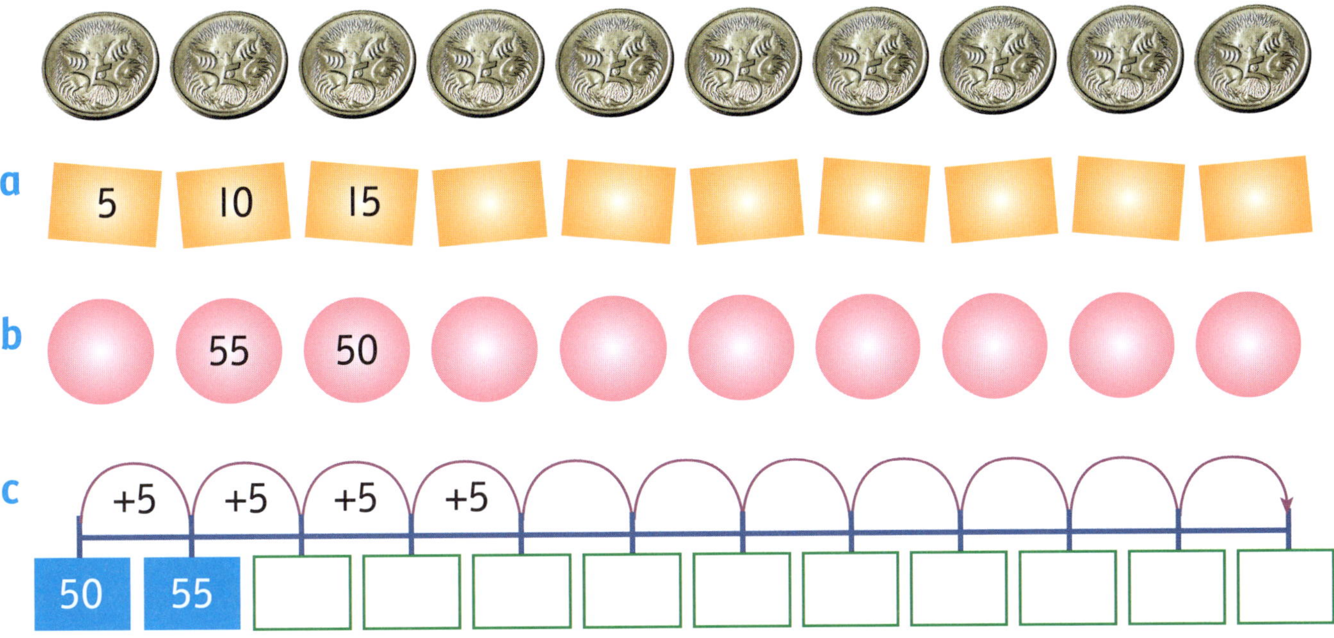

2 Write the new price.

a 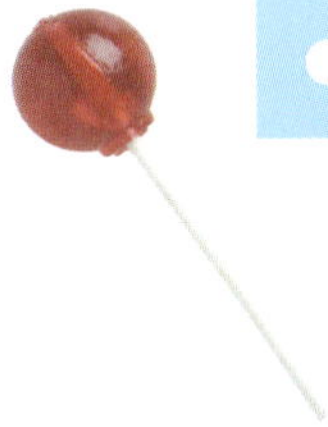 25c 5c off

b 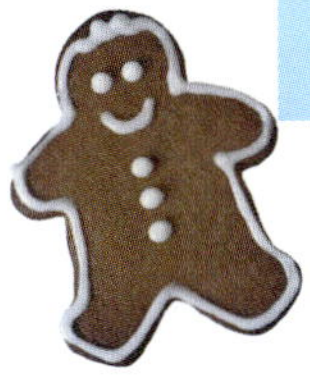 15c 5c off

c 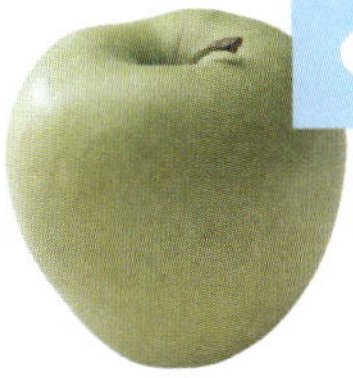 30c 5c off

d 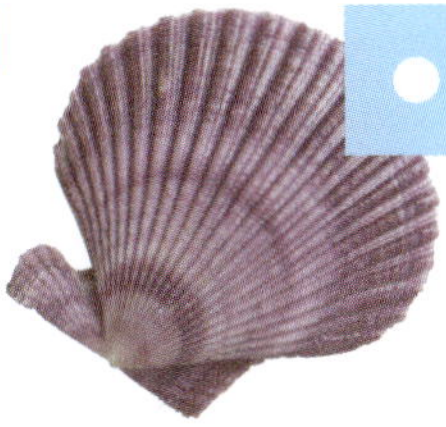 50c 5c off

e 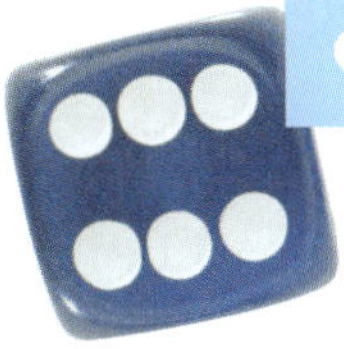 60c 10c off

f 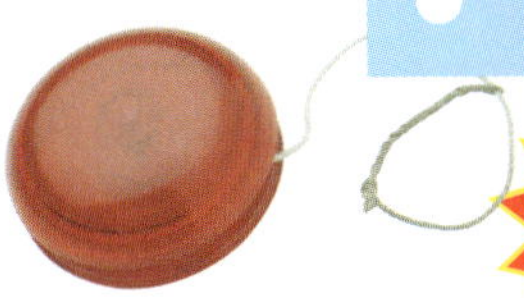 75c 10c off

g 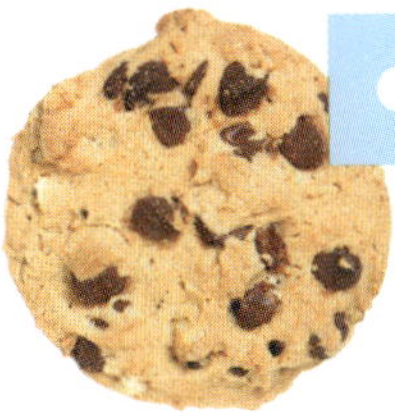 45c 10c off

h 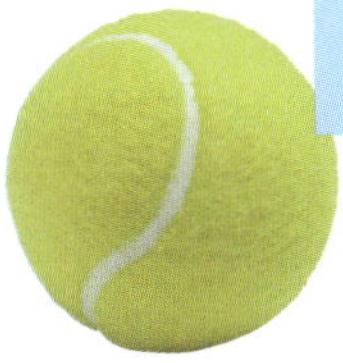 $1 10c off

Multiplication as repeated addition

1

2 + 2 + 2 = ☐

☐ twos are ☐

2

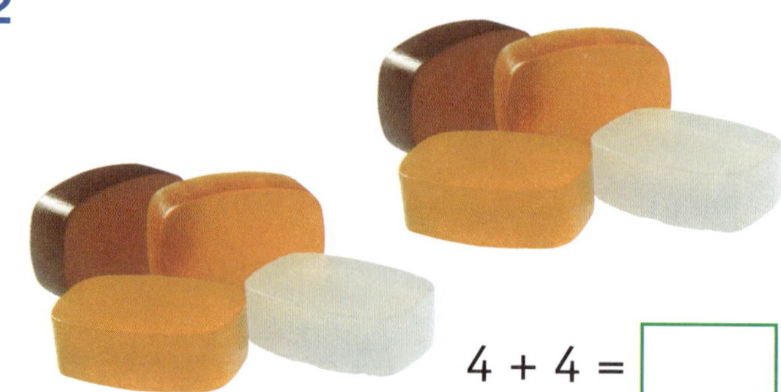

4 + 4 = ☐

☐ fours are ☐

3

3 + 3 + 3 + 3 = ☐

☐ threes are ☐

4

5 + 5 + 5 = ☐

☐ fives are ☐

5

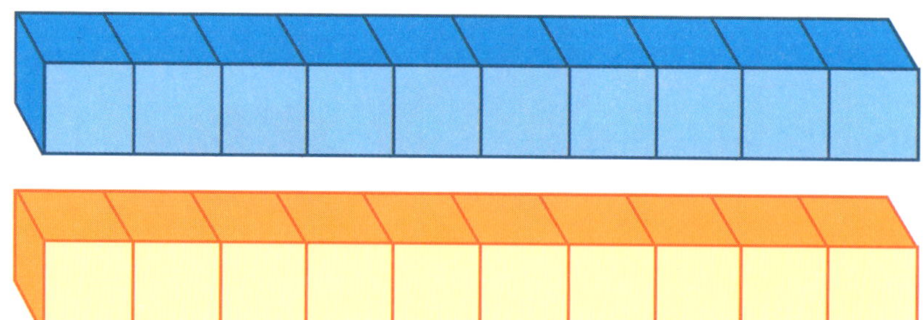

10 + 10 = ☐

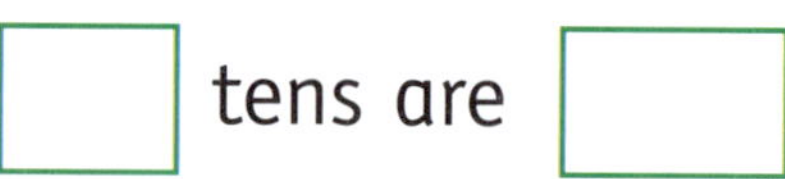

☐ tens are ☐

use counters to model equal groups

6 Use counters to help you.

a 5 twos are ☐ 

b 3 threes are ☐ 

c 3 fours are ☐ 

d 5 fives are ☐ 

e 5 threes are ☐ 

f 8 twos are ☐

g 4 twos are ☐ 

h 4 threes are ☐ 

i 4 fives are ☐ 

The multiplication sign

× is the sign that tells us to multiply

1

4 groups of two are ☐

$4 \times 2 =$ ☐

2

3 groups of three are ☐

$3 \times 3 =$ ☐

3

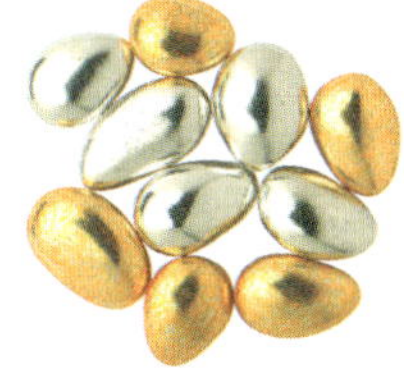

2 groups of ten are ☐

$2 \times 10 =$ ☐

4

3 groups of fives are ☐

$3 \times 5 =$ ☐

5

3 groups of four are ☐

$3 \times 4 =$ ☐

6

4 groups of ten are ☐

$4 \times 10 =$ ☐

7

5 groups of three are ☐

$5 \times 3 =$ ☐

8

2 rows of five are ☐

$2 \times 5 =$ ☐

9

2 rows of six are ☐

$6 \times 2 =$ ☐

Draw a diagram

6 bowls with 2 fish in each bowl.
1 bowl with 5 fish.

How many fish altogether? ☐

Multiplying by ten

1 a

$3 \times 10c =$ ☐ c

b

$5 \times 10c =$ ☐ c

c

$4 \times 10c =$ ☐ c

d

$7 \times 10c =$ ☐ c

e

$6 \times 10c =$ ☐ c

f

$8 \times 10c =$ ☐ c

g

$10 \times 10c =$ ☐ c

h

$9 \times 10c =$ ☐ c

2 a $10 \times 2 =$ ______ b $10 \times 5 =$ ______ c $10 \times 3 =$ ______

d $10 \times 4 =$ ______ e $10 \times 1 =$ ______ f $10 \times 0 =$ ______

g $10 \times 7 =$ ______ h $10 \times 9 =$ ______ i $10 \times 8 =$ ______

Challenge!

a In each question, how much more to make $1?

b How much money is there altogether? ☐

Patterns on the number line

1 Make equal jumps along the number line.
Write the numbers you land on.

a

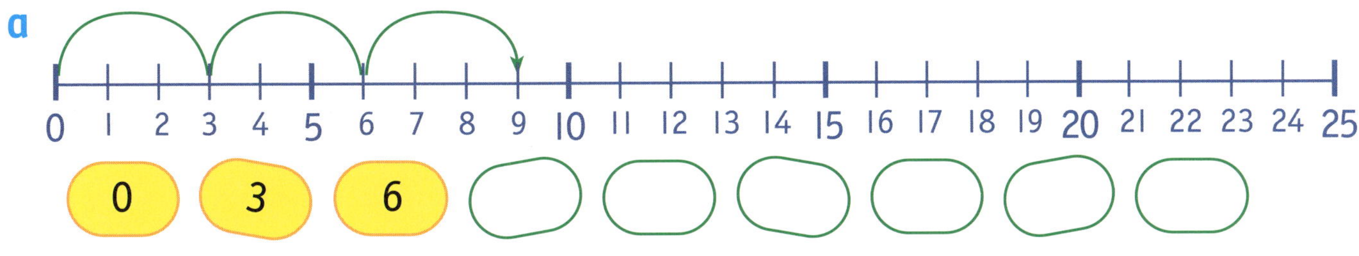

The rule is ______________ .

b

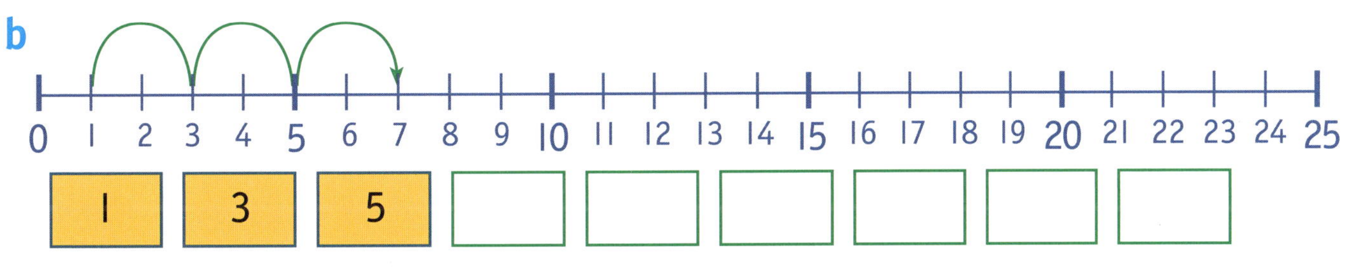

The rule is ______________ .

c

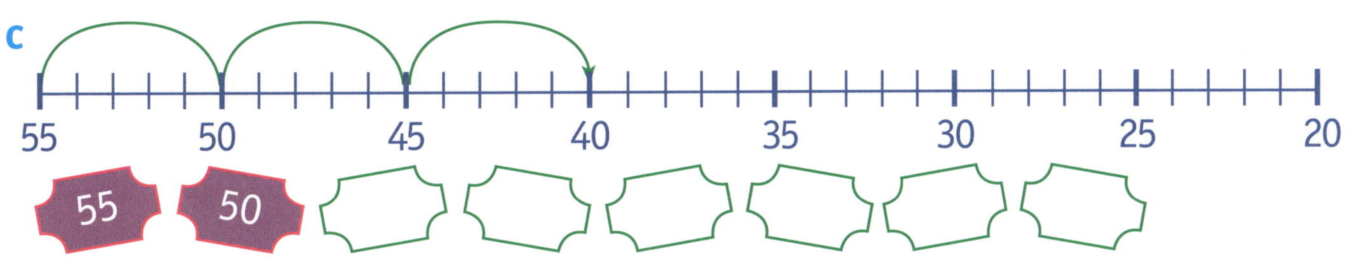

The rule is ______________ .

d

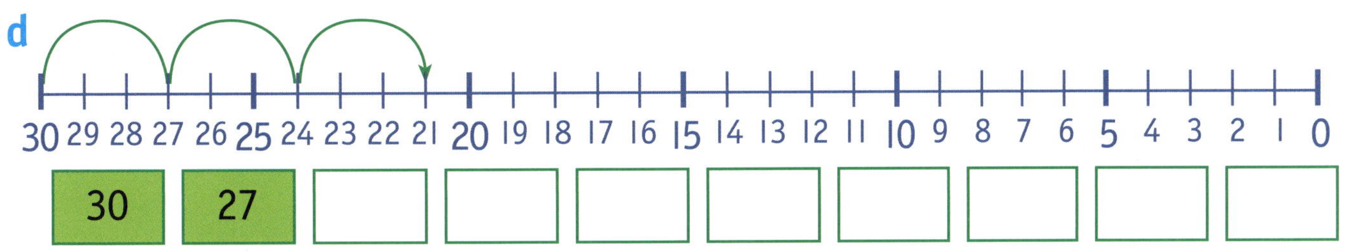

The rule is ______________ .

Looking for patterns

Keep counting by 5.

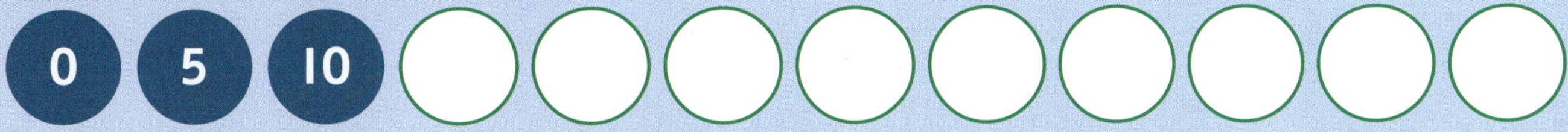

When I count in fives from zero, the numbers end in ☐ or ☐ .

Counting in 2s, 3s and 5s

1 Continue each counting pattern.

a 2 4 6 8

b 5 10 15 20

c 22 24 26

d 0 3 6

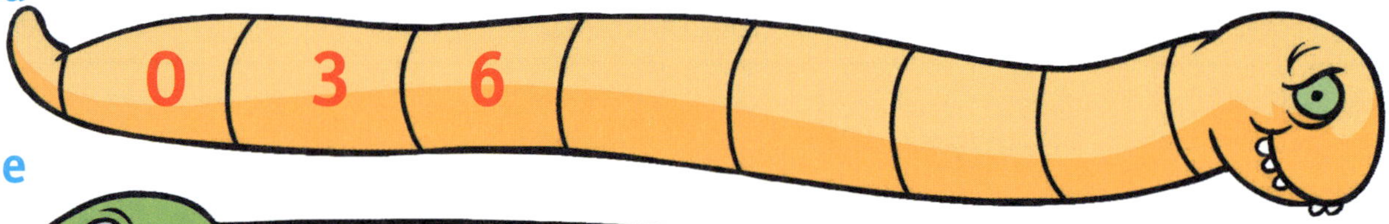

e 25 30 35 40

f 12 15 18

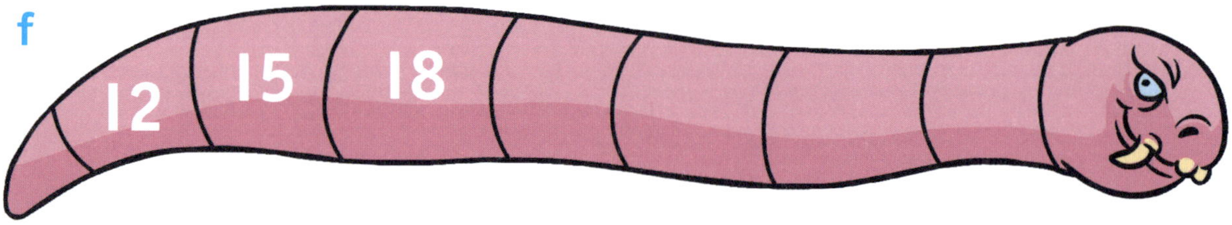

Looking for patterns

Describe each pattern. Write +2, +3 or +5 in the box.

Mastery Checklist

I can:
- ☐ count forwards and backwards by 5s, 10s, 3s, 2s.
- ☐ use repeated addition to find a total of equal groups.
- ☐ write a multiplication equation for a total of equal groups.
- ☐ solve multiplication problems.

Multiplication Problems

Draw a picture to help you.

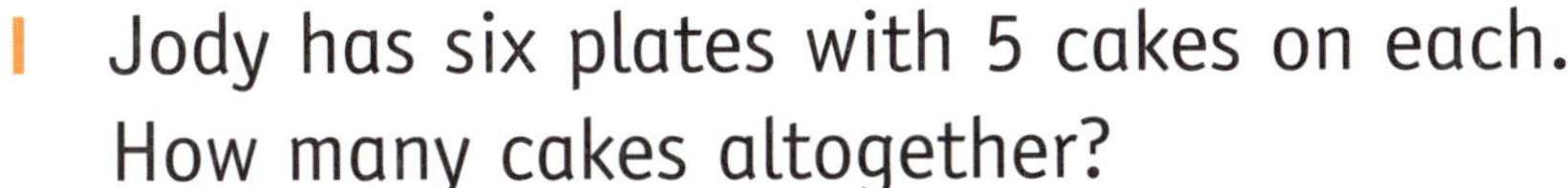

1 Jody has six plates with 5 cakes on each.
How many cakes altogether?

☐ cakes

2 Josh puts bugs in his pockets.
He has 4 pockets in his pants,
3 in his shirt and one in his backpack.
He puts 3 bugs in every pocket.
How many bugs altogether?

☐ bugs

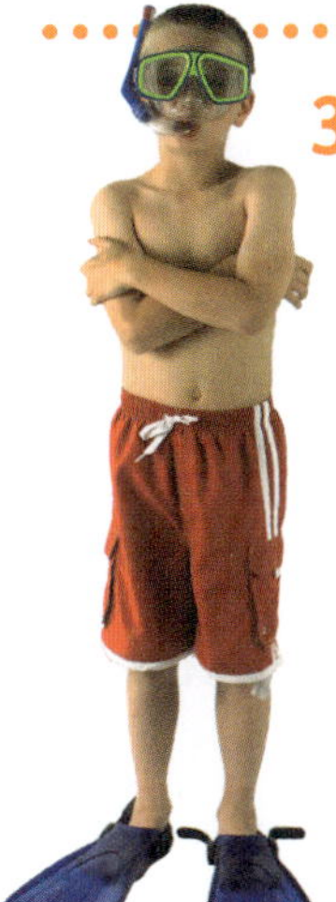

3 On days that start with T,
Lee swims 4 laps of the pool.
How many laps does he swim
in two weeks?

☐ laps

I can solve a problem by:
☐ multiplying. ☐ drawing a picture or diagram.

Data and graphing

Tally marks
卌 = 5

1 Every child in 2A coloured a shirt their favourite colour.
How many?

Colour	Tally	Total
green		
red		
blue		
pink		
yellow		
black		

2 Colour a block for each child.

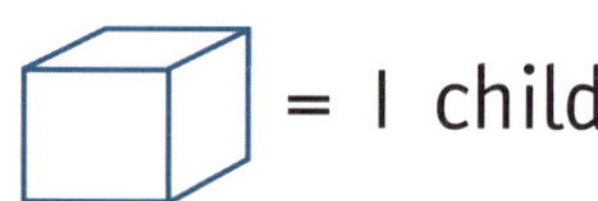

2A's favourite shirt colour

3 Which colour was:

a most popular? ____________ b least popular? ____________

4 How many children are in 2A? ________

Tally table

1 Where do people go for their holidays? Here is a tally of one group's answers. Make it into a graph.

Places People Visit

Cities ||||
Mountains 𝍸 |
Farms |||
Overseas ||
Beaches 𝍸 ||

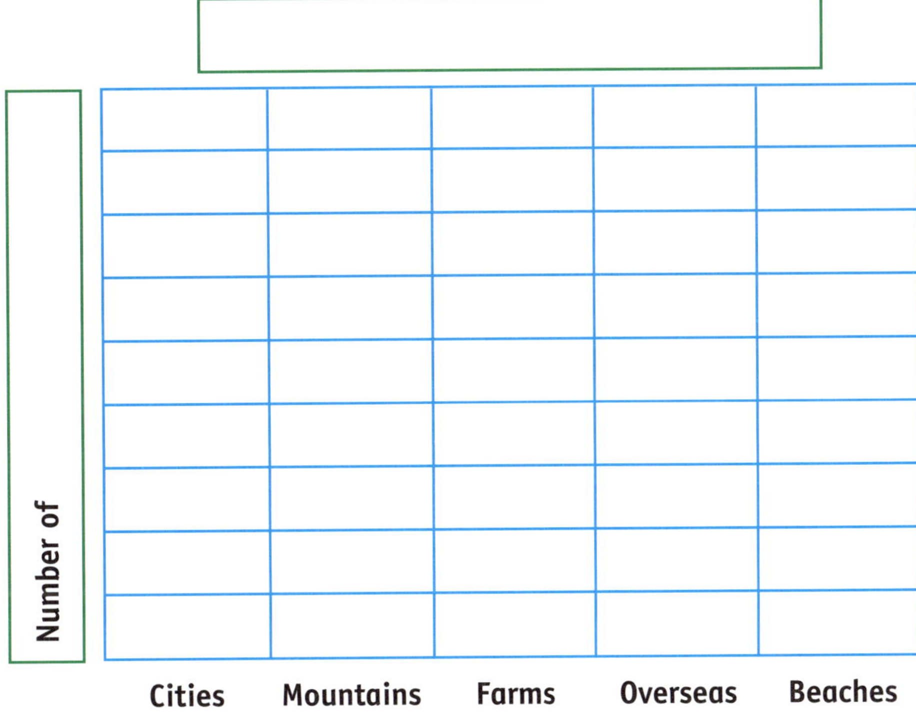

2 What question would you like to ask your class?

List the possible answers.

3 Survey your class and fill in this tally table.

survey the class

Answers	Tallies	Totals

Problem solving

Missing Data

1 Flick the dog chewed this graph. He ate some of it.

What is missing on the graph? What do you think the graph is about?

2 Redraw this graph with the missing parts filled in.

I can solve a problem by:

☐ identifying the features of a graph. ☐ drawing a graph.

AAC9M2ST02 Statistics **MA1-WM-01** Working mathematically • Apply mathematical techniques to solve problems • Communicate their thinking and reasoning coherently and clearly **MA1-DATA-01** • **MA1-DATA-02** Data B • Identify a question of interest and gather relevant data • Create displays of data and interpret them

More or less likely

In each pair, label one event **more likely** and the other **less likely**.

1 a

b

2 a

b

3 a

b

Chance

Use one of these to describe each event.

impossible | **unlikely** | **uncertain**

possible | **likely** | **very likely** | **certain**

Today

you blow up balloons

[ ]

your hair grows

[ ]

you walk up stairs

[ ]

This week at school

your class goes swimming

[ ]

you sing a song

[ ]

your teacher grows green hair

[ ]

This weekend

you move house

[ ]

you walk your dog

[ ]

it rains

[ ]

Challenge! Write or draw your own events to match the labels.

impossible | **likely** | **unlikely** | **certain**

Chance

1 Join each sentence to the right place on the line.

a unlikely — likely — very likely

Today

You go home on a bus. | You read a 200 page book. | You watch TV. | You eat lunch.

b impossible — certain

Tomorrow

There are clouds in the sky. | The sky is green. | The sun rises. | You sleep until 8 o'clock.

c You flip a 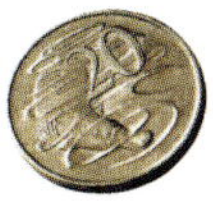 coin. What is the chance of the coin:

impossible — even chance — certain

landing on heads. | landing on its thin edge. | landing on tails. | landing on either heads or tails.

2 Write your own sentences.

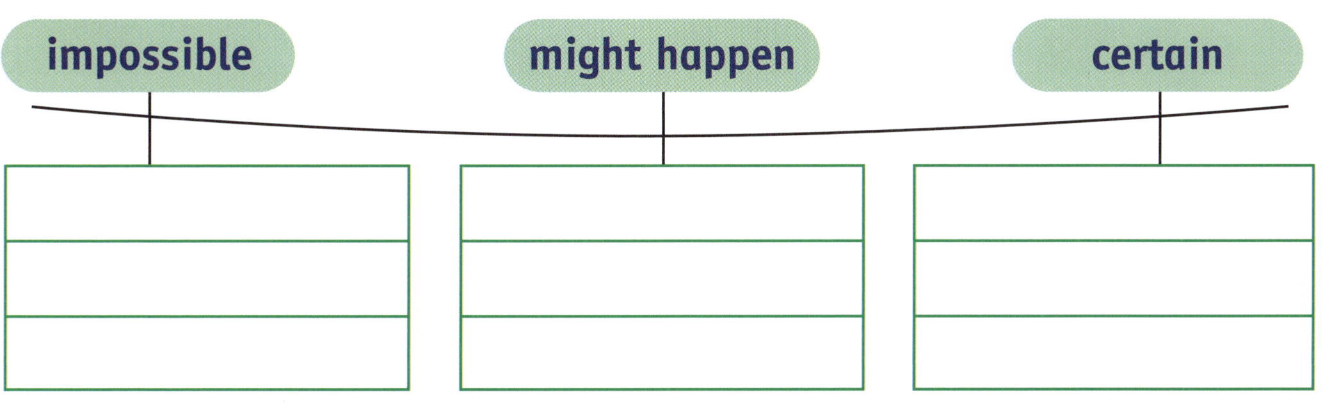

Position

1 Draw what is:

a above

b below

c next to

d below

e beside

f under

2 Draw:

a a fish under the starfish.

b a tree next to the leaf.

c a bird above the ladybird.

d a worm beside the spider.

3 Draw what is to the left and right.

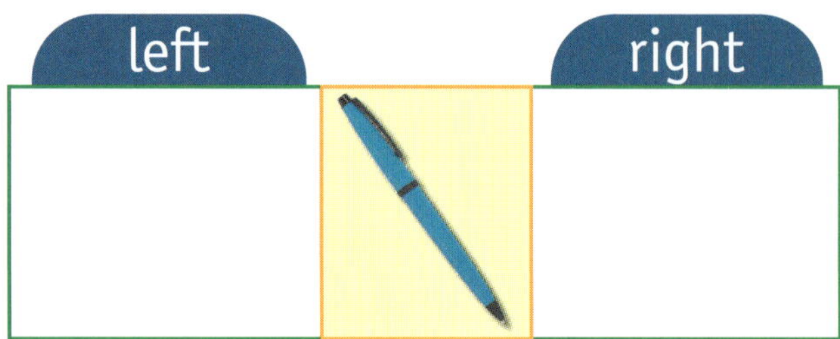

4 Do you write with your right or left hand?

Following directions

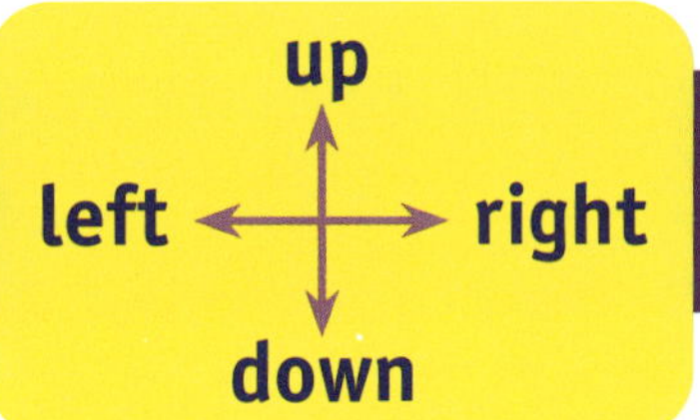

1 Follow the directions. Start at ☺.

Move:
up 3
left 2
up 4
right 5
down 2
right 2
up 4
left 3

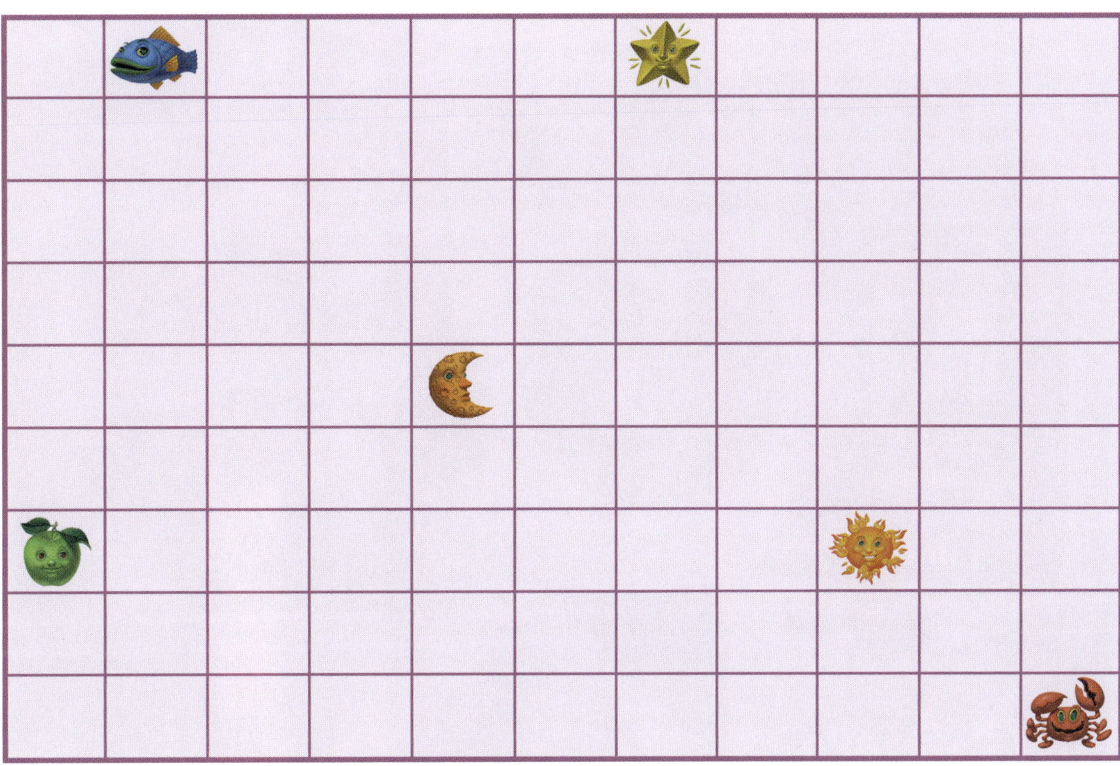

Where did you end up?

____

2 Draw your own path. Write the directions.

____
____
____
____
____
____
____
____
____
____

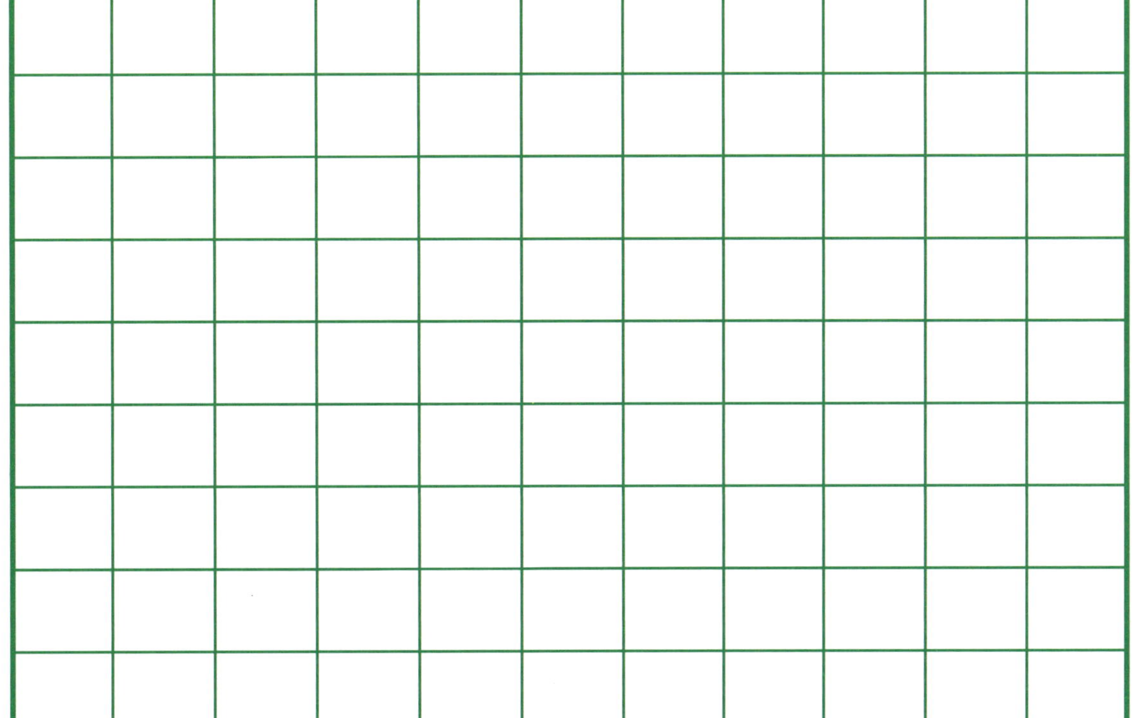

Drawing paths

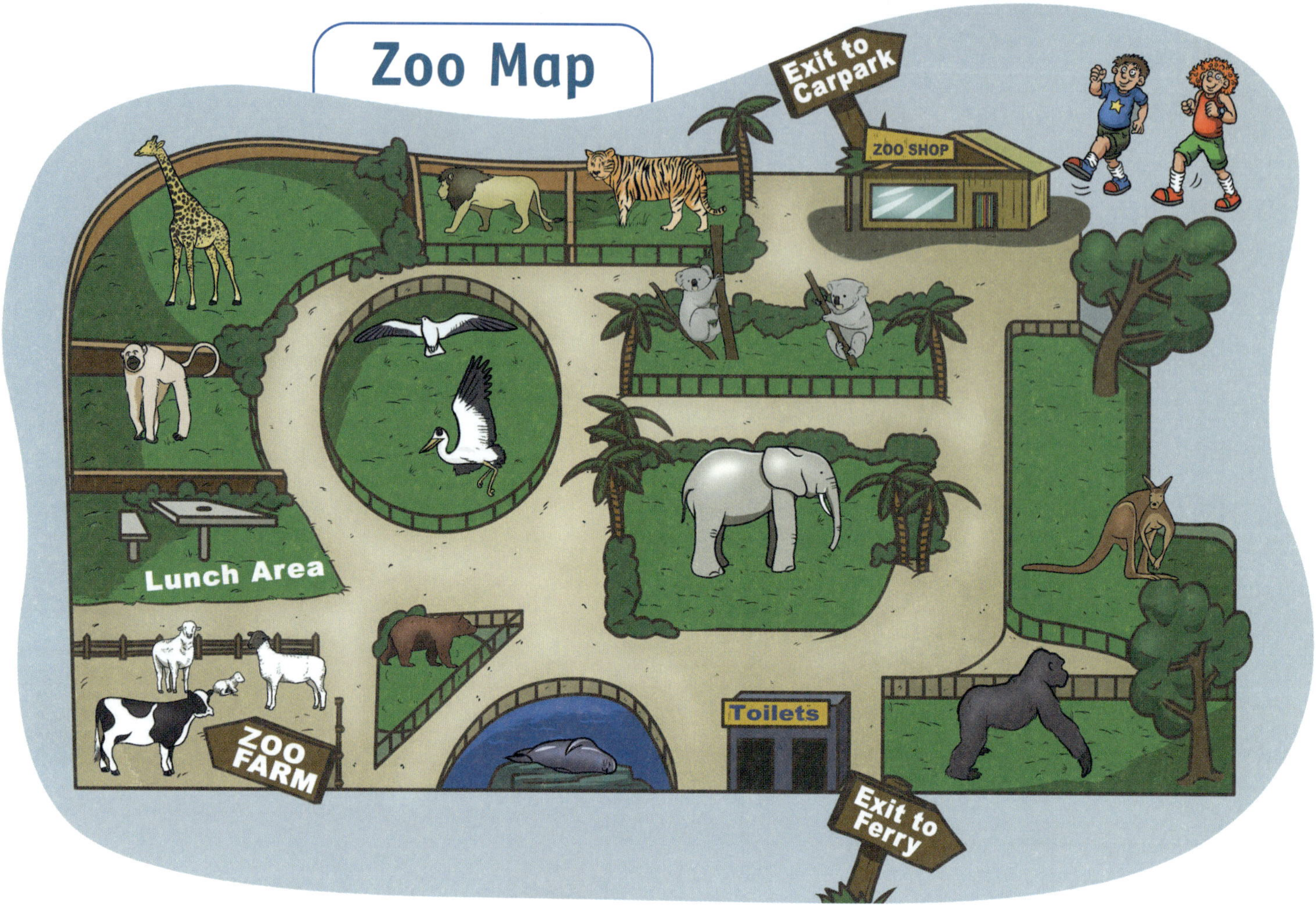

Zoo Map

Draw Katy's path in red. Draw Paul's path in blue.

1 Katy wants to see the elephants, lions and giraffes. Then she will stop for lunch.

2 Paul wants to see the birds, kangaroos and bears. Then he will stop for lunch.

3 After lunch, Katy wants to see the bears and the koalas. Then she will look in the shop before going home by car.

4 After lunch, Paul wants to see the farm and the seals. Then he will go to the toilet before going home by ferry.

Challenge!

What animals would you like to see? Draw your own path in green. Write where you went.

Mastery Checklist

I can:

- [ ] organise data and make a graph.
- [ ] describe the chance of an event happening.
- [ ] describe position.
- [ ] write and follow directions.

Problem solving

School map

1 Draw a simple map of your school below.

2 Mark the path from your classroom to the office on the map.

3 Write directions.

I can solve a problem by:

☐ knowing the features of a place. ☐ drawing a map.

Revision • Term 2

1

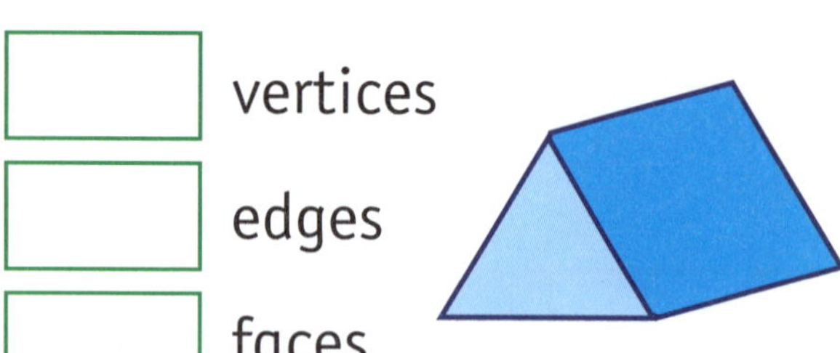

2 a $3 + 8 + 7 =$ ☐

b $5 + 9 + 15 =$ ☐

c $12 + 13 + 8 =$ ☐

3 How many more to make 20?

a

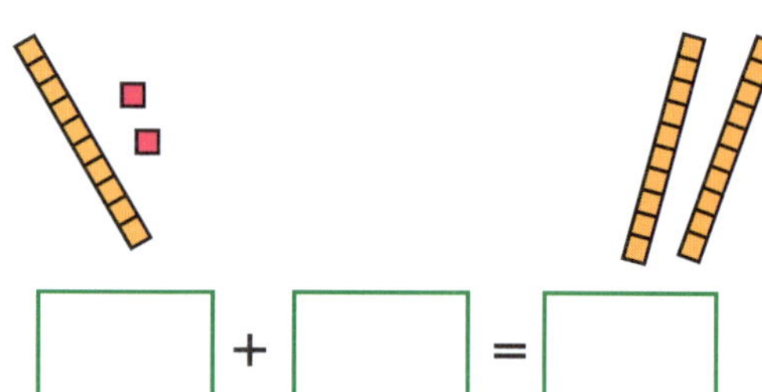

☐ + ☐ = ☐

b How much more to make $20?

☐

4 Take away.

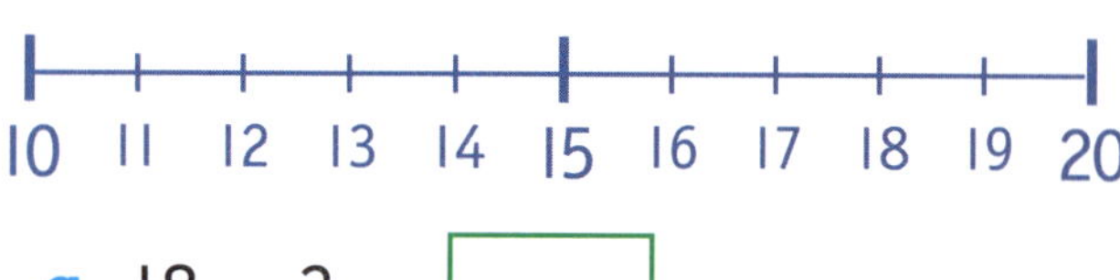

a $18 - 3 =$ ☐

b $15 - 4 =$ ☐

c $19 - 6 =$ ☐

5 How much change from $20?

a

b

6 a

$4 + 4 =$ ☐

☐ fours are ☐

b

3 threes are ☐

$3 \times 3 =$ ☐

c

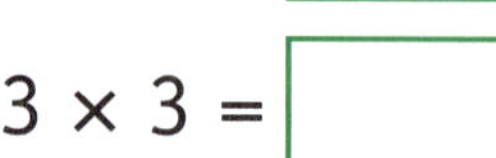

$4 \times 10c =$ ☐ c

7 Colour to make symmetrical.

8 Colour the face that is a rectangle.

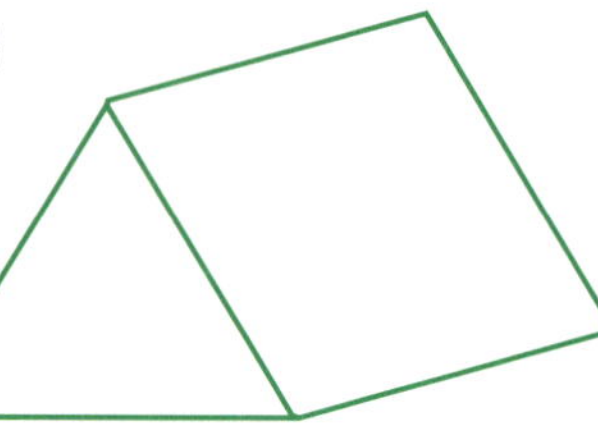

9 Continue each pattern.

a 5, 10, 15, ☐, ☐

b 2, 4, 6, ☐, ☐

c 3, 6, 9, ☐, ☐

10

a Draw what is below .

☐

b Draw a leaf above the moon.

c Start at the star.

Move up 2 then left 1.

Draw a ✗ where you land.

11 What is the top view?

☐ circle

☐ square

☐ rectangle

12 Match.

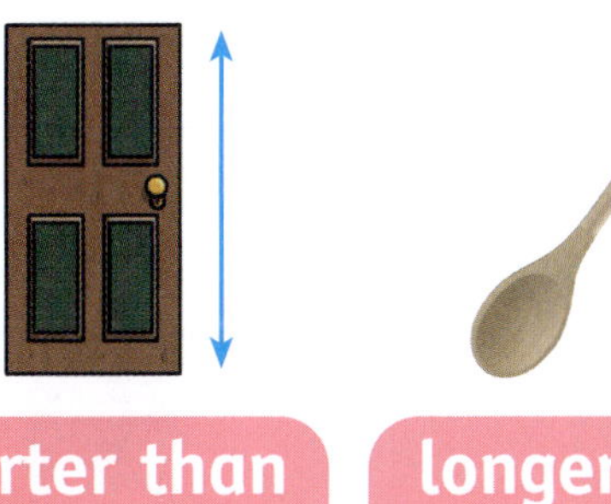

shorter than 1 metre

longer than 1 metre

13

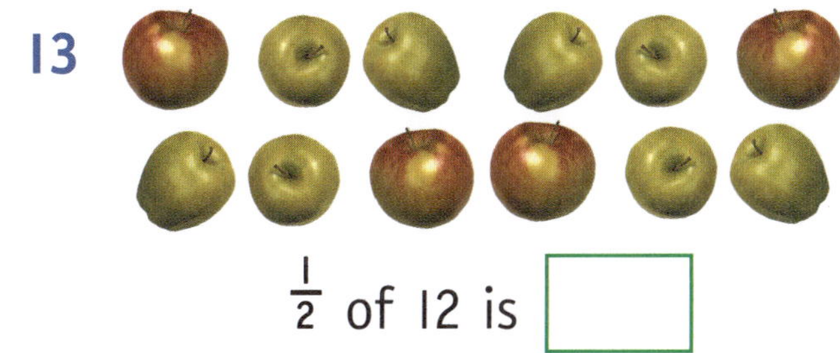

$\frac{1}{2}$ of 12 is ☐

14 Join to the right spot on the line.

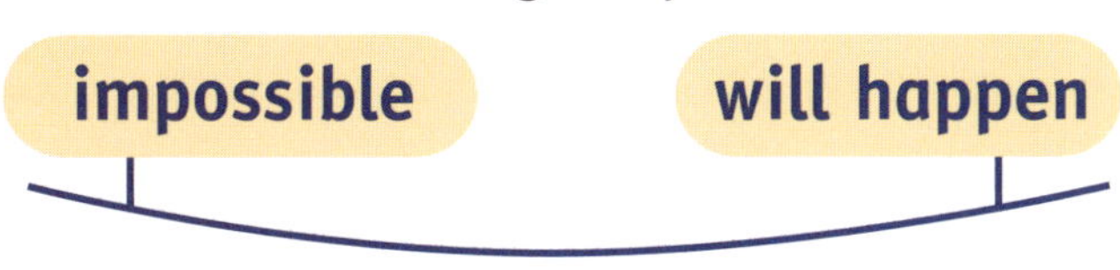

A coin lands on heads.

15 Make a tally.

Colour	Tally	Total
orange		
blue		

16 Continue each pattern.

a 16, 14, 12, ☐ ☐ ☐

b 55, 45, 40, ☐ ☐ ☐

Number lines to 1000

1 Write the next 5 numbers.

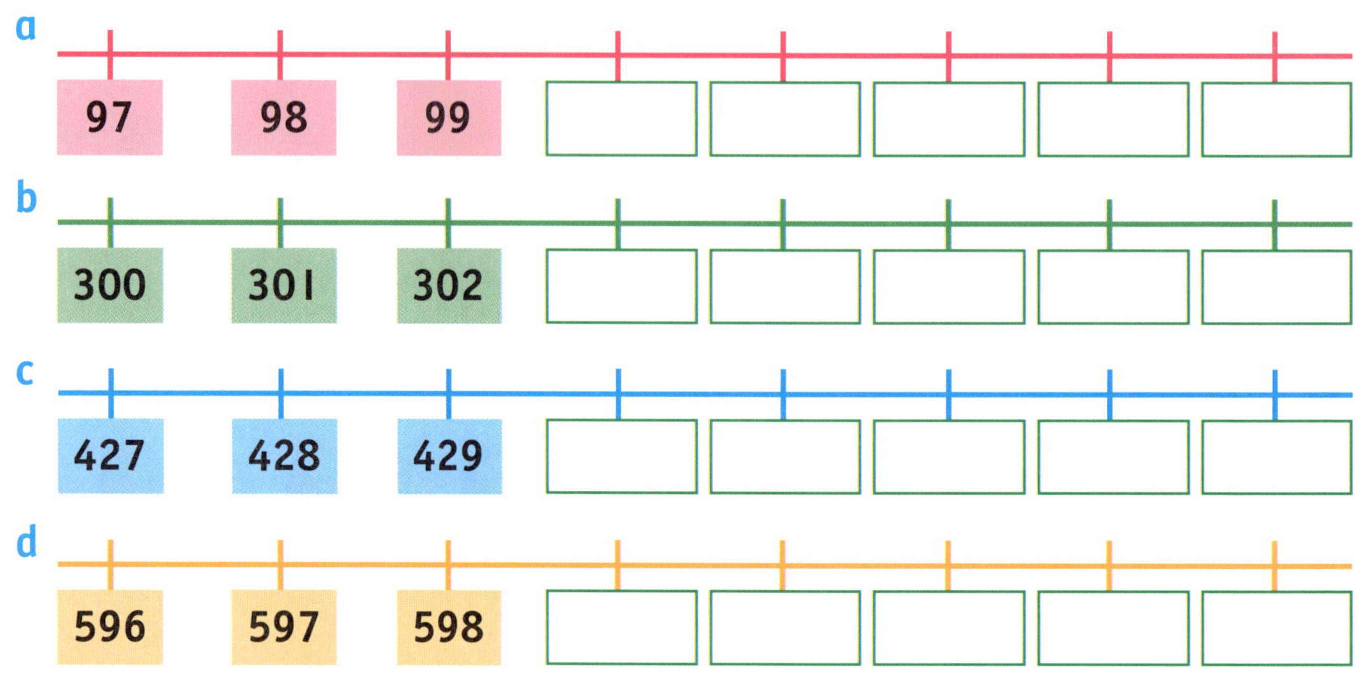

2 Match.

605 620 635 646 659

600 610 620 630 640 650 660

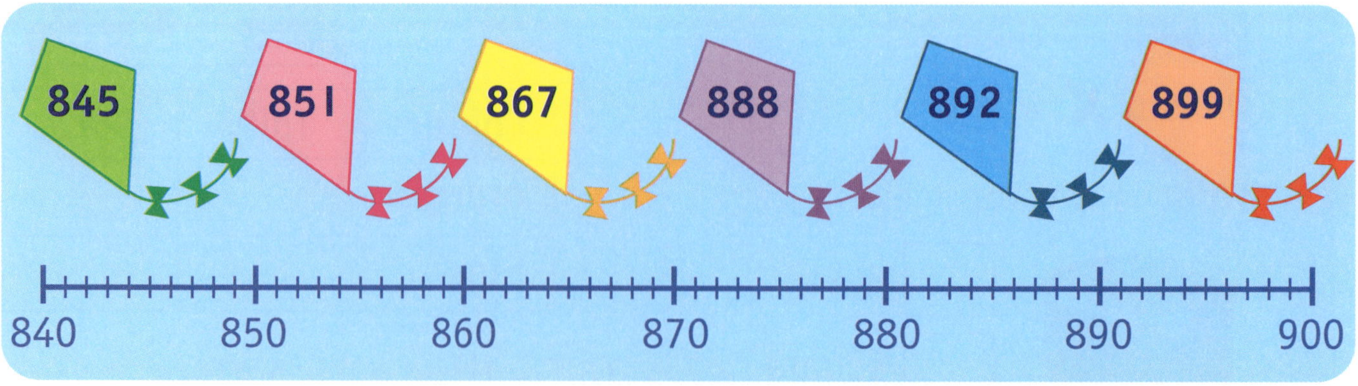

845 851 867 888 892 899

840 850 860 870 880 890 900

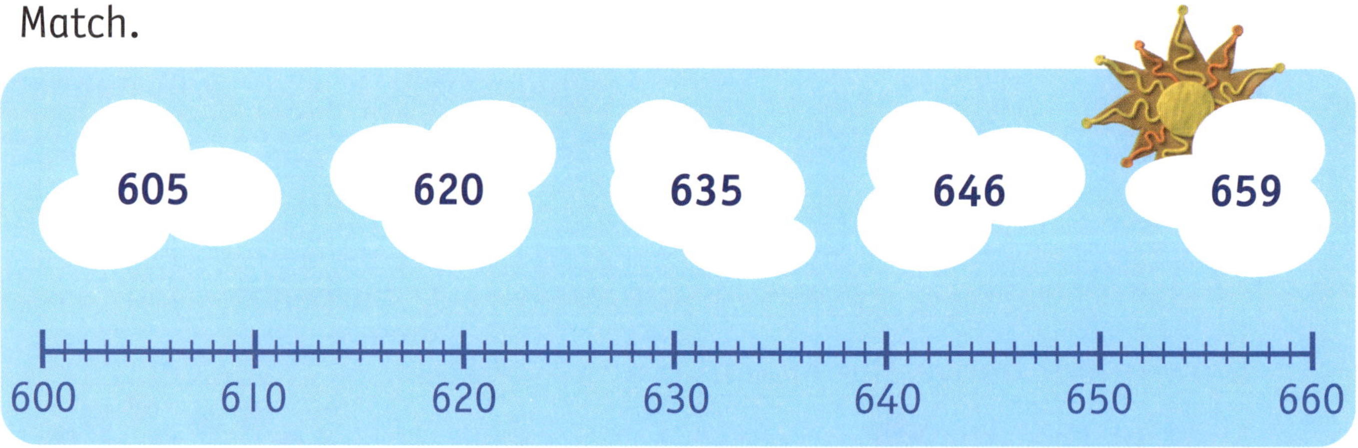

Challenge!

Which number is halfway between 620 and 640?

Counting in hundreds

1 Write the next three numbers.

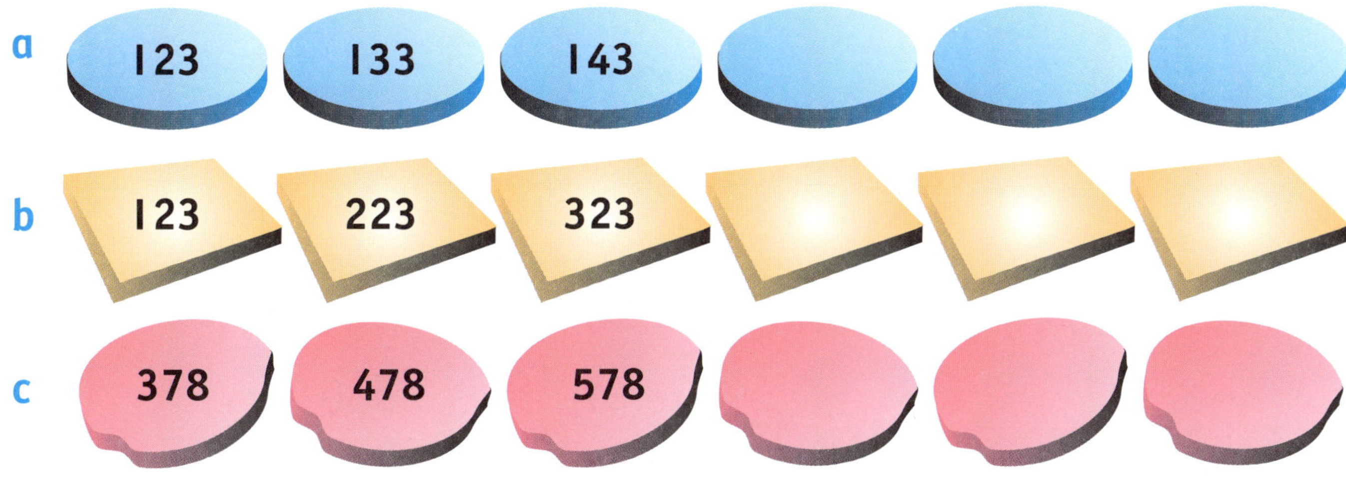

2 Write the number 100 **more** than.

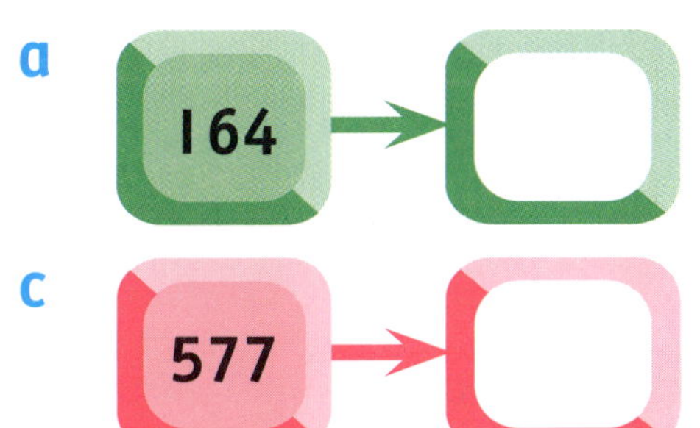

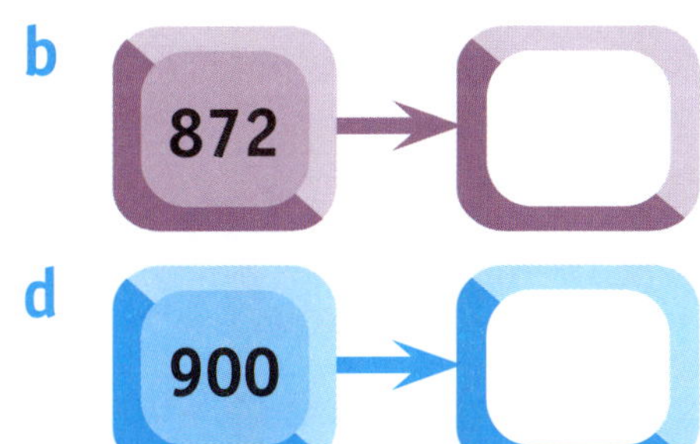

3 Write the number 100 **less** than.

a 484

b 869

c 611

d 722

4 Round to the nearest hundred.

c number of students in your school

d number of days in a year

Counting to 1000

1 Count in tens.

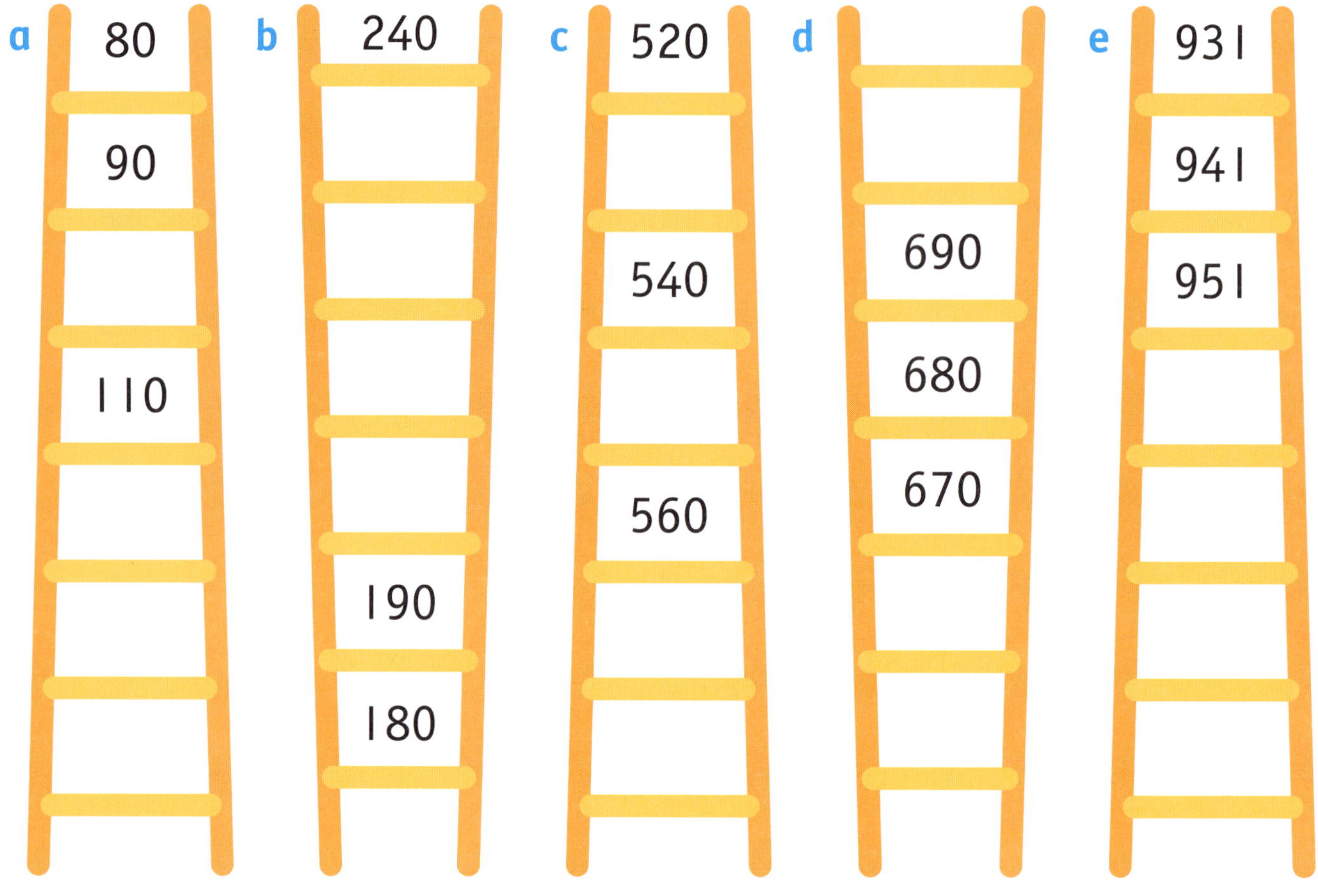

a
80
90
110
b
240
190
180
c
520
540
560
d
690
680
670
e
931
941
951

2 How many? = 100 = 10 ▪ = 1

a

b

c

d

e

f

AC9M2N01 • AC9M2N02 Number **MA1-RWN-01 • MAE-RWN-02** Representing whole numbers B • Use counting sequences of ones and tens flexibly
• Form, regroup, and rename three-digit numbers

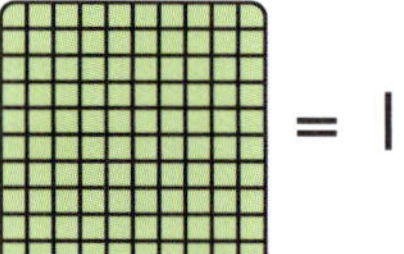

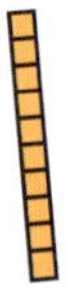

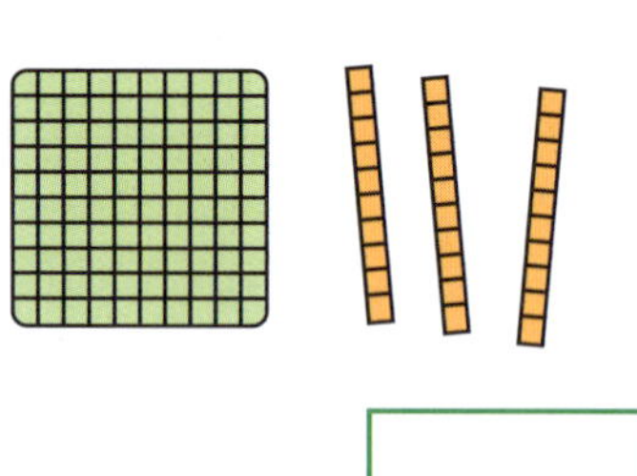

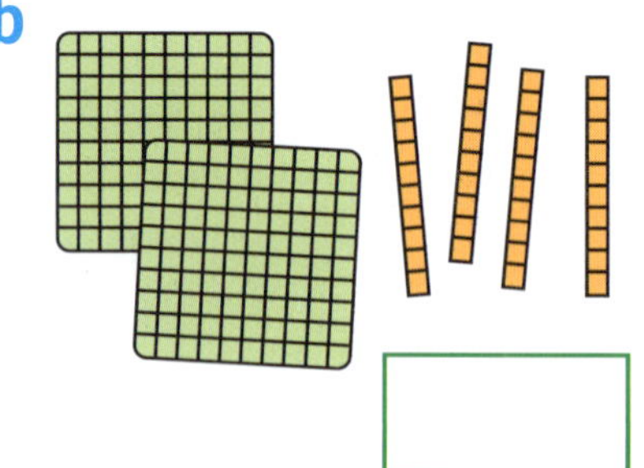

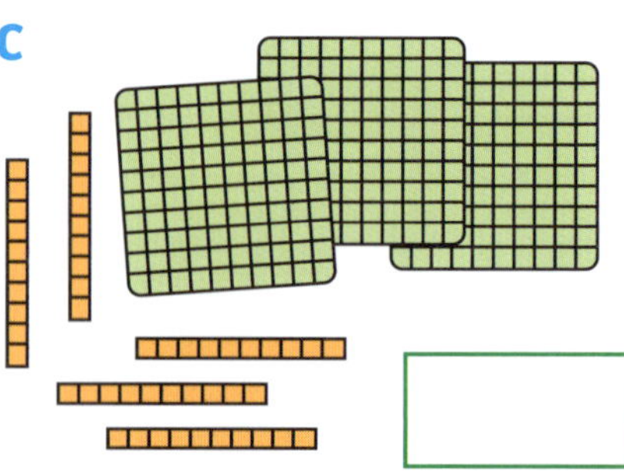

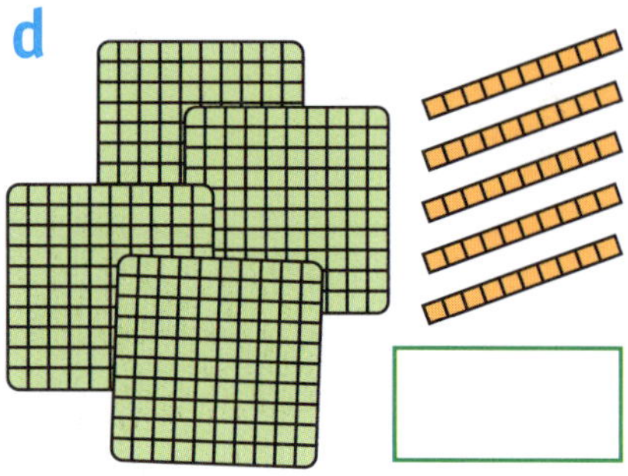

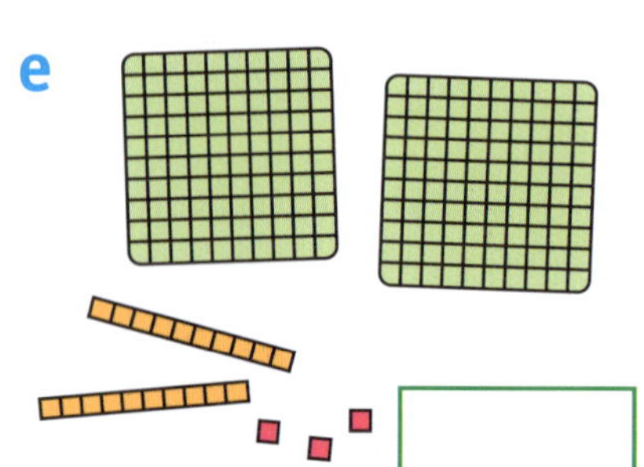

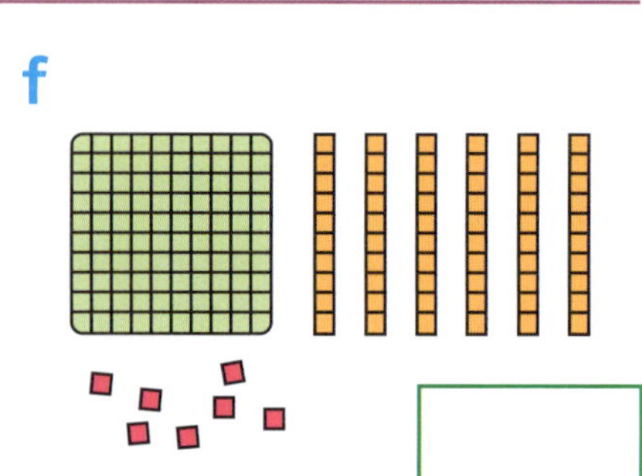

Place value

1

2 hundreds 4 tens 3 ones

200 + 40 + ☐ = ☐

2

____ hundreds ____ tens ____ ones

☐ + ☐ + ☐ = ☐

3

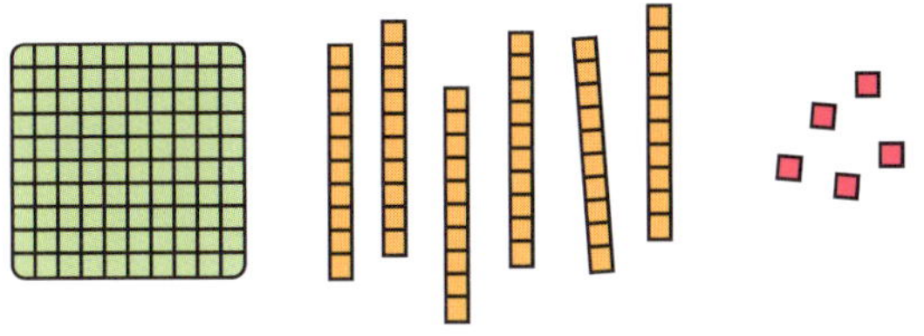

____ hundreds ____ tens ____ ones

☐ + ☐ + ☐ = ☐

4

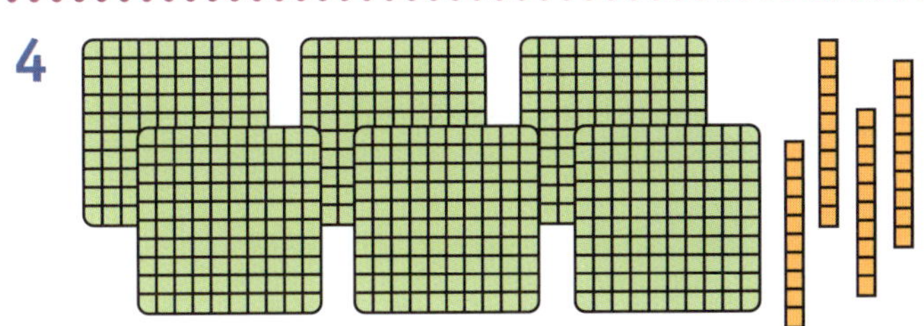

____ hundreds ____ tens ____ ones

☐ + ☐ + ☐ = ☐

5

____ hundreds ____ tens ____ ones

☐ + ☐ + ☐ = ☐

6

____ hundreds ____ tens ____ ones

☐ + ☐ + ☐ = ☐

7 a 300 + 90 + 1 = ☐

b 700 + 20 + 0 = ☐

c 900 + 0 + 9 = ☐

d 800 + 40 + 1 = ☐

Challenge! Colour the number with:

a 6 hundreds **red**

b 82 tens and 7 ones **blue**

c 3 hundreds and 1 ten **green**

594 625 827 319

Hundreds, tens and ones

Number words

1 How many?

a

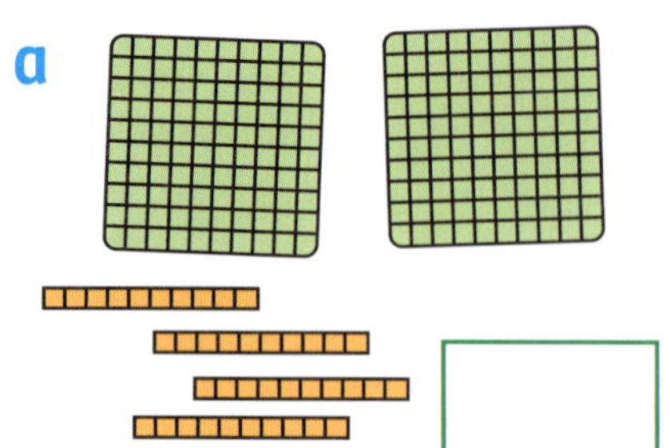

☐

b

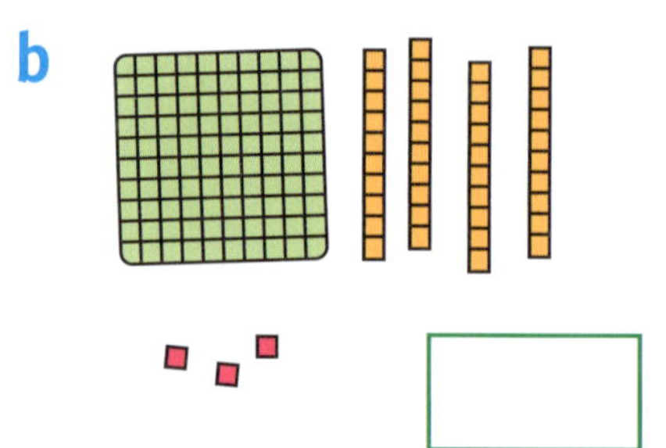

☐

c

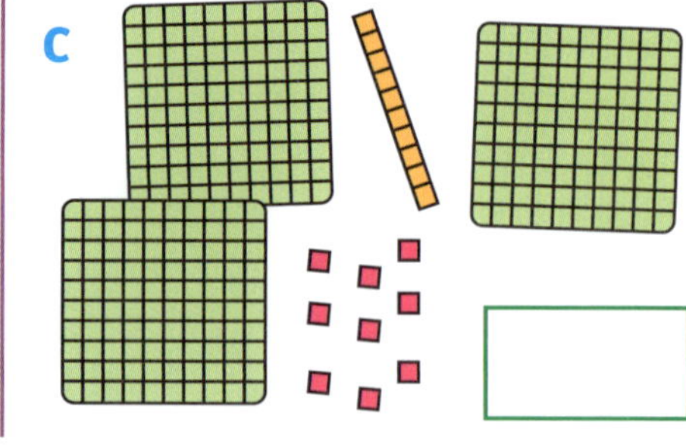

☐

2 Complete.

a 356 = 300 + 50 + ☐

b 724 = ☐ + 20 + ☐

c 431 = ☐ + ☐ + ☐

d 168 = 100 + ☐ + ☐

e 942 = ☐ + ☐ + ☐

f 605 = ☐ + ☐ + ☐

g 220 = ☐ + ☐ + ☐

h 811 = ☐ + ☐ + ☐

3 Write in numerals.

a two hundred and thirty-five ☐

b nine hundred ☐

c seven hundred and ten ☐

d one hundred and two ☐

e four hundred and nineteen ☐

f ninety-three ☐

g eight hundred and twenty-one ☐

h one thousand ☐

4 Write in words.

a 612 ______________________________

b 950 ______________________________

c 348 ______________________________

Trial and error

How many 3-digit numbers can be made with

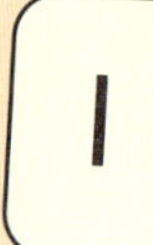

Write them in order from smallest to largest.

☐

Knowing numbers

1 What number am I?

567	385	242	809	172	497	600	905	86

I am the largest. __________ I have 2 hundreds. __________

I have 9 ones. __________ I have no hundreds. __________

I am all hundreds. __________ I am a little less than 500. __________

2 These are the prize-winning numbers. Match.

A computer game — one hundred	780
A plane ticket — eight hundreds and twenty-two ones	100
Free movies — 5 less than two hundred and fifty	604
A new bike — four more than six hundred	430
A scooter — nine hundred and sixty-one	245
The latest game pad — a number less than one hundred	822
A Whizkid Game — seven hundreds and eight tens	961
Two years of chocolates — forty-three tens	75

3 Which number matches?

Students in a class	Pages in a dictionary	People at a big concert	Words on this page	Days in a year
3000	365	270	25	145

Mastery Checklist

I can:
- ☐ count forwards and backwards by ones, tens and hundreds.
- ☐ use place value to partition three-digit numbers.
- ☐ read and write three-digit numbers in words.

Problem solving

What is my number?

1 I have 3 digits. They are all odd. **1 3 5 7 9**

All my digits have a curve in them.

My digits go from left to right, largest to smallest.

What is my number?

2 I have 3 digits. They are all even. **0 2 4 6 8**

If you double my 1s digit you get my 10s digit.

If you double my 10s digit you get my 100s digit.

What is my number?

3 I have 3 digits. My 100s digit is as large as can be.

My 10s digit is 3 smaller than my 100s digit.

My 1s digit is 3 smaller again.

What is my number?

I can solve problems by:

☐ understanding place value and odd and even numbers. ☐ using logical thinking.

AC9M2N02 Number **MA1-WM-01** Working mathematically • Apply mathematical techniques to solve problems
MA1-RWN-01 • **MAE-RWN-02** Representing whole numbers B • Form, regroup, and rename three-digit numbers

Area

1 How many blocks cover each book? 

a 

b 

c 

d 

2 Which book has:

a the smallest area? ______________ b the largest area? ______________

3 **Estimate** Which covers a larger area, your hand or your foot? ______________

4 Use squared paper. Draw around your hand and your foot. Count the squares.

hand

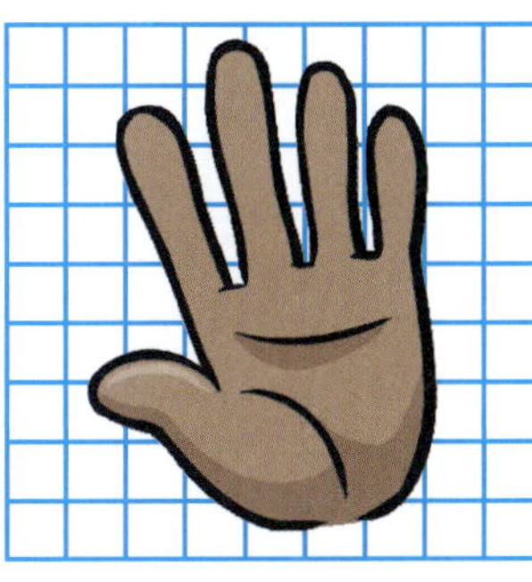

Number of squares.

foot

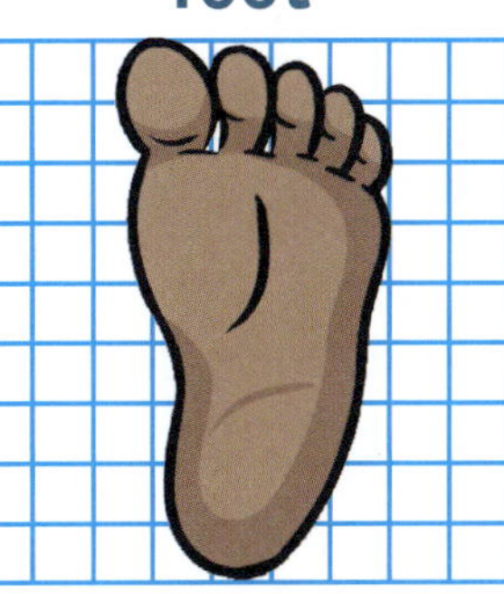

Number of squares.

My ______________ covers a larger area.

Grid area

Area is the size of a surface.

1 What is the area of each shape in squares?

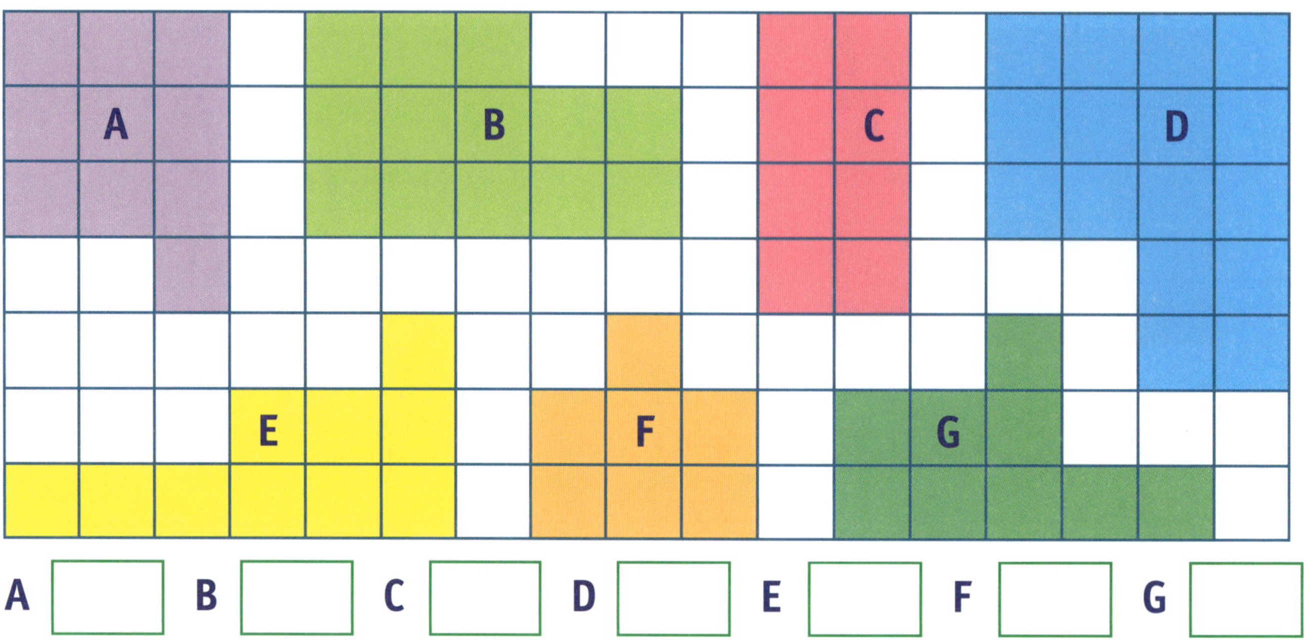

A ☐ B ☐ C ☐ D ☐ E ☐ F ☐ G ☐

2 Which shape has:

a the smallest area? __________ b the largest area? __________

3 Which 2 shapes have the same area? __________

4 a Draw and colour 4 different shapes with an area of 12 squares:

A B C D

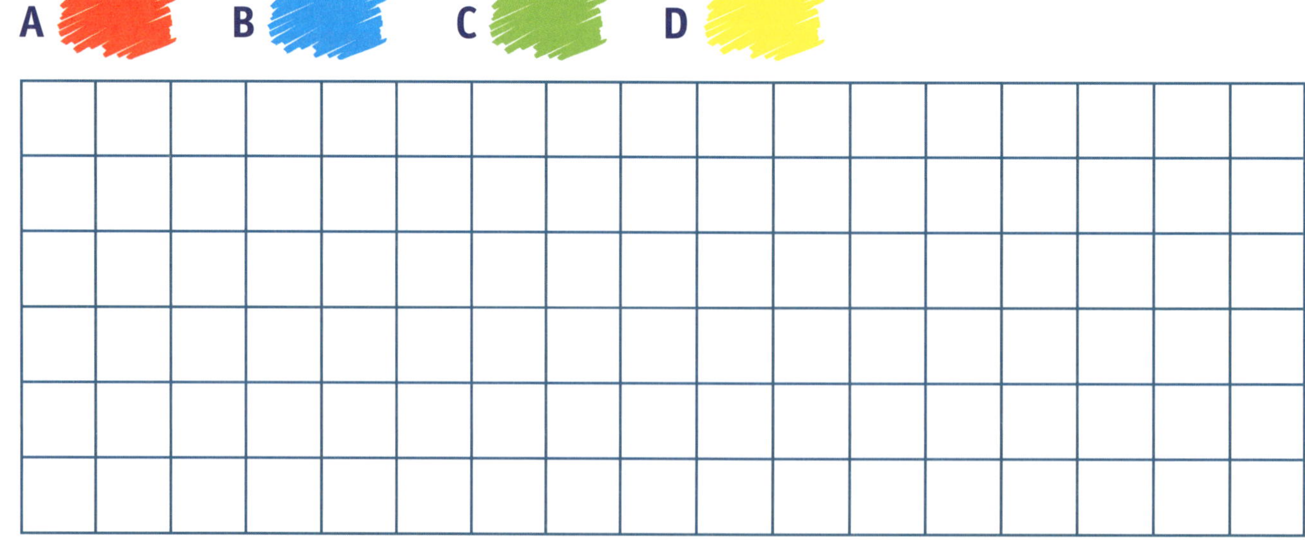

b Does each shape cover the same area? __________

Challenge! What is the area not coloured:

a in question 1? ☐ squares b in question 4? ☐ squares

Problem solving

Sally's Zoo Animals

3 frogs

5 lizards

2 crocodiles

In Sally's Zoo each animal has its own yard. Frog yards cover 2 squares. Lizard yards cover 5 squares. Each crocodile needs 8 squares. Draw Sally's Zoo.

Every square has one metre long sides. How far is it around each yard?

frogs ____________ lizards ____________ crocodiles ____________

What did you find out? ______________________________

I can solve a problem by:

☐ measuring area in squares. ☐ drawing a diagram.

Half-metre

1 Cut a one metre piece of string or paper in half.

half-metre | $\frac{1}{2}$ metre

2 Find things that are about half a metre long.

____

____

____

____

____

You can write metre as m.
3 metres = 3 m

$\frac{1}{2}$ m

3 Measure these lengths. Match to a label.

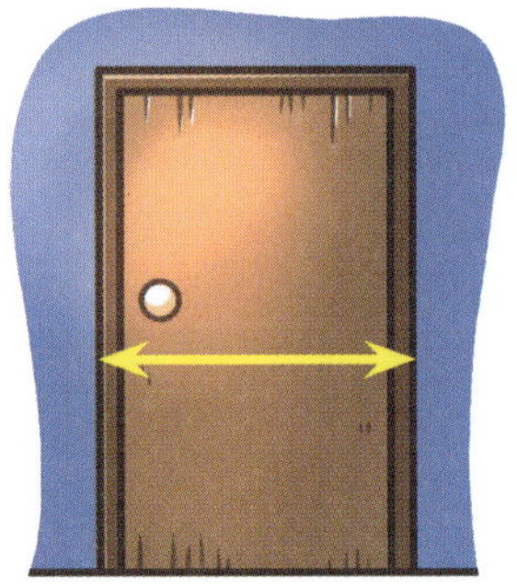

shorter than $\frac{1}{2}$ m

longer than $\frac{1}{2}$ m

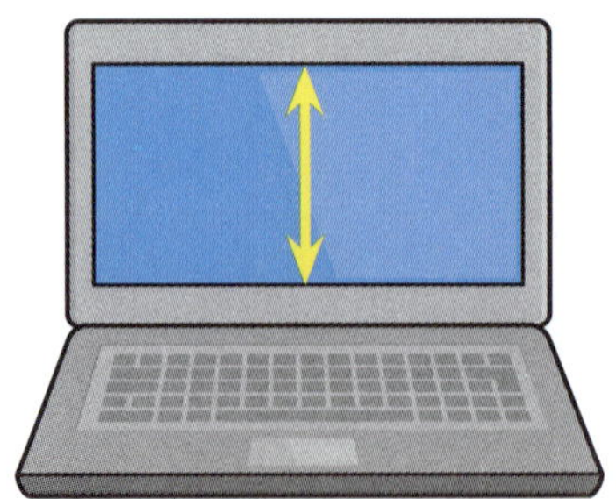

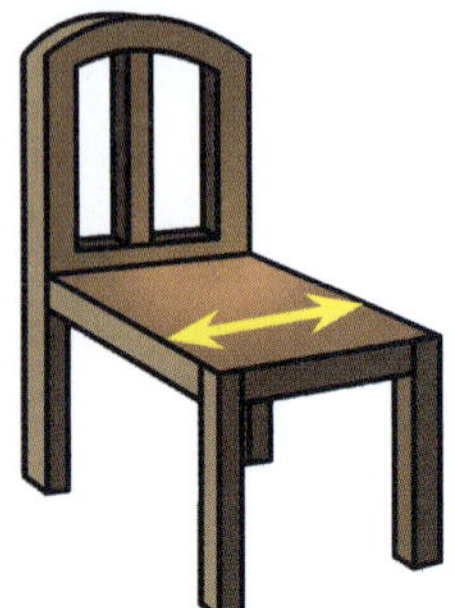

Challenge! Are you closer to 1 m or $1\frac{1}{2}$ m tall?

Measure to check.

Making 1 metre

measure with informal units

1 How many pencils make 1 metre?

a **Estimate:** ______

Lay out that number of pencils.

b Do they make 1 metre? Yes No

Add or take away pencils to make 1 metre.

c **Measure:** How many pencils make 1 metre? ______

2 How many of your feet in 1 metre?

a **Estimate:** ______

Lay out a 1 metre ruler or string.

Step along that length, heel to toe, with no gaps. Count them.

b **Measure:** How many feet in 1 metre? ______

c Was your estimate right? Yes No

Body units – how many make 1 metre?

Body unit	a **Estimate**	b **Measurement**	c **Was your estimate right?**
3 Finger length			Yes No
4 Handspan			Yes No
5 Forearms			Yes No
6 Arm length			Yes No

7 Did you get better at estimating 1 metre? ______

Centimetres

This pencil is 15 centimetres long. That's 15 cm.

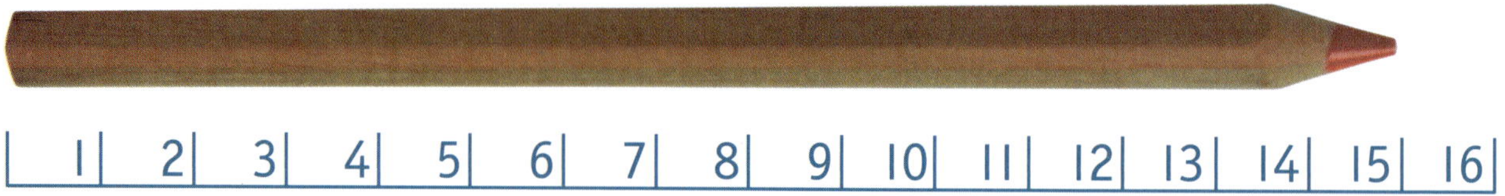

1 How long in centimetres (cm)?

a  ______

b ______

To measure small things we use the centimetre.
cm = centimetre

c  ______

d  ______

e ______

2 Draw lines:

a 6 cm long.

b 3 cm long.

c 11 cm long.

d 8 cm long.

Mastery Checklist

I can:
- ☐ compare areas using square units.
- ☐ measure lengths to the nearest metre or half-metre.
- ☐ measure lengths to the nearest centimetre.

AC9M2M01 Measurement **MA1-GM-02** Geometric measure B • Length: Recognise and use formal units to measure the lengths of objects

Problem solving

Two new fish tanks

You have two new fish tanks. Put a different set of fish in each tank. Make sure the total fish length in each tank adds up to 20 cm.

| cm | 2 cm | 3 cm | 4 cm | 5 cm |

Fill each tank with fish.

I can solve a problem by:

☐ adding to 20. ☐ drawing a diagram.

Tessellating shapes

Tessellating shapes fit together without any gaps or overlaps.

1 How many more tiles are needed? Guess first, then check by drawing in the missing tiles.

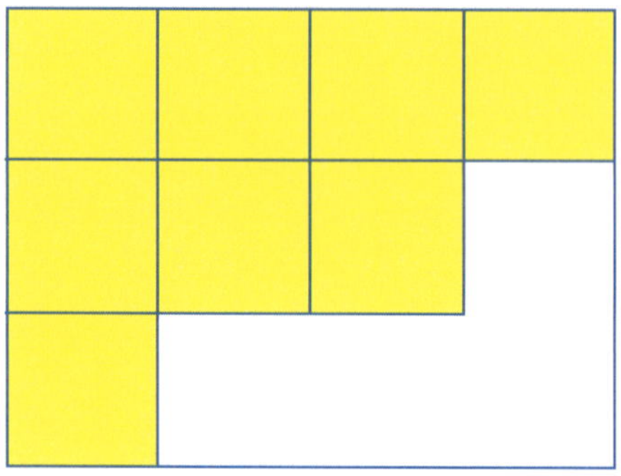

a guess check

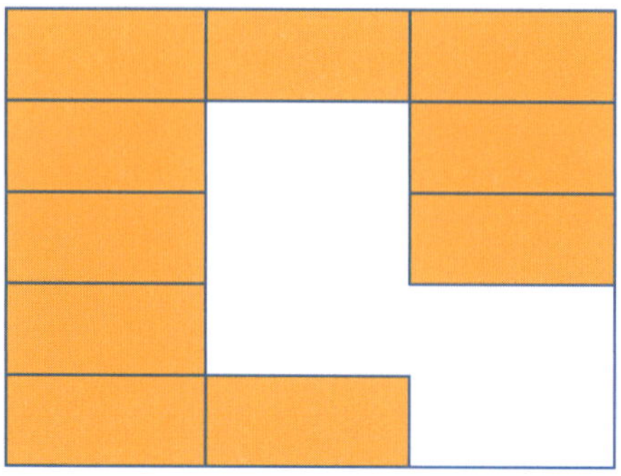

b guess check

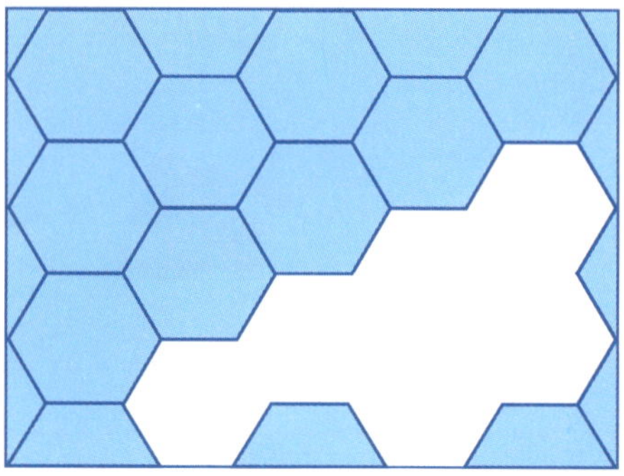

c guess check

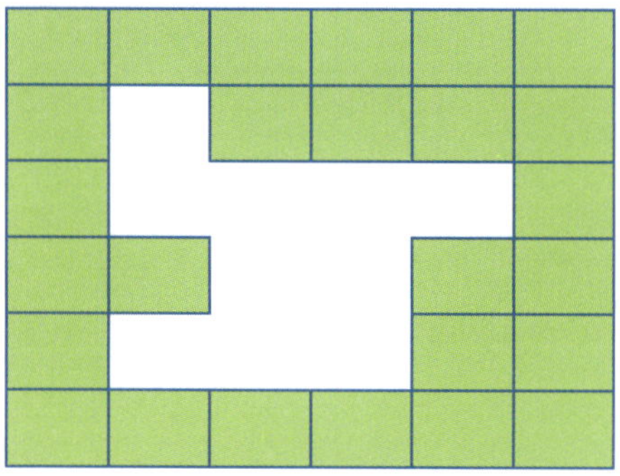

d guess check

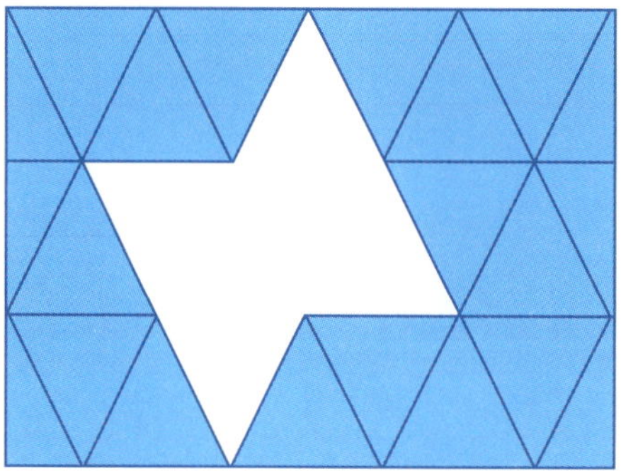

e guess check

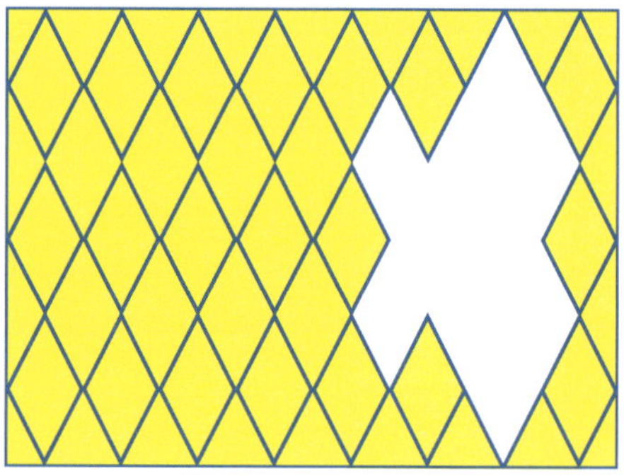

f guess check

2 Draw your own tessellating pattern.

Splitting shapes

1 These shapes have been split. Name the smaller shapes.

a
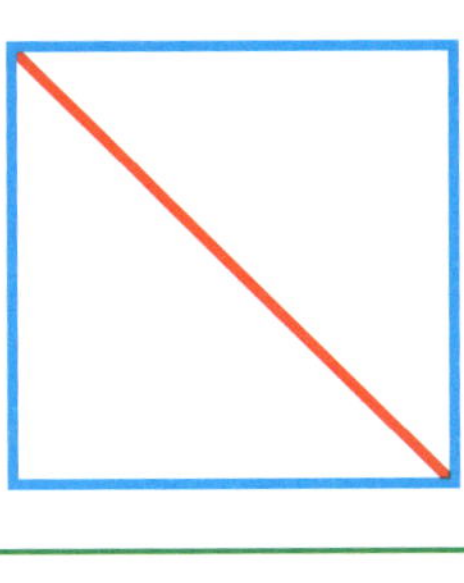

b
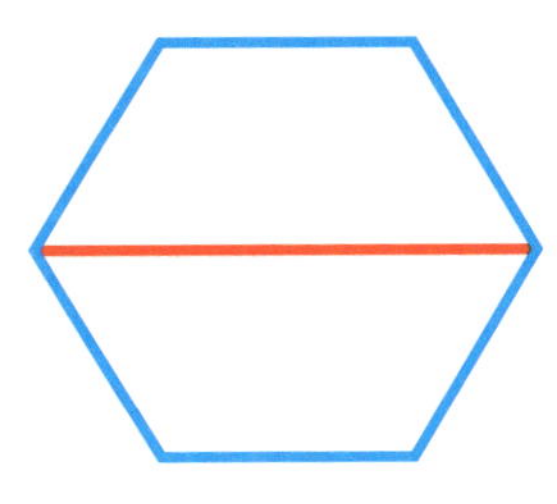

c
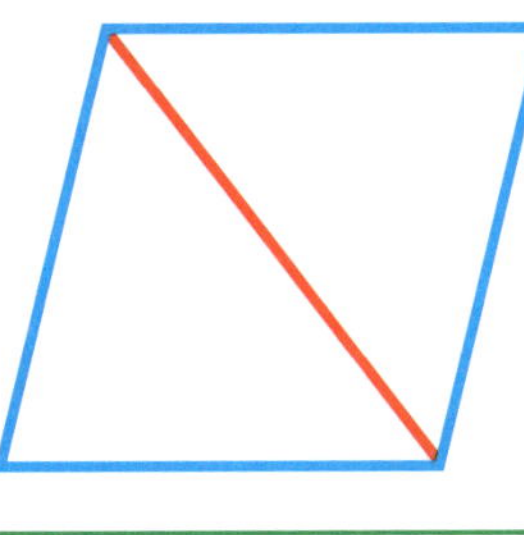

d
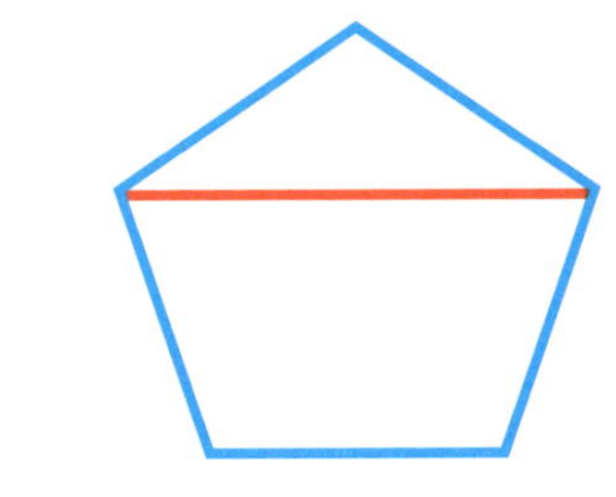

e
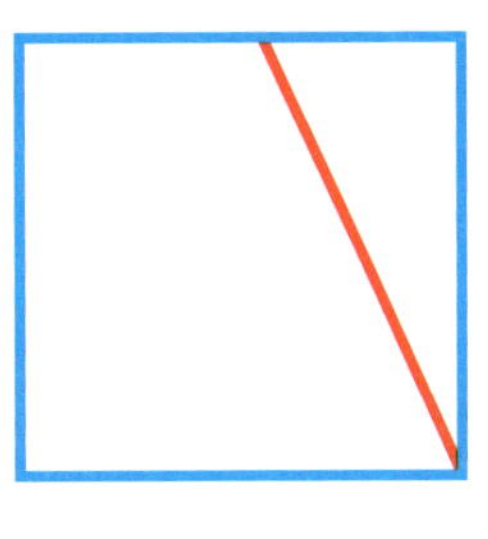

f
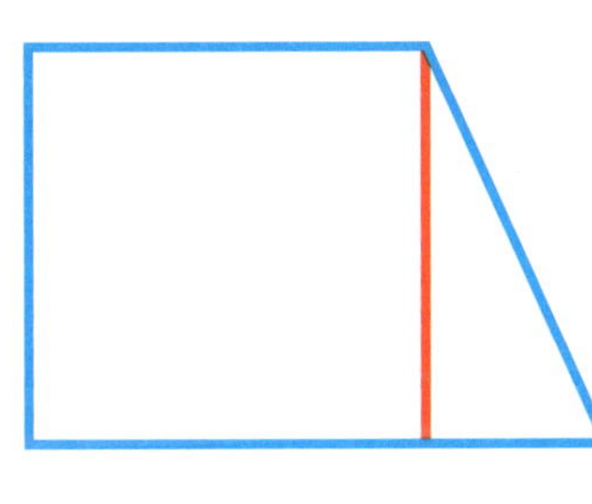

2 Split these shapes into:

a 2 triangles.

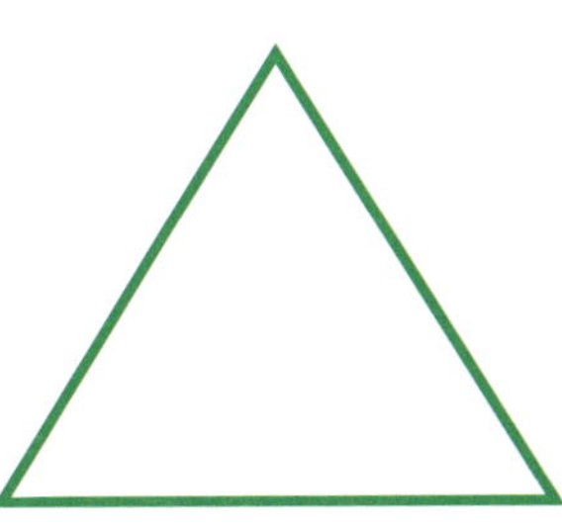

b 2 triangles.

c 2 squares.

d 1 triangle and 1 trapezium.

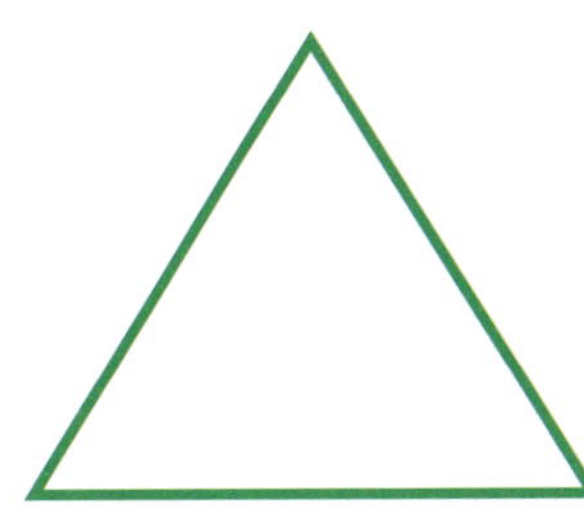

e 1 triangle and 1 trapezium.

f 2 triangles and 1 square.

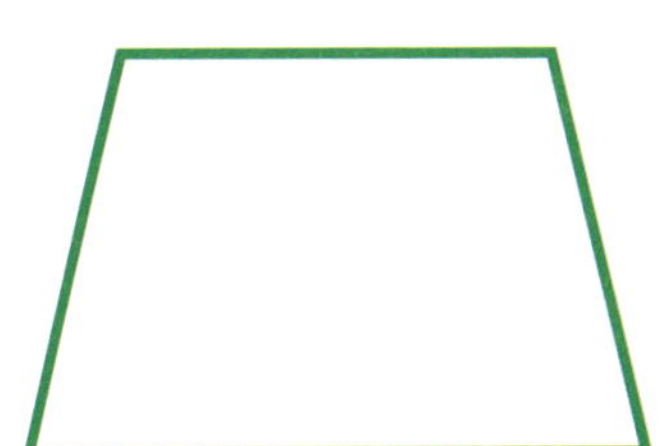

Combining shapes

1 Combine these 2D shapes to make a larger shape. Draw it.

a trapezium	**b** square	**c** hexagon
d trapezium	**e** triangle	**f** triangle
g rectangle	**h** rhombus	**i** pentagon

Problem solving

Hexagon split

Can you find 6 ways to split a hexagon into smaller shapes?

Name the smaller shapes you make.

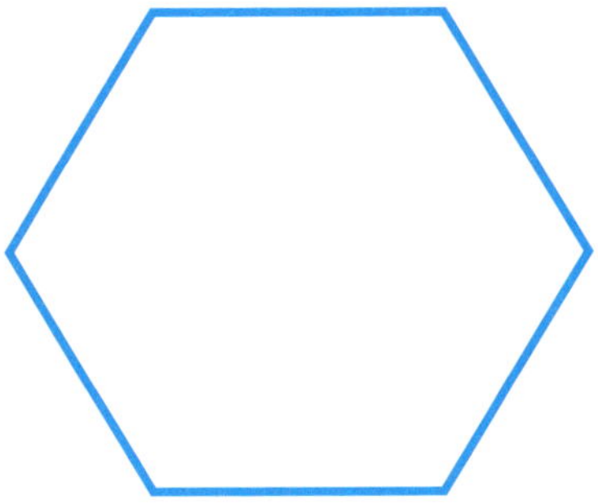

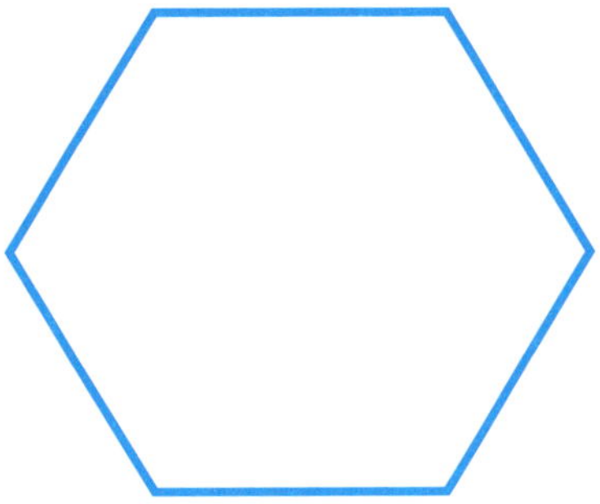

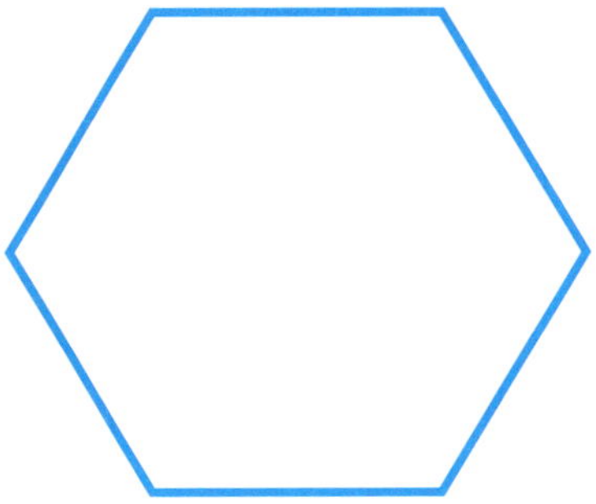

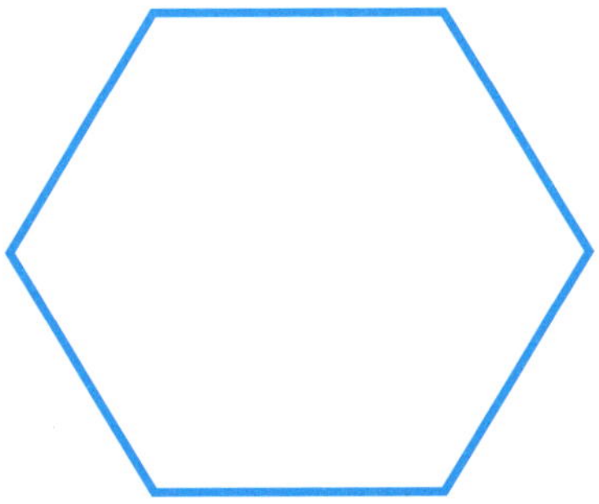

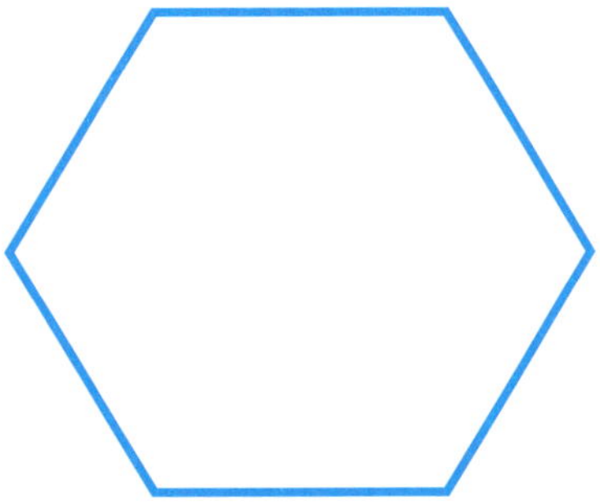

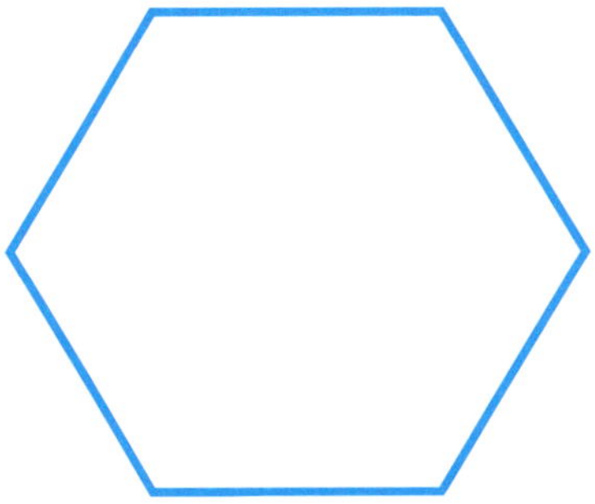

I can solve problems by:

☐ splitting 2D shapes into smaller shapes. ☐ drawing diagrams.

Multiplying by five

1 How many fingers?

a 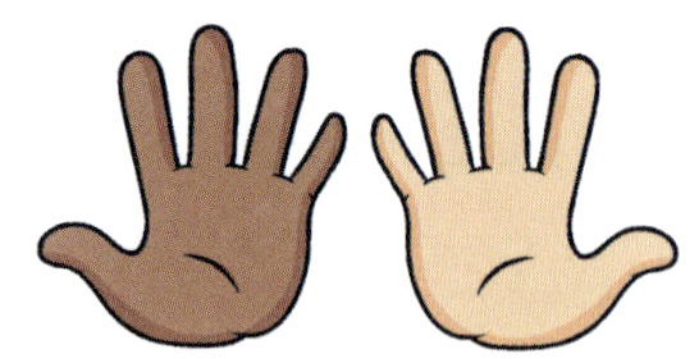

$2 \times 5 =$ ☐

b 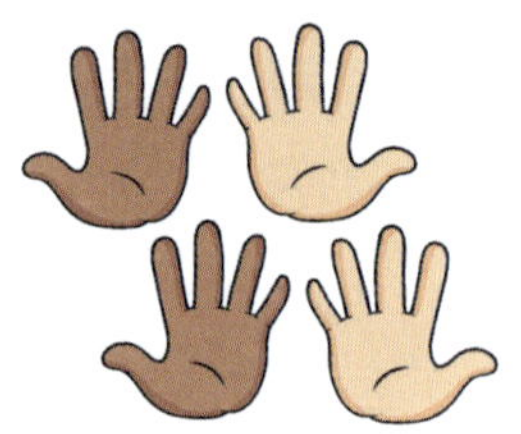

$4 \times 5 =$ ☐

c 

$1 \times 5 =$ ☐

d 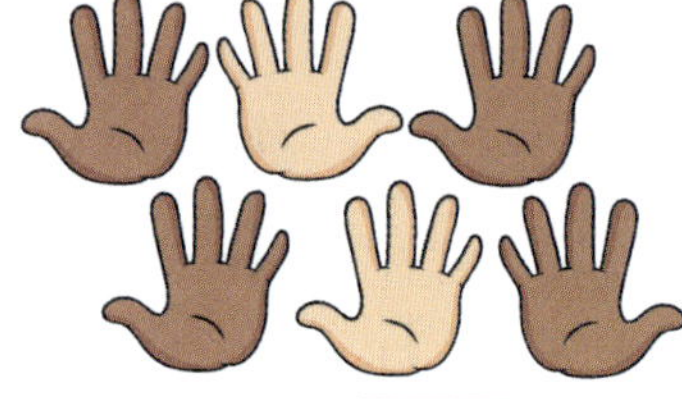

$6 \times 5 =$ ☐

e 

$3 \times 5 =$ ☐

f 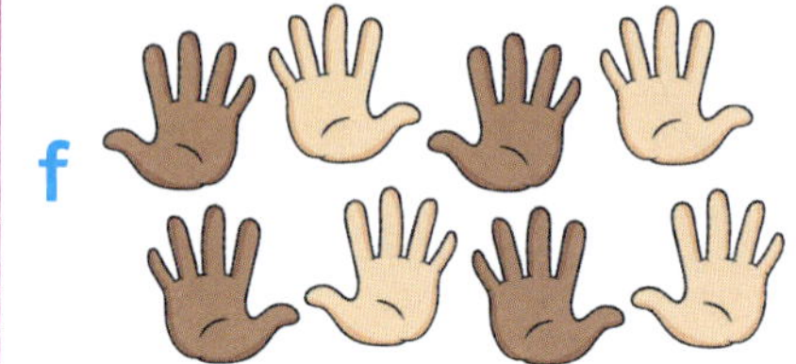

$8 \times 5 =$ ☐

g 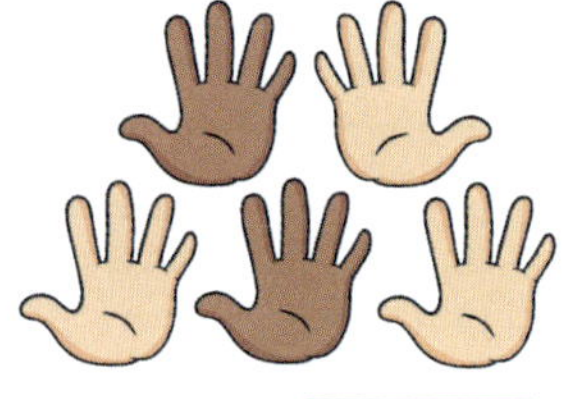

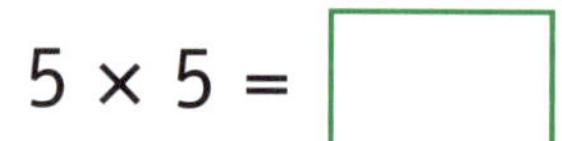

$5 \times 5 =$ ☐

h 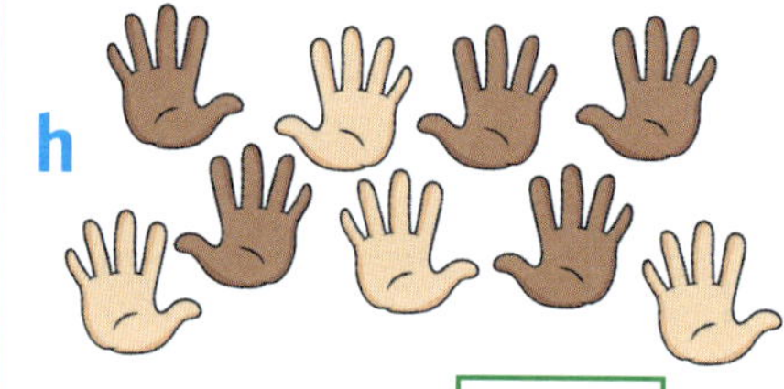

$9 \times 5 =$ ☐

i 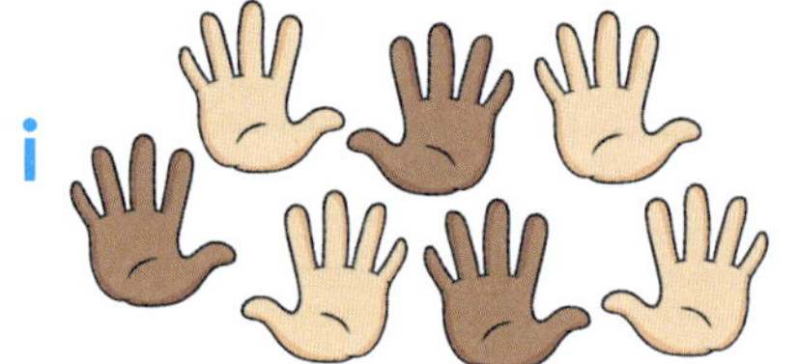

$7 \times 5 =$ ☐

2 Write the answer then write each as a multiplication.

a 3 fives are ______

______ × ______ = ______

b 2 fives are ______

______ × ______ = ______

c 4 fives are ______

______ × ______ = ______

d 5 fives are ______

______ × ______ = ______

e 10 fives are ______

______ × ______ = ______

f 6 fives are ______

______ × ______ = ______

3 Count by fives.

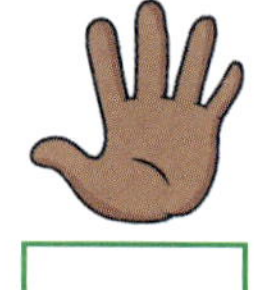 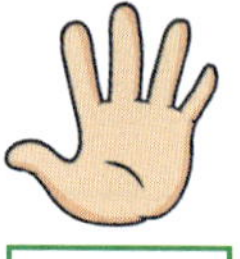 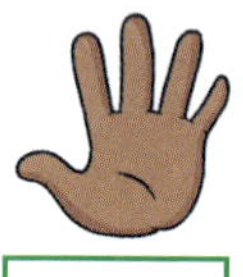      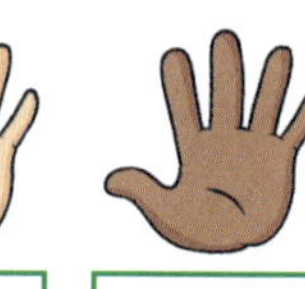 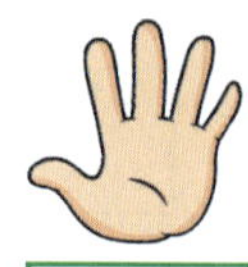

☐ ☐ ☐ ☐ ☐ ☐ ☐ ☐ ☐ ☐

$10 \times 5 =$ ☐

Challenge! In question 3 double each number.
Write the new counting pattern.

Doubling

Count the doubles.

1

double 2 is ☐

2

double 3 is ☐

Double the numbers.

3

double 4 is ☐

4

double 5 is ☐

5

double 6 is ☐ 

☐ × 2 = ☐

6

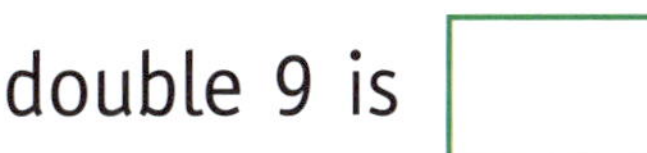

double 9 is ☐

☐ × 2 = ☐

7 Jenny has 7 hamsters and 7 rats. How many altogether?

☐ × 2 = ☐

8 Matty has 8 snakes and 8 lizards. How many altogether?

☐ × 2 = ☐

Patterns in the hundred chart

1	2	3	4	5	6	7	8	9	10
11	12	13	14	15	16	17	18	19	20
21	22	23	24	25	26	27	28	29	30
31	32	33	34	35	36	37	38	39	40
41	42	43	44	45	46	47	48	49	50
51	52	53	54	55	56	57	58	59	60
61	62	63	64	65	66	67	68	69	70
71	72	73	74	75	76	77	78	79	80
81	82	83	84	85	86	87	88	89	90
91	92	93	94	95	96	97	98	99	100

1 Colour:

a the counting by 2s pattern yellow.

b the counting by 5s pattern blue.

2 Complete.

a $2 \times \square = 10$

b $5 \times \square = 10$

c $2 \times \square = 20$

d $5 \times \square = 20$

3 a Write the counting by 10s pattern.

b These numbers are also part of the counting by ☐ pattern.

4 a Colour your own counting pattern in red.

b Write your counting pattern here.

☐ ☐ ☐ ☐ ☐ ☐ ☐ ☐ ☐ ☐

Looking for patterns

Which number pattern does this show?

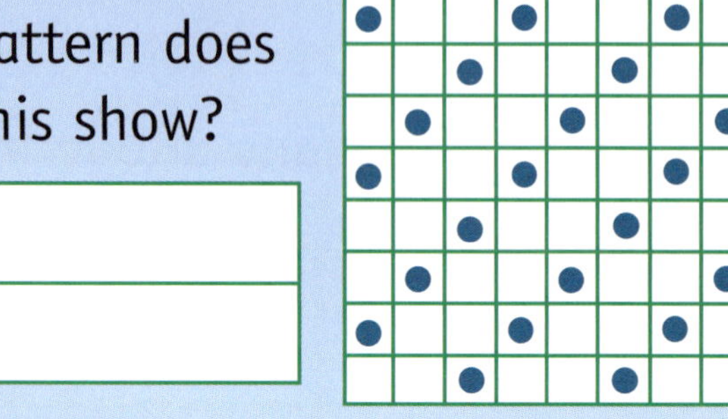

Colour your own pattern.

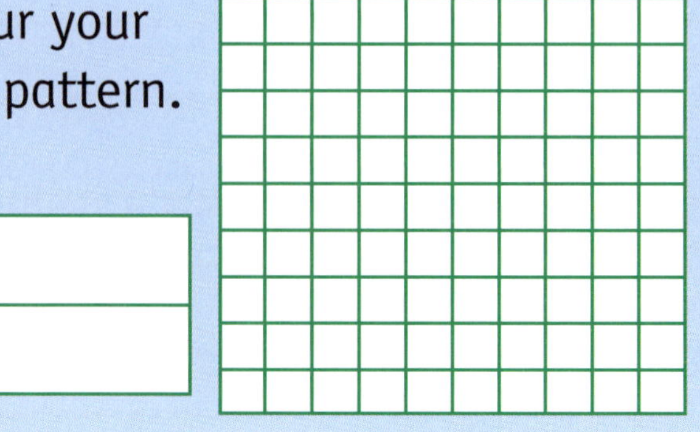

Counting in 2s, 3s and 5s

1 Continue each number pattern. What is the rule?

2 Write the missing numbers.

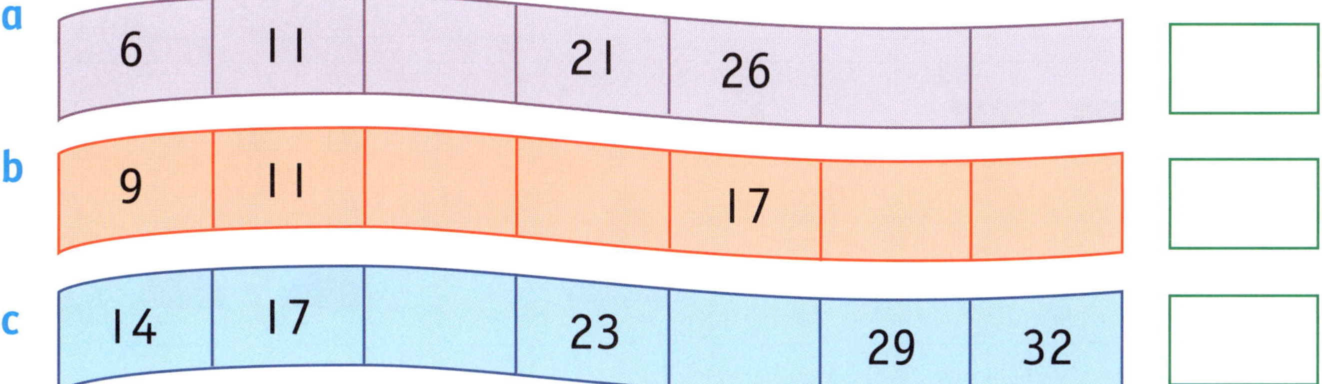

3 Write your own number patterns.

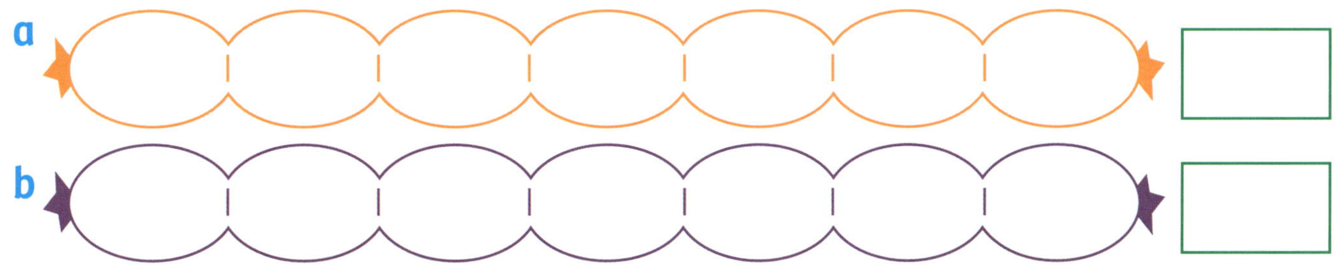

Challenge!

Use all the numbers to complete the sums.

1 2 3 4 5 6

☐ + ☐ = ☐ ☐ + 3 = 6

10 – ☐ = ☐ 8 – ☐ = 7

Multiplying by three

2 and 3 tables

1 How many corners?

a $2 \times 3 =$ ☐

b $4 \times 3 =$ ☐

c $6 \times 3 =$ ☐

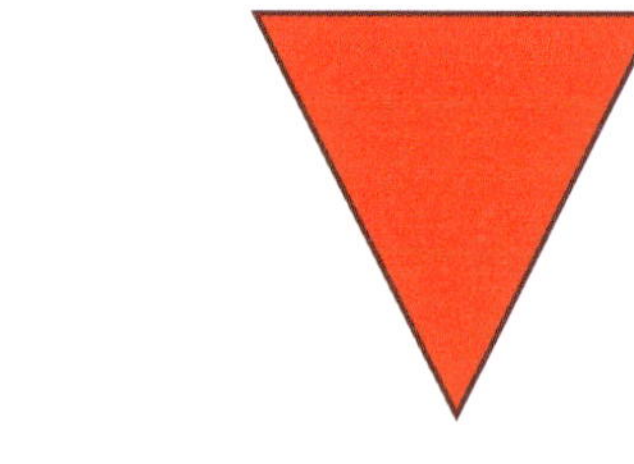

d ☐ × ☐ = ☐

e ☐ × ☐ = ☐

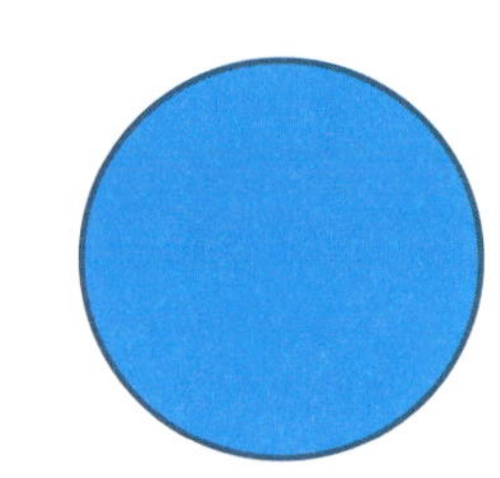

f ☐ × ☐ = ☐

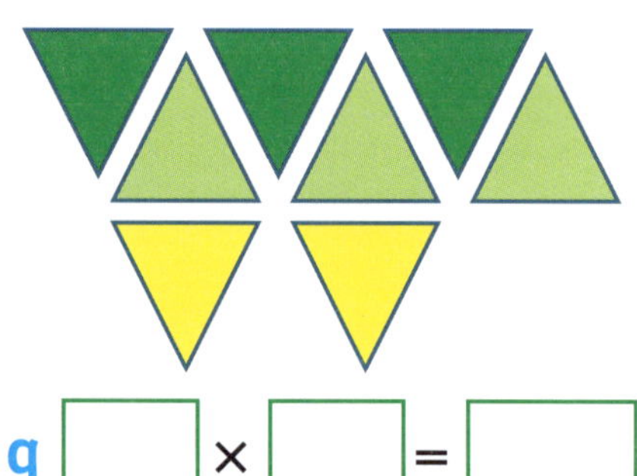

g ☐ × ☐ = ☐

h ☐ × ☐ = ☐

i ☐ × ☐ = ☐

2 Jump in threes.

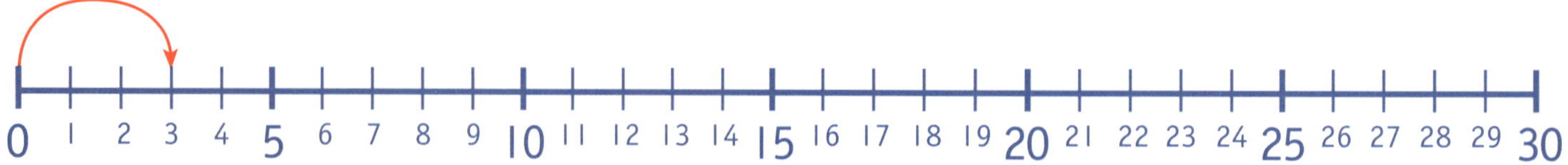

Draw a diagram

Each child has 3 lollies.
There are 7 children.

How many lollies? ☐

Multiplying

Write two multiplications for each.

1

3 × 2 = ☐

2 × 3 = ☐

2

☐ × ☐ = ☐

☐ × ☐ = ☐

3

☐ × ☐ = ☐

☐ × ☐ = ☐

4

☐ × ☐ = ☐

☐ × ☐ = ☐

5

☐ × ☐ = ☐

☐ × ☐ = ☐

Draw a diagram

Use 24 counters.
Draw them on squared paper.
How many different rectangles can you make?

☐

Write 2 multiplications for each.

Mastery Checklist

I can:

- ☐ make tessellating patterns of shapes.
- ☐ combine and split shapes to form new shapes.
- ☐ count by 5s, 2s, 10s, 3s.
- ☐ multiply by 5, 3, 2 and double numbers.

Your pet dragon

Investigation 3

It would be very exciting to have a dragon for a pet!

1 Draw your dragon here. Make it as long as the one metre ruler. If your dragon is one metre long, how long are its head, body and tail?

My dragon's name is ______________________________

1 metre

2 Now design a home for your dragon. Draw it here. Name all the rooms and what they will be used for.

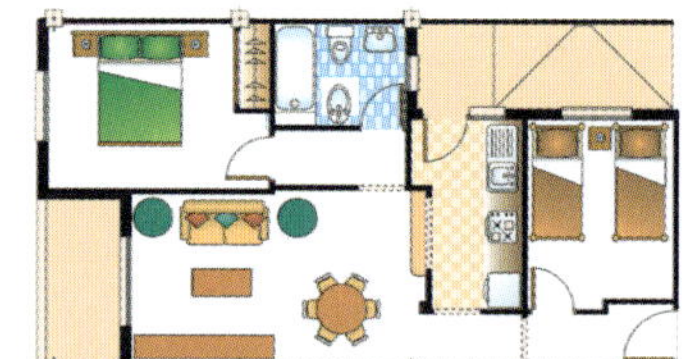

AC9M2M01 Measurement **MA1-GM-02** Geometric measure B • Length: Recognise and use formal units to measure the lengths of objects
MA1-WM-01 Working mathematically • Apply mathematical techniques to solve problems • Communicate their thinking and reasoning coherently and clearly

Your pet dragon

Investigation 3

3 Your dragon will need food and bedding. What else?
Write a shopping list of things your dragon needs.

4 How much will it cost to feed a dragon every week?

5 There are many things you need to do to look after a dragon.
Write a timetable. Write how long it takes to do each job.

Job	Day of the week	How long it takes

To complete these tasks I needed to:

- ☐ draw a plan.
- ☐ make lists of money amounts and times.
- ☐ add money.
- ☐ add lengths to 1 metre.
- ☐ decide how much time it takes to do different jobs.

I enjoyed this task!

☆☆☆☆☆

Revision

Shade one bubble.

1

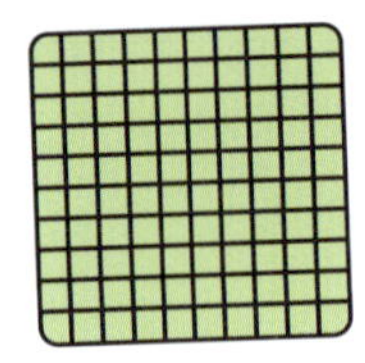
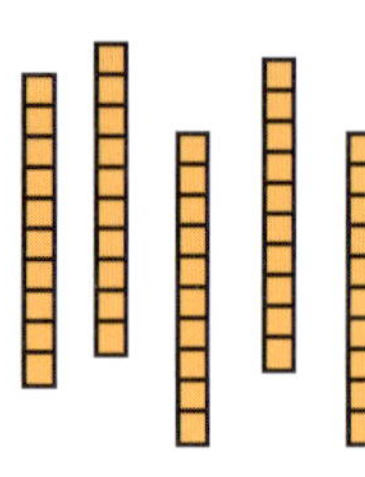

This number is:

532 ◯ 253 ◯ 352 ◯ 523 ◯

2 Which 2 shapes will make a trapezium?

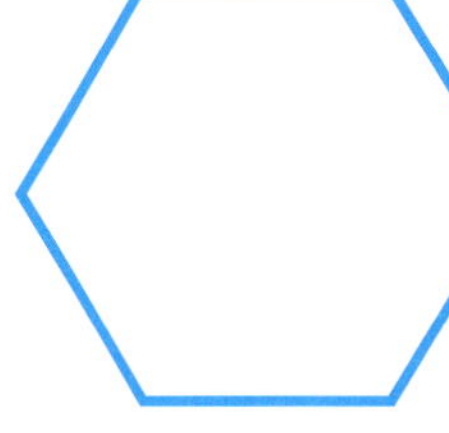
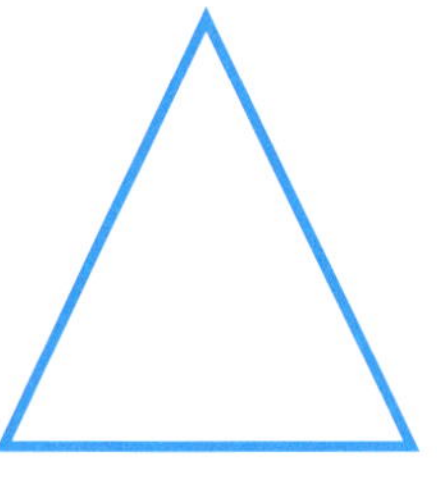
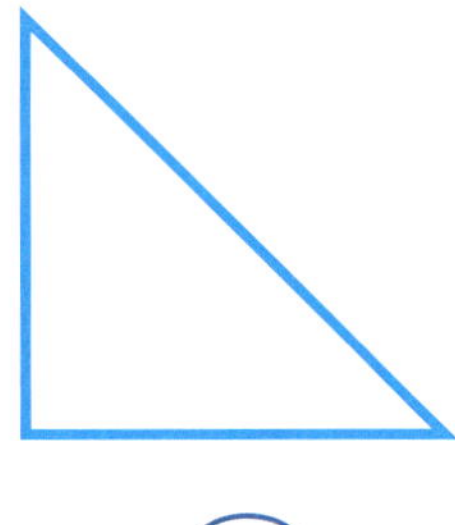

◯ ◯ ◯ ◯

3

10c × 9 = 90c ◯ 9c × 10 = 90c ◯ 9 × \$1 = \$9 ◯ 10c + 9 = 90c ◯

4 Which 2 multiplications match the array?

4 × 2 = 8 ◯ 5 × 2 = 10 ◯ 2 × 4 = 8 ◯ 2 × 5 = 10 ◯

Revision

Shade one bubble.

5

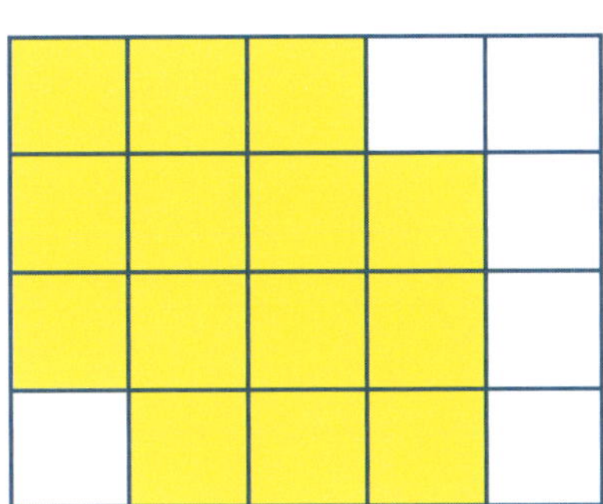

The coloured area covers:

9 squares	14 squares	6 squares	12 squares
◯	◯	◯	◯

6 The number with 3 tens is:

370	273	437	63
◯	◯	◯	◯

7 How long is the pencil?

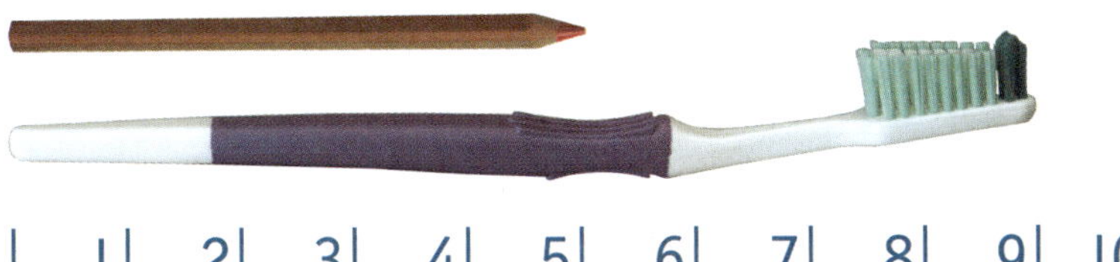

1	2	3	4	5	6	7	8	9	10	11	12	13	14	15	16

9 cm	8 cm	10 cm	5 cm
◯	◯	◯	◯

8

Write your answers in the boxes.

a double 7 = ☐

b 3 × 8 = ☐

c 1, 3, 5, ☐

d 9 × 5 = ☐

e 2 × ☐ = 20

f 3 × 5 = ☐ × ☐

Split to add

Split Strategy +

To add 12, add the 10, then add 2.

1 13 + 12 = ☐

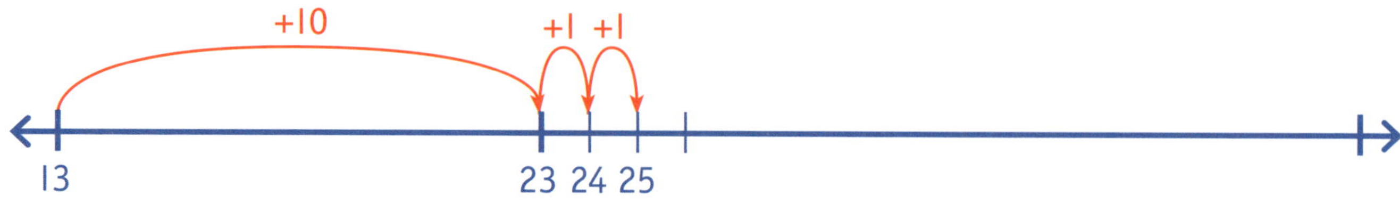

To add 22, add the 20, then add 2.

2 27 + 22 = ☐

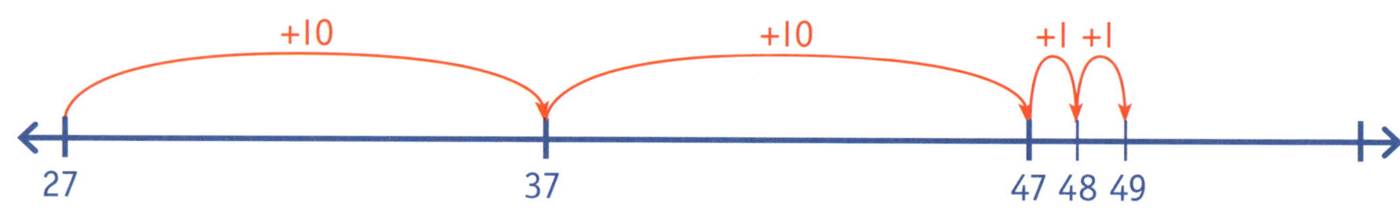

3 35 + 15 = ☐

4 48 + 16 = ☐

5 52 + 25 = ☐

Addition using algorithms

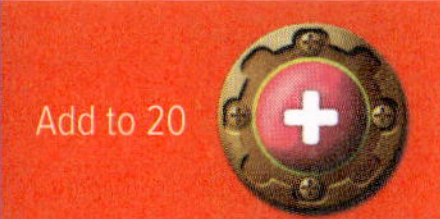

1

tens	ones
1	1
+	7

11 + 7 = ☐

2 Here are some more.

a

tens	ones
1	0
+	6

b

tens	ones
1	2
+	5

c

tens	ones
1	5
+	3

d

tens	ones
1	7
+	2

e

tens	ones
1	1
+	4

f

tens	ones
1	6
+	3

3

a 13 + 3 = ____

b 17 + 2 = ____

c 11 + 6 = ____

d 10 + 8 = ____

e 12 + 7 = ____

f 14 + 5 = ____

g 18 + 2 = ____

h 13 + 7 = ____

Challenge! How many ways can you add to 20?

Using 2 numbers.

13	15	9
11	16	10
5	7	4

Using 3 numbers.

4	7	11
3	5	8
6	9	10

Using 4 numbers.

5	1	9
7	4	8
2	3	6

Estimating addition

Estimate, then calculate the total cost for each list.

estimate

Shopping list	Price
bread	
milk	
cheese	
Total cost	

estimate

Shopping list	Price
eggs	
milk	
potatoes	
Total cost	

estimate

cheese	
potatoes	
lettuce	
2 apples	
bread	
Total cost	

estimate

milk	
4 apples	
chocolates	
strawberries	
milk	
Total cost	

Challenge! Make your own shopping list. Buy 8 things.
Estimate, then work out how much they will cost.

More addition algorithms

Add the ones, then the tens.

1 **a**

tens	ones
1	4
+ 1	3

b

tens	ones
2	6
+ 1	1

c

tens	ones
2	5
+ 2	2

d

tens	ones
3	7
+ 1	2

e

tens	ones
3	1
+ 2	8

f

tens	ones
3	0
+ 3	9

2 **a** $43 + 46$

b $54 + 24$

c $65 + 31$

d $36 + 22$

e $41 + 37$

f $54 + 45$

g $37 + 40$

h $68 + 11$

i $75 + 23$

Challenge! How many different 2-digit additions can you make using just the digits 1 and/or 2?

11 + 11, 11 + 12, 11 + 21 ...

What if you had the digits 1, 2 and/or 3 to work with?

Addition patterns

Complete. Look for the pattern.

1

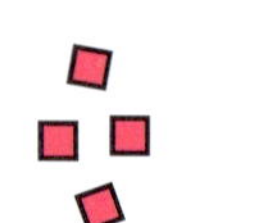 4 + 2 = ☐

 14 + 2 = ☐

 24 + 2 = ☐

2

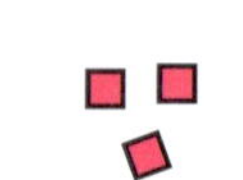 3 + 5 = ☐

 13 + 5 = ☐

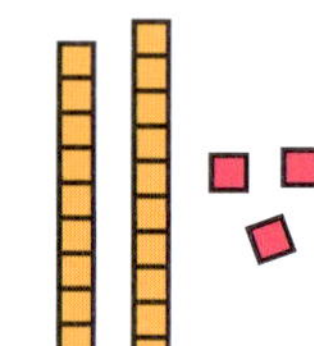 23 + 5 = ☐

3

 5 + 4 = ☐

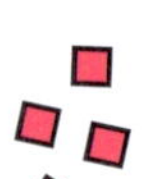 15 + 4 = ☐

 25 + 4 = ☐

4

a 5 + 2 = ☐
15 + 2 = ☐
25 + 2 = ☐

b 4 + 4 = ☐
14 + 4 = ☐
24 + 4 = ☐

c 6 + 3 = ☐
16 + 3 = ☐
26 + 3 = ☐

d 2 + 7 = ☐
12 + 7 = ☐
22 + 7 = ☐

Challenge! Continue one pattern until you reach more than 100.

Mastery Checklist

I can:
- ☐ partition by place value to add two-digit numbers.
- ☐ use an algorithm to add.
- ☐ explore addition patterns.
- ☐ solve addition problems.

Problem solving

Length problems

For each problem:

a Draw a diagram. **b** Show your working. **c** Write your answer.

1 Flappy Bird flew 16 metres before lunch and 12 metres after lunch. How many metres did he fly altogether?

2 Super Cat jumped 42 metres to the shed and then another 21 metres to the back fence. How many metres did she jump altogether?

3 Wiggly Worm wriggled 18 metres. Then she wriggled another 11 metres. She then turned and went back 6 metres. How far is she from where she started? Draw it.

I can solve a problem by:

☐ adding 2-digit numbers. ☐ drawing a diagram or using an algorithm.

AC9M2N06 Number **MA1-WM-01** Working mathematically • Apply mathematical techniques to solve problems
MA1-CSQ-01 Combining and separating quantities B • Form multiples of ten when adding and subtracting two-digit numbers

One minute

Time yourself. Use a one-minute timer.

1 Write numbers in order.

How many can you write in one minute?

2 Thread beads. Colour the number used in one minute.

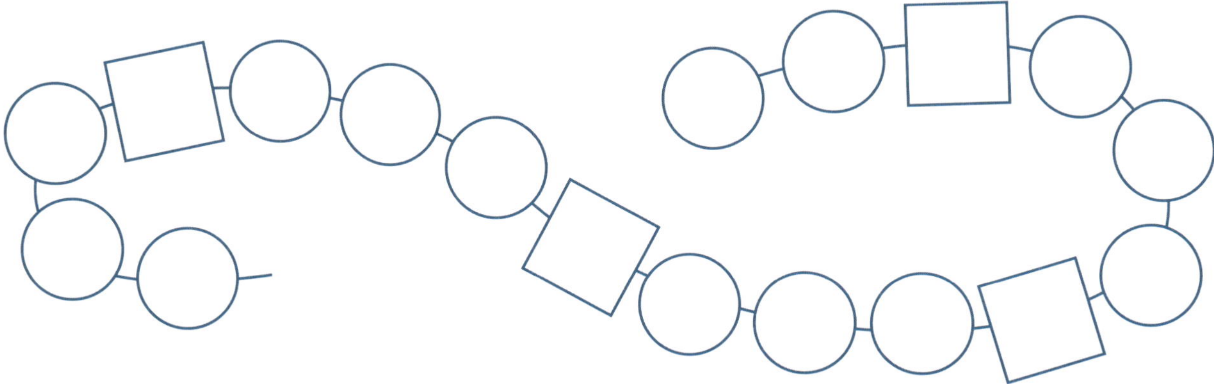

3 Roll a dice. Tick each number as you roll it. Did you get them all within 1 minute?

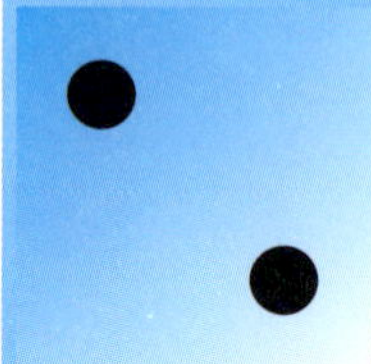
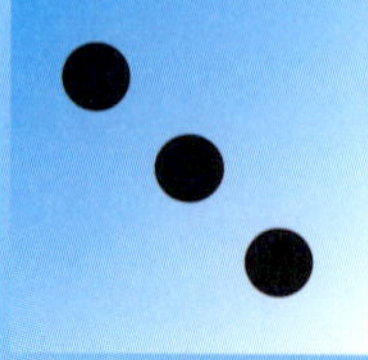
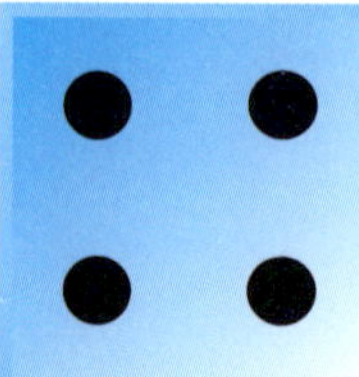
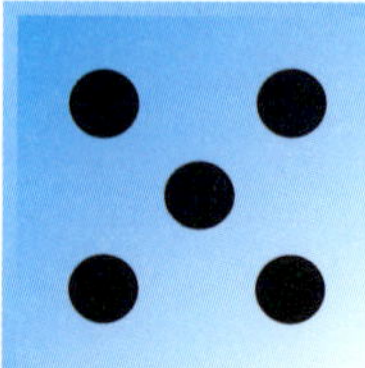
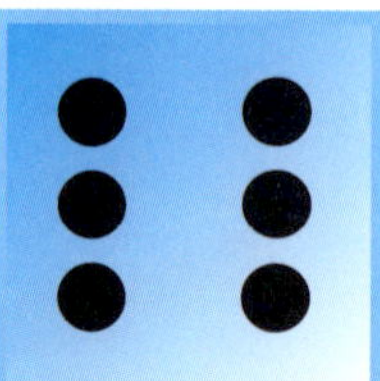

Challenge! How many cubes can you join in one minute?

Hours, minutes and seconds

1 Match.

Movie

hours

minutes

seconds

zzzZZ

2 How long does it take? Write hours, minutes or seconds.

travel to school	
write your name	
a birthday party	
blink your eyes	
go to the pool	

Time taken

1 Will it take hours, minutes or seconds?

a 

b 

c 

d 

e 

f 

2 Write the missing numbers.

a There are ☐ minutes in 1 hour.

b There are ☐ minutes in half an hour.

c There are ☐ months in one year.

d There are ☐ days in one week.

e There are ☐ days in two weeks.

3 Draw something that takes:

a seconds	b minutes	c hours

Challenge! How many months old are you? ☐

100 months? More than 100 months? Less than 100 months?

One and two minutes

time yourself doing things

Use a one-minute timer.

1 In one minute, how many times can you:

a write your name? __________ b bounce a ball? __________

c flip a coin? __________ d draw a hexagon? __________

2 In two minutes, how many:

a cubes can you join? __________ b dogs can you draw? __________

c numbers can you write? __________ d push-ups can you do? __________

3 Tick the activities that take about 5 minutes.

read 2 pages of a book

draw a picture of a house

sing the national anthem

walk to the park

eat a piece of cake

watch a movie

fill a bucket of water

have a bath

sleep

Mastery Checklist

I can: ☐ explore the duration of a minute.
☐ compare hours, minutes and seconds.

Half of a collection

Halves are two equal parts.

1 Circle two equal halves.

a

☐ is half of 8.

b

☐ is half of ☐

c

☐ is half of ☐

d

☐ is half of ☐

2 Here is half. How many in a whole? Draw and write the answer.

a

☐ is half of ☐

b

☐ is half of ☐

Challenge!

28 in a class.
Half are girls.
How many boys? ☐

Half of the girls
have black hair.
How many girls have black hair? ☐

Quarter of a collection

Quarters are four equal parts.

1

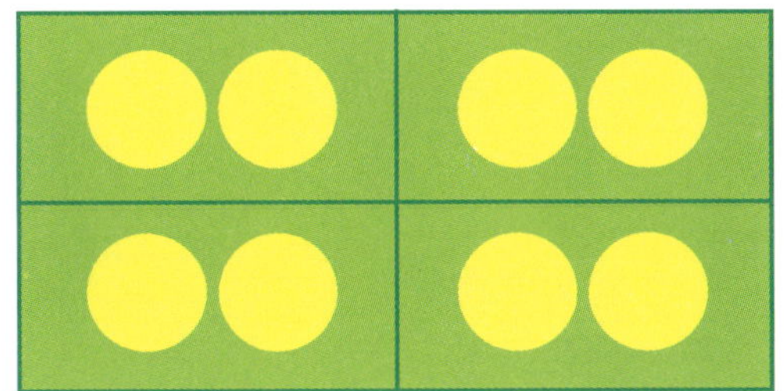

one quarter of 8 is ☐

2

one quarter of 12 is ☐

3

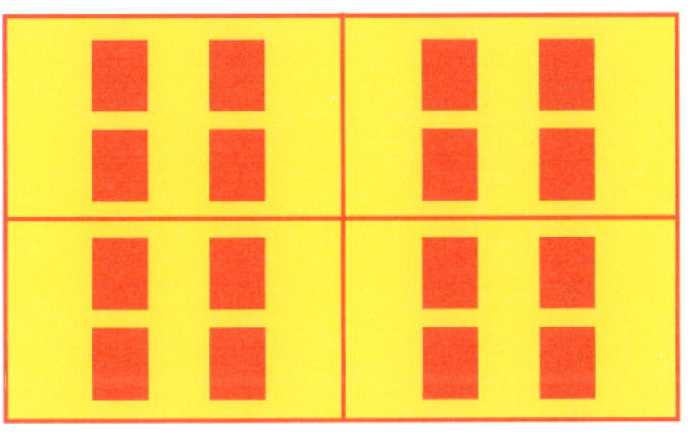

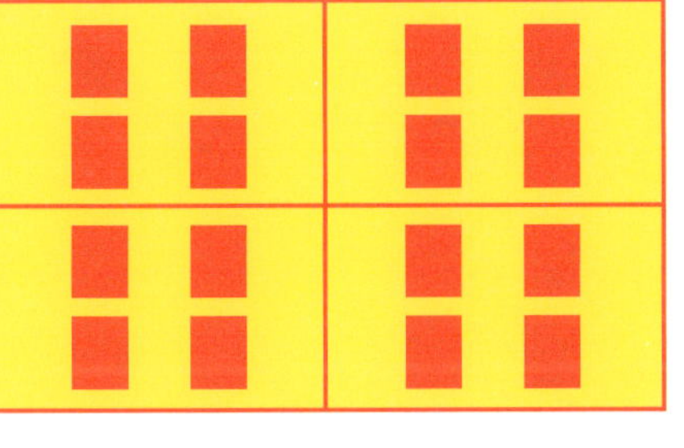

one quarter of ☐ is ☐

4

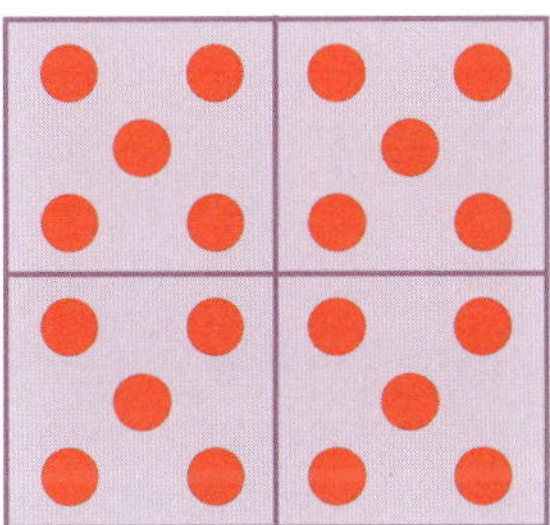

one quarter of ☐ is ☐

5

one quarter of ☐ is ☐

6 Use counters. $\frac{1}{4}$ **= one quarter**

a $\frac{1}{4}$ of 4 = ☐

b $\frac{1}{4}$ of 8 = ☐

c $\frac{1}{4}$ of 12 = ☐

d $\frac{1}{4}$ of 16 = ☐

e $\frac{1}{4}$ of 20 = ☐

f $\frac{1}{4}$ of 24 = ☐

Challenge! Colour $\frac{1}{4}$ red, $\frac{1}{4}$ blue, $\frac{1}{2}$ yellow.

Halves and quarters

1 **a** Jess had 4 balloons.
She gave half to Alex.
Jess gave Alex
☐ balloons.

b George had 8 cars.
He gave half to Ross.
George gave Ross
☐ cars.

c Katy had 12 cherries.
She gave half to Jarrah.
Katy gave Jarrah
☐ cherries.

d Lee had 10 pencils.
He gave half to Adam.
Lee gave Adam
☐ pencils.

2 **a** Mel had 8 marbles.
She lost a quarter of them.
How many did she lose? ☐
How many left? ☐

b Ravi had 12 pencils.
A quarter of them broke.
How many broke? ☐
How many left? ☐

c Tan had 16 cards.
He gave Ned a quarter of them.
How many did Ned get? ☐
How many did Tan keep? ☐

d Mia had 20 lollies.
She gave Li a quarter of them.
How many did Li get? ☐
How many did Mia keep? ☐

Challenge! There are 24 children.
Each child will be given 1 piece of apple and 1 piece of orange.
Oranges are cut into quarters. Apples are cut into halves.

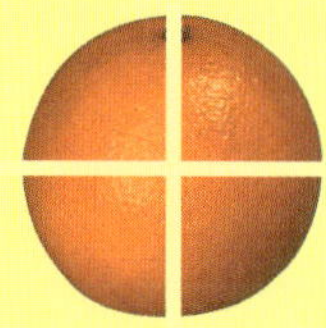

How many whole apples and oranges do they need?
☐ whole apples ☐ whole oranges

Eighths

1 Circle one eighth of each group.

a

$\frac{1}{8}$ of 8 is ☐

b

$\frac{1}{8}$ of 16 is ☐

c

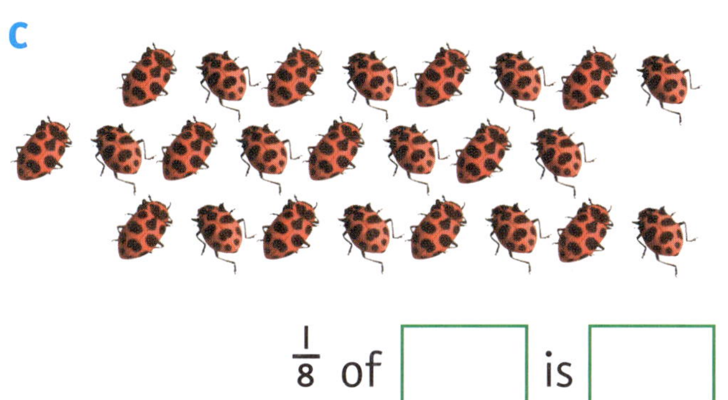

$\frac{1}{8}$ of ☐ is ☐

d

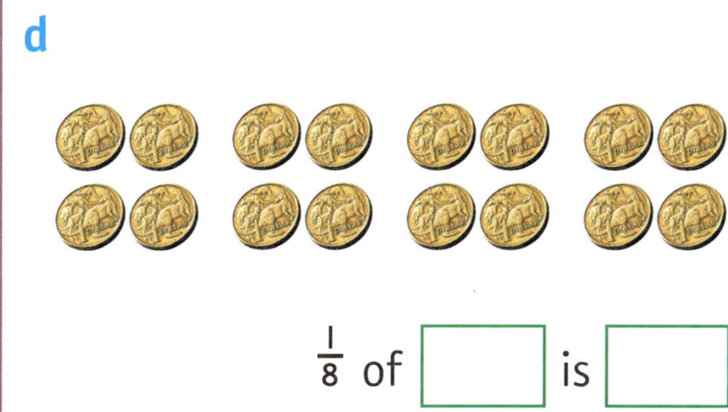

$\frac{1}{8}$ of ☐ is ☐

2 Cut this length into half. Then cut each half into half.
Then cut each part into half again.

3 What fraction is the length cut into? ☐

Challenge! Colour each one $\frac{1}{2}$ blue, $\frac{1}{4}$ green, $\frac{1}{8}$ red.
Make each one different.

Collecting data

Tally marks can help you keep count.

What is our favourite sandwich filling?

1 Ask the class and tally the results.

Sandwich filling	Tally	Total
Vegemite		
cheese		
salad		
chicken		
other		

2 Graph the results.

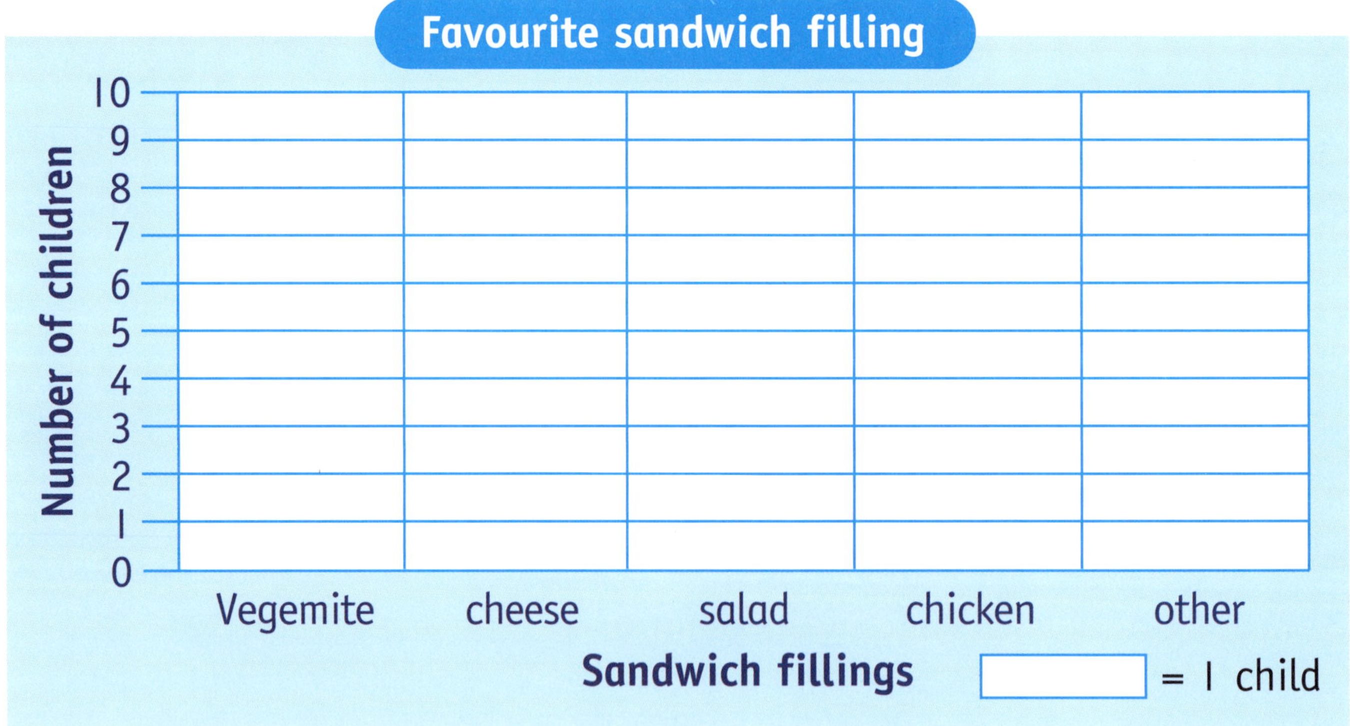

3 Which sandwich filling was:

a most popular? ______________ b least popular? ______________

4 How many children liked:

a chicken? ________ b cheese? ________ c Vegemite? ________

5 How many children altogether? ________

Tables and graphs

Ned collected five different things.

1 Use tally marks to count each thing.

2 What is the total for each thing?

3 Record the information on this column graph.

Things collected	Tally	Total
cards	𝍸 ||||	
shells		
stickers		
leaves		
marbles		

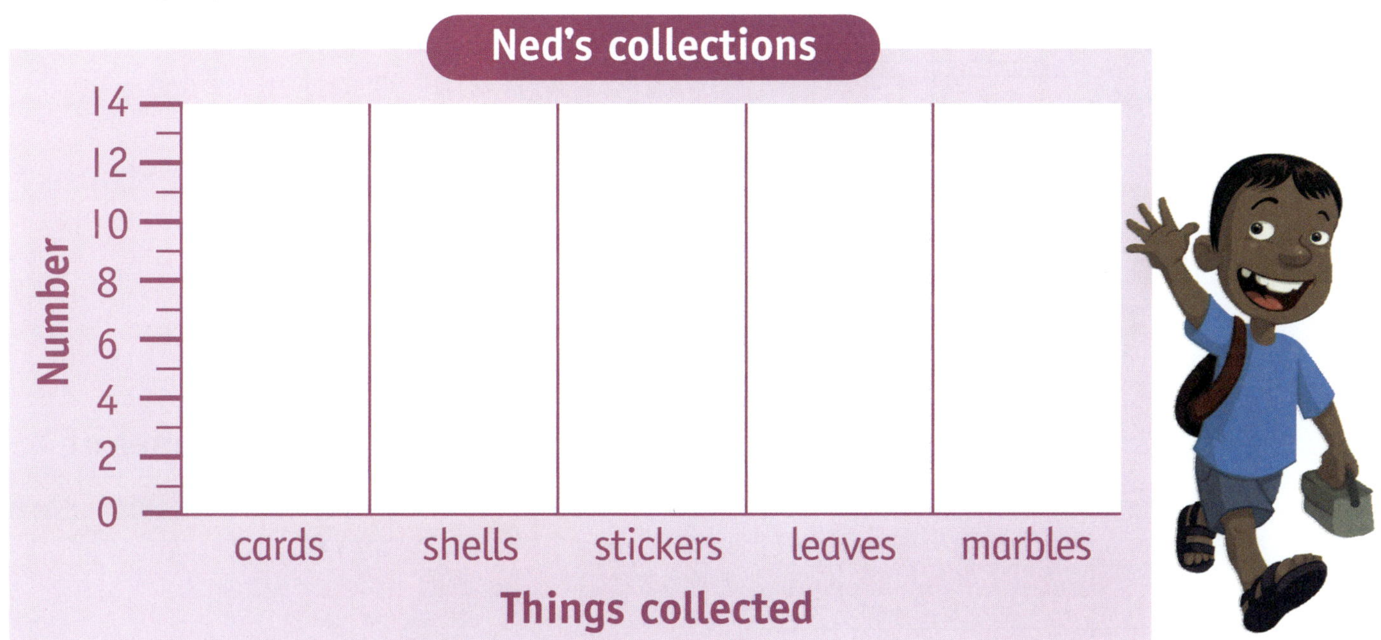

Mastery Checklist

I can:

- ☐ find a half, a quarter or an eighth of a collection.
- ☐ find the whole given half.
- ☐ halve a length multiple times to make eighths.
- ☐ collect, record and display data.

Revision • Term 3

1 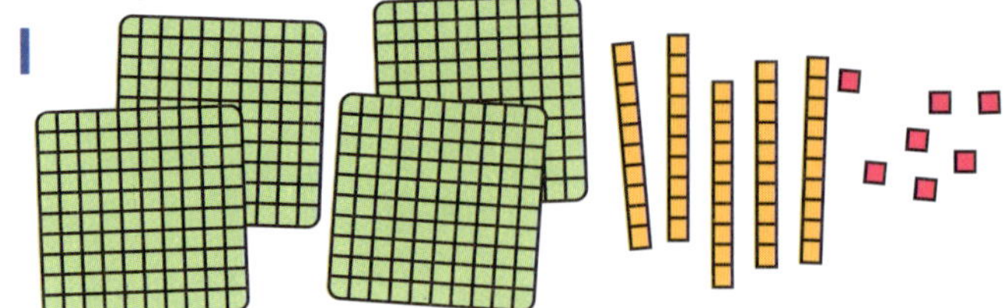

_____ hundreds _____ tens ____ ones

_____ + _____ + _____ = _____

2 Write in numerals.

a six hundred and ninety-seven _____

b eight hundred and fifty _____

3 Write 260 in words.

_____

4 Continue each pattern.

a 1, 3, 5, ☐ ☐ ☐

b 0, 3, 6, ☐ ☐ ☐

5 Write number sentences.

a _____ + _____ = _____

b _____ + _____ = _____

c _____ − _____ = _____

d _____ − _____ = _____

6 a

$$\begin{array}{r} 16 \\ +\ 13 \\ \hline \end{array}$$

b

$$\begin{array}{r} 24 \\ +\ 33 \\ \hline \end{array}$$

7   

a 2 groups of 5 = _____

b 3 × 5 = _____

c 4 × 5 = _____

8  10c

Jim has 50c.

He can buy ☐ lollies.

9 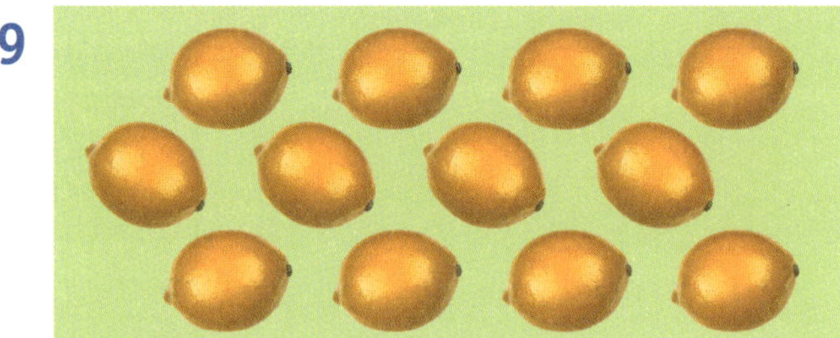

a One half of 12 = _____

b One quarter of 12 = _____

10 How long is your textbook?

Estimate: _____ cm

Measure: _____ cm

11 Number of

	faces	edges	corners
(triangular prism)			
(rectangular prism)			

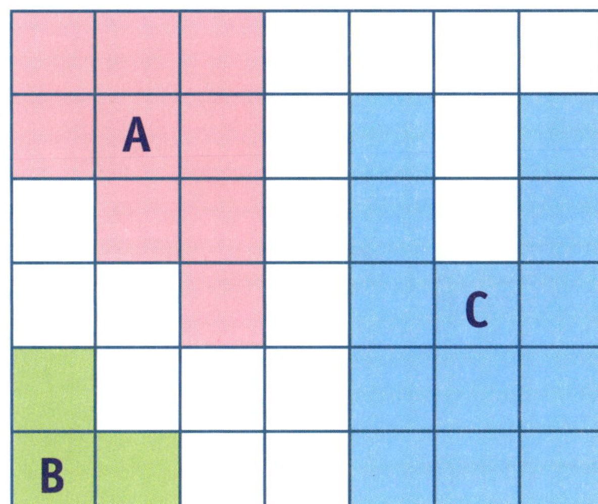

12 What is the area in squares of:

a A ☐ B ☐ C ☐

Which shape has:

b the smallest area? ______

c the largest area? ______

13 Split this shape into 2 triangles.

14 The pencil weighs 5 blocks. The scissors weigh 10 blocks.

a The pencil weighs ________ than the scissors.

b The difference is ________ blocks.

15 Circle the one that takes about 5 minutes.

16 Circle 4 equal quarters.

$\frac{1}{4}$ of 8 = ☐

17 Use the tallies to complete the table and the graph.

	Tally	Total
dogs	||||	
fish	~~||||~~ |||	
cats	~~||||~~ |	

Pets of 2A

Number of animals	dogs	fish	cats
8			
7			
6			
5			
4			
3			
2			
1			

Comparing numbers

1 How many?

a

b

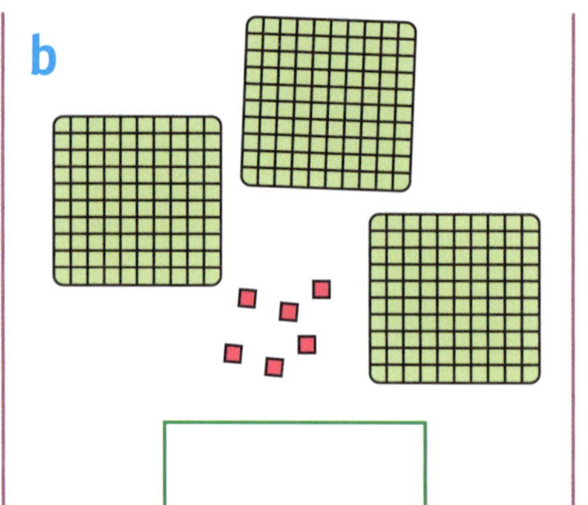

c

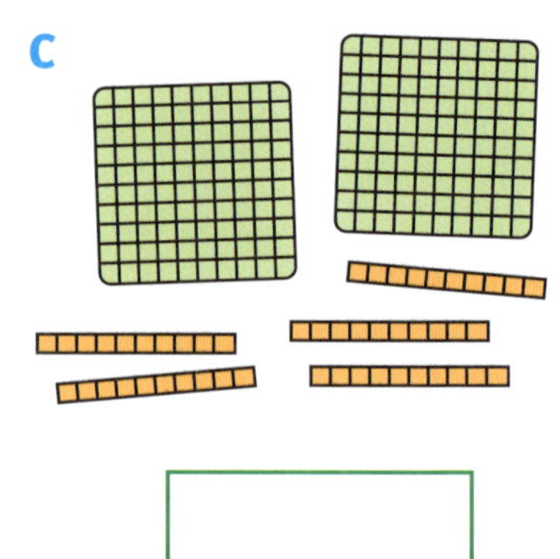

d Tick the largest number.

2 a

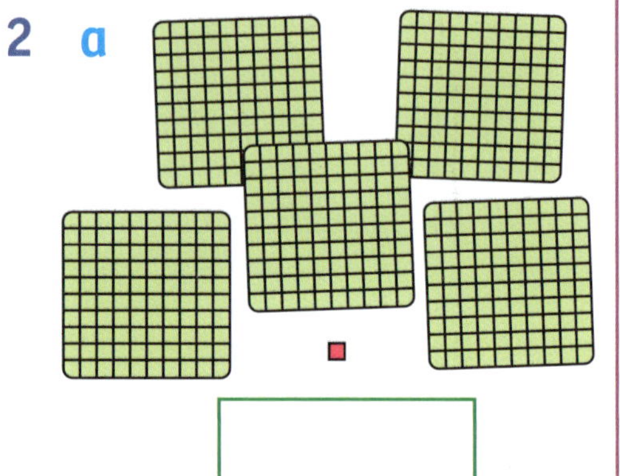

b

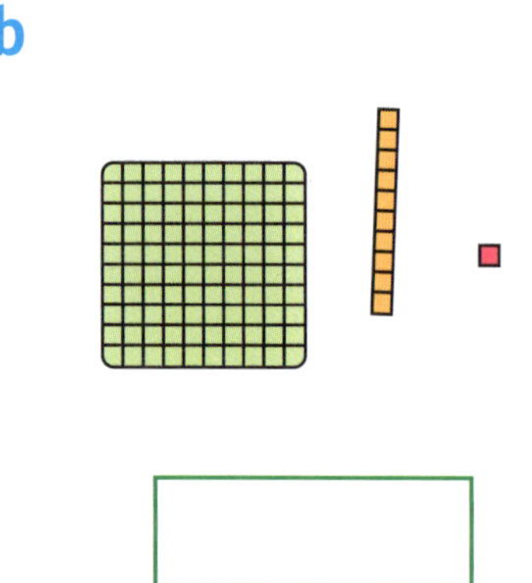

c

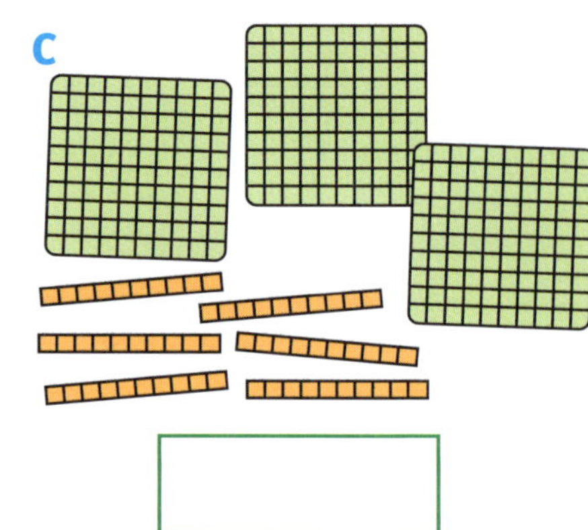

d Tick the smallest number.

3 a Circle the larger number.

b Circle the smaller number.

Challenge! Find the smallest and largest number on this page.

smallest **largest**

Counting in tens and hundreds

1 How many cents?  = 100 cents 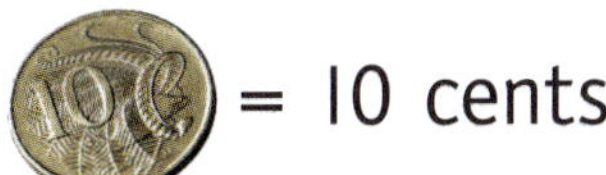 = 10 cents  = 5 cents

a ☐ + ☐ = ☐ c

b ☐ + ☐ = ☐ c

c ☐ + ☐ = ☐ c

d ☐ + ☐ = ☐ c

e ☐ + ☐ = ☐ c

f ☐ + ☐ = ☐ c

2 Write the number.

a 700 → 50 → 8 → ☐

b 500 → 80 → 7 → ☐

c 900 → 60 → 4 → ☐

d 300 → 30 → 3 → ☐

e 200 → 90 → 9 → ☐

f 600 → 10 → 1 → ☐

Challenge! In question 1, how much altogether? ☐

Number lines

1 Count by 1s.

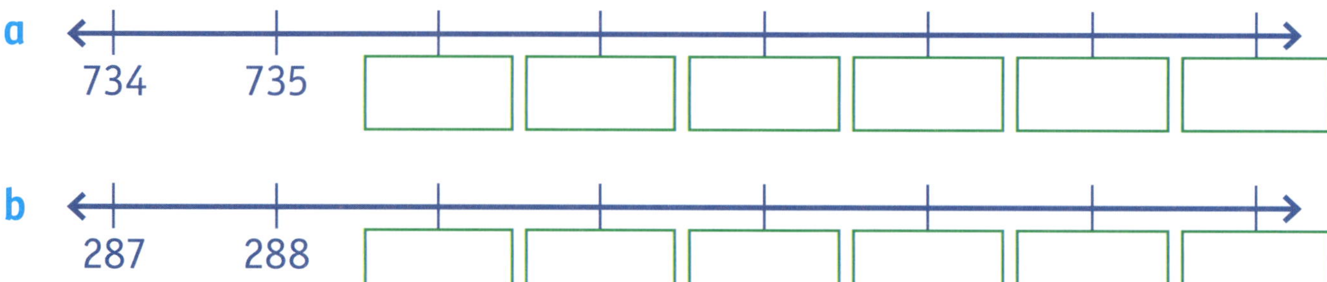

2 Count by 10s.

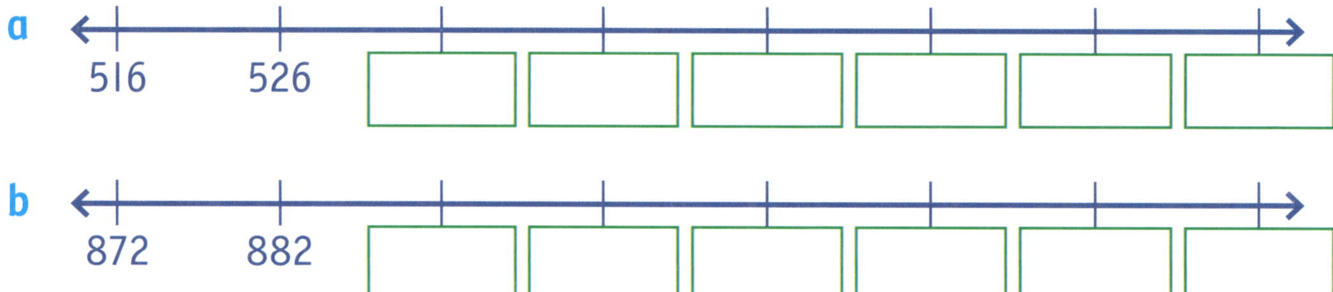

3 Count by 100s.

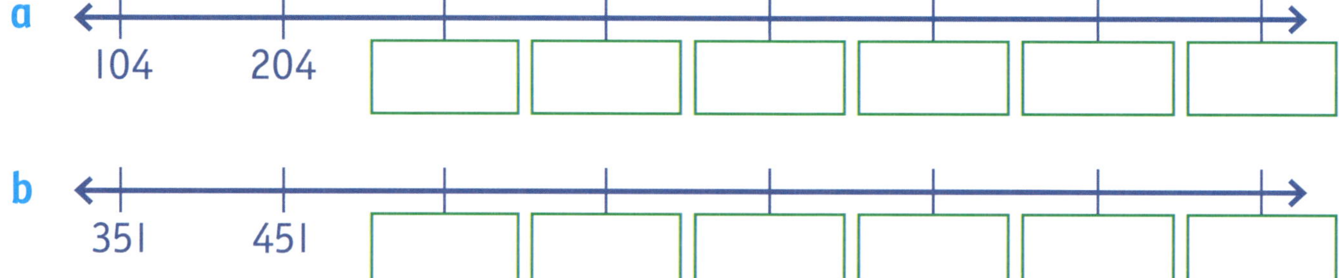

4 Fill in the missing numbers.

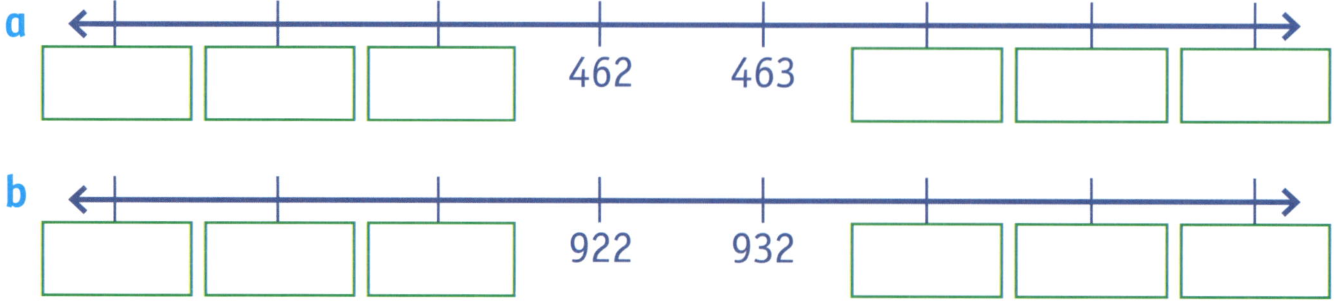

Nearest ten or hundred

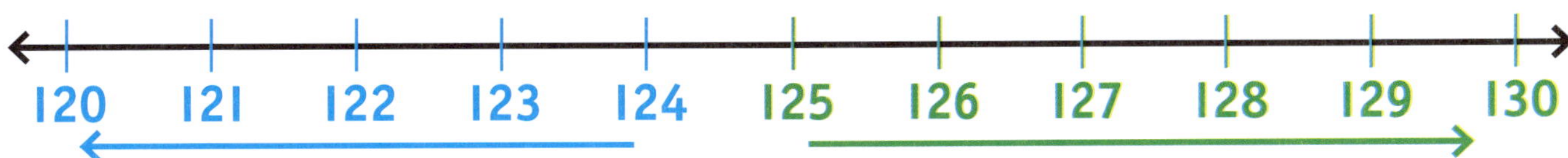

1 Circle the nearest 10.

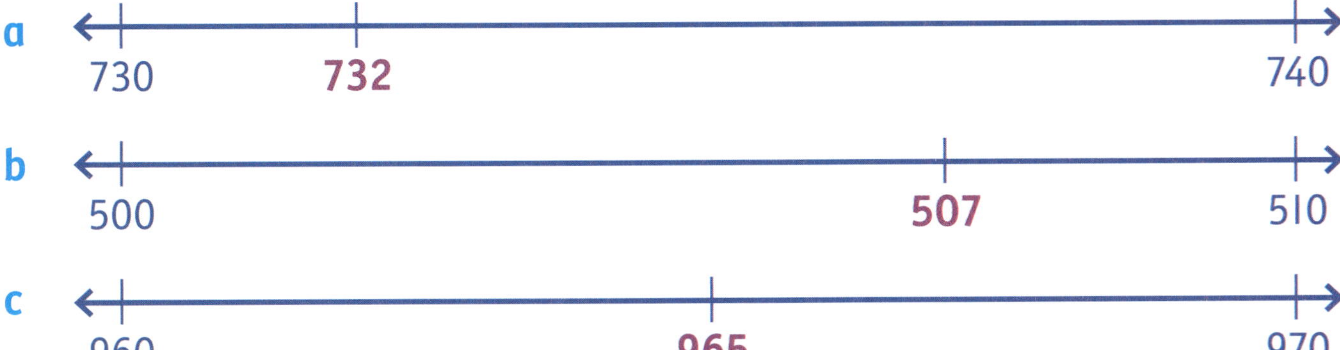

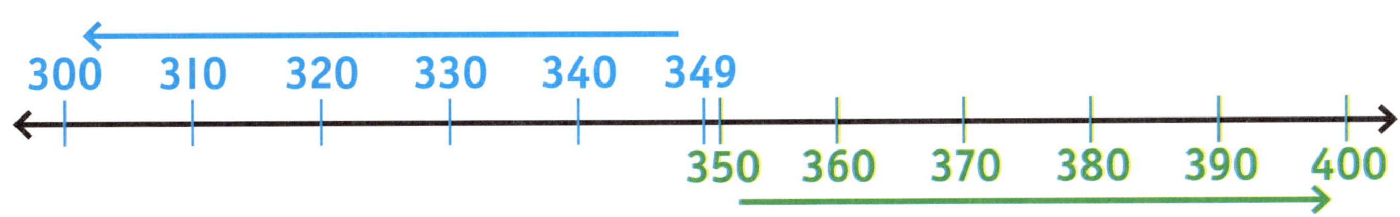

2 Circle the nearest 100.

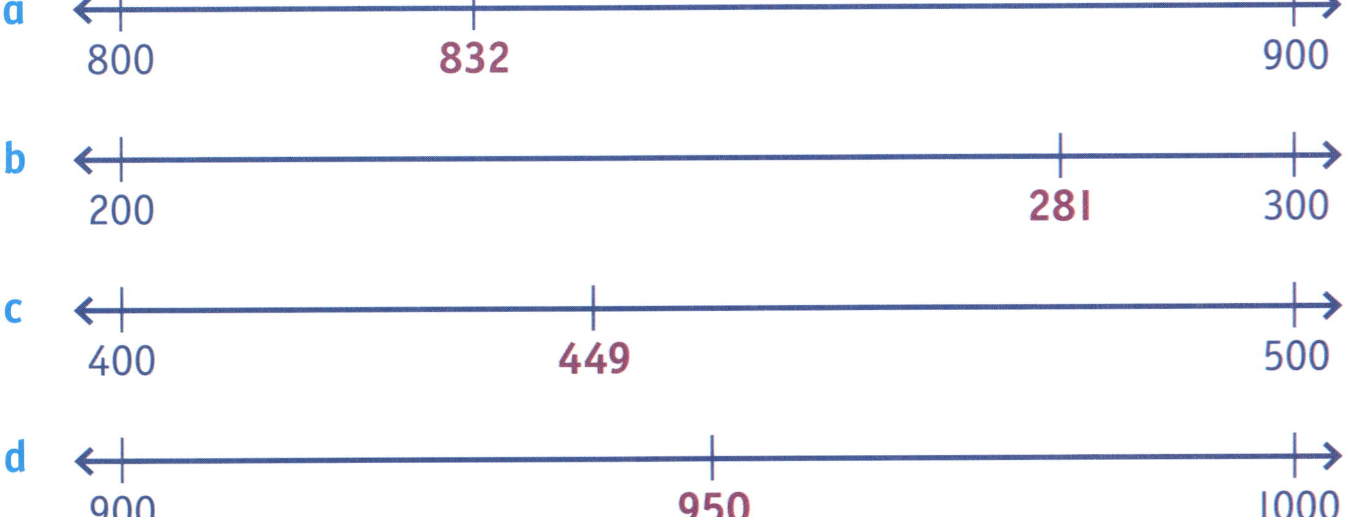

Mastery Checklist

I can:
- ☐ count by 1s, 10s, 100s.
- ☐ compare numbers using place value.
- ☐ round to the nearest 10 or 100.

Problem solving

Tall Star building

The Tall Star building is 10 floors high.

The even numbered floors have 2 flats.

The odd numbered floors have 3 flats.

How many flats are in the Tall Star building? ________

I can solve a problem by:

☐ knowing the odd and even numbers. ☐ writing a list, or using an algorithm.

AC9M2N01 Number MA1-WM-01 Working mathematically • Apply mathematical techniques to solve problems

Time

Morning bus

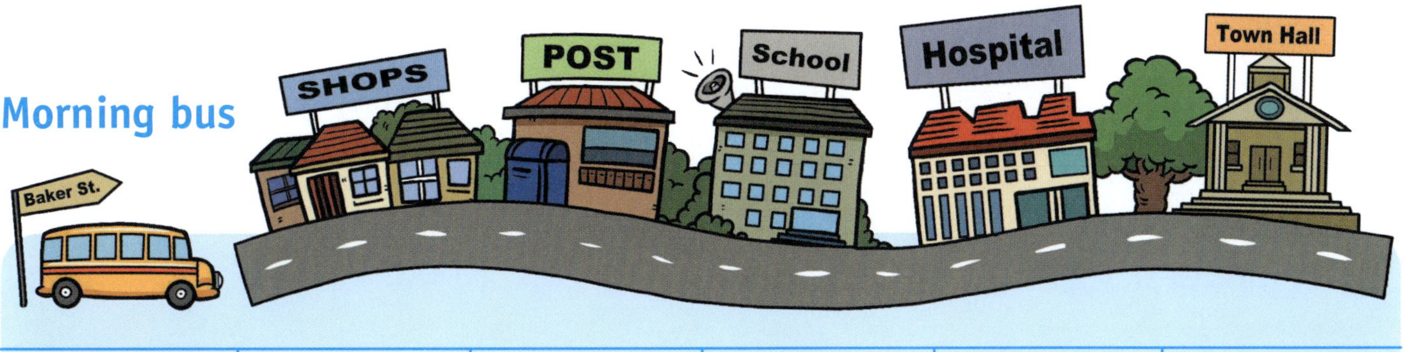

Begins at Baker Street	Shops	Post Office	School	Hospital	Ends at Town Hall
7:00	7:30	8:00	8:30	9:00	9:30

1 What time does the bus get to the:

a school? ______________ b Town Hall? ______________

2 Write these times both ways. eg 6:00, 6 o'clock.

The bus a begins at [:] ______________________

b ends at [:] ______________________

3 How long does the bus take to get from:

a Baker Street to the Post Office? ______________

b the school to the hospital? ______________

c the beginning to the end? ______________

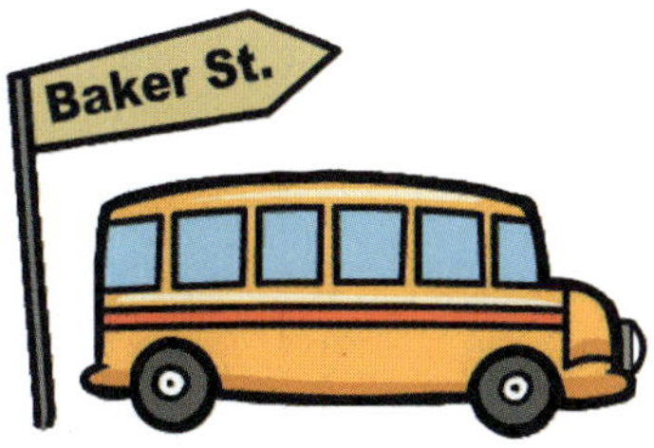

4 My favourite TV show is: [   ]

It goes for [   ] minutes.

If it starts at [:]

it will end at [:]

Start time

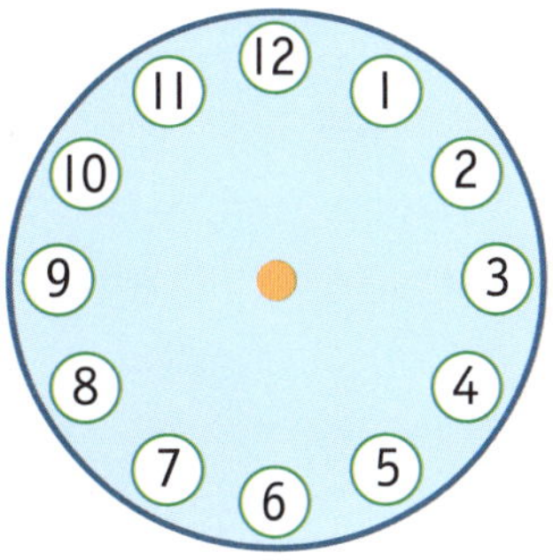

End time

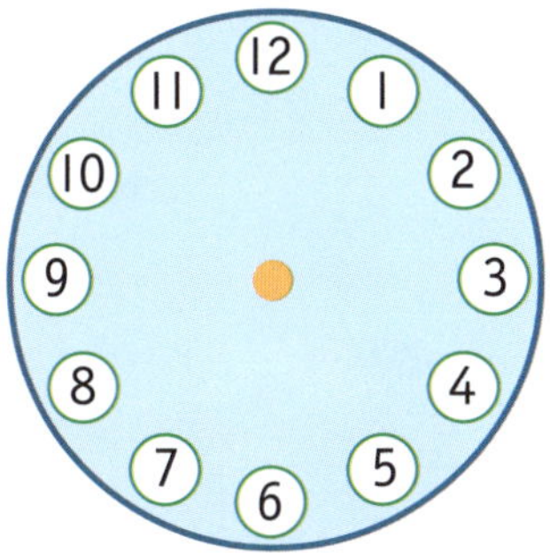

Quarter past and quarter to

At a quarter past, the big hand has moved a quarter of the way around to the number 3.

The small hand is just past the hour.

At a quarter to, the big hand sits on 9. It has a quarter of the way still to go.

The small hand is near the next hour.

1 Write the time.

a

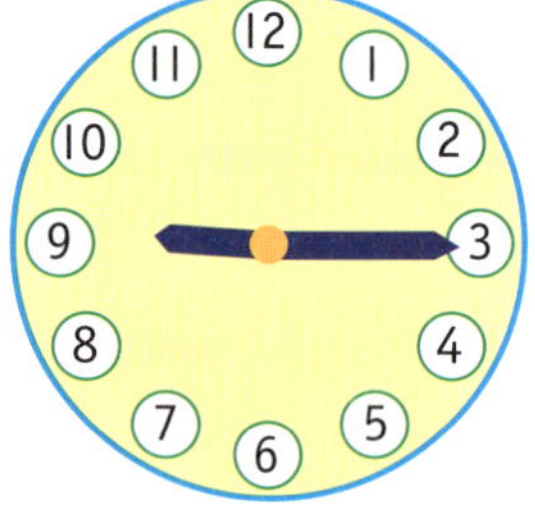

b

c

2 Draw the big hand to show the time.

a

b

c

d

e

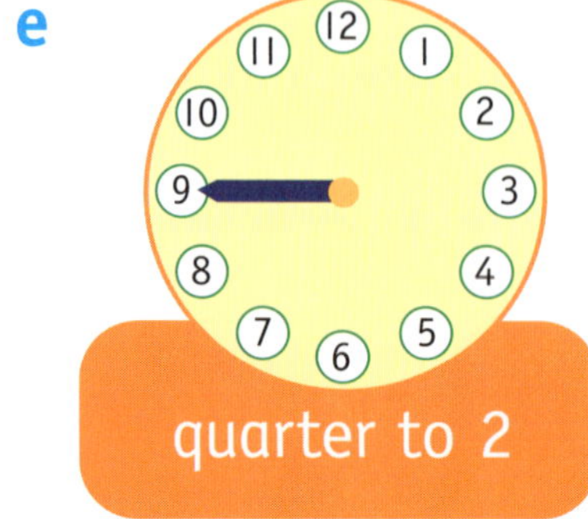

f

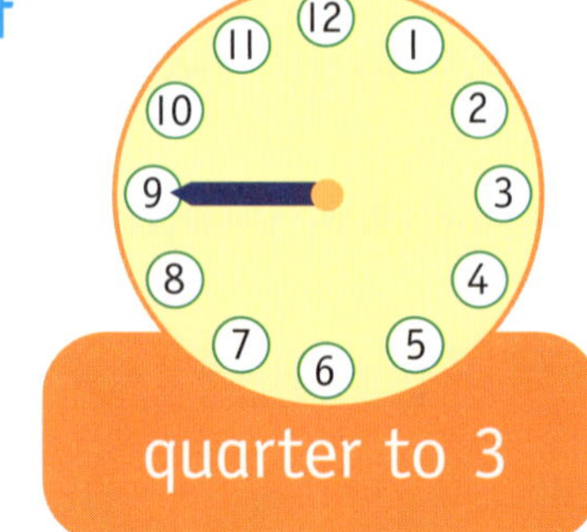

Reading clocks

There are 60 mins in an hour.

There are **15 mins** in a **quarter of an hour.**

1 o'clock | quarter past 1 | half past 1 | quarter to 2

Fill in the matching times.

1

2

quarter past 3

3

4

quarter to 10

5
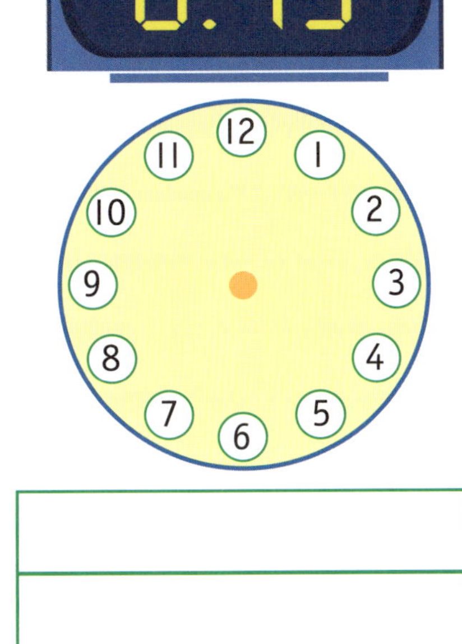

6

A special day

Make a timetable for a special day where you can do all your favourite activities. You can choose the things you want to do. Use pictures, words and times.

Activity	Start Time	How long it takes	End time

Mastery Checklist

I can:
- ☐ read and make a timetable.
- ☐ calculate duration in hours and minutes.
- ☐ read time in quarter hours on analog and digital clocks.
- ☐ measure time in informal units.

Problem solving

Time units

You will need a **partner** for this activity. Choose a quick and easy body movement, like a clap or a stamp. This will be your time unit.

One person completes the activity listed while the other person makes as many of the body movements as possible. Count how many movements are made. That's your time measured in your units.

1 What is your chosen unit? ____________________

2 Find the amount of time each activity takes.

Activity	My time in units	Partner time in units
a Walk across the room		
b Say the alphabet		
c Move from 1 chair to another		
d Write the alphabet		
e Drink a full glass of water		

3 Put the activities in order from shortest to longest time.

____

4 Now swap roles and record a set of times for the other person.

5 Highlight the shortest time for each activity.

6 Who was fastest at most things?

____

I can solve a problem by:

☐ using informal time units. ☐ using a table.

Split to subtract

Split Strategy –

To subtract 13, take away 10, then take away 3.

1   27 − 13 = ☐

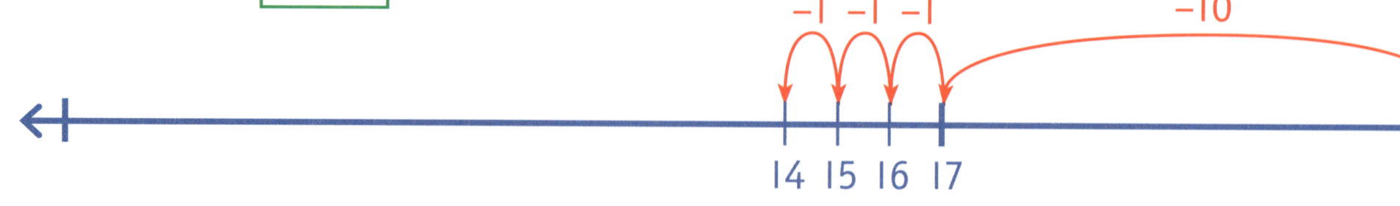

To subtract 22, take away 20, then take away 2.

2   35 − 22 = ☐

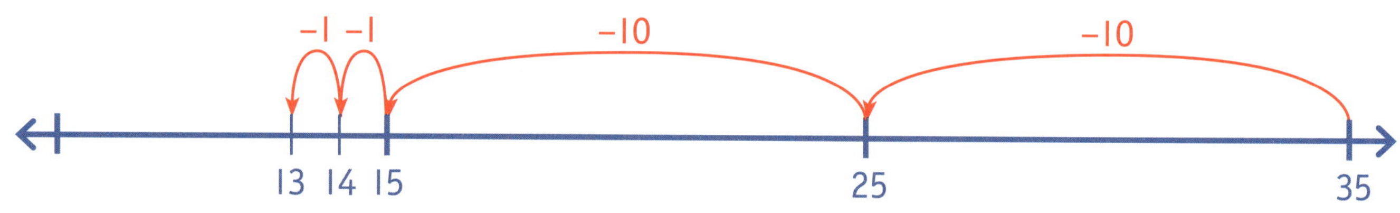

3   48 − 15 = ☐

4   54 − 16 = ☐

5   62 − 25 = ☐

AC9M2N04 Number **MA1-CSQ-01** Combining and separating quantities B • Form multiples of ten when adding and subtracting two-digit numbers

Subtraction using algorithms

Subtract to 50

1

	tens	ones
	1	6
–		4

We read this as 16 – 4.

16 – 4 = ☐

2 Here are some more.

a

	tens	ones
	1	8
–		2

b

	tens	ones
	1	5
–		3

c

	tens	ones
	1	9
–		7

d

	tens	ones
	1	7
–		5

e

	tens	ones
	1	4
–		4

f

	tens	ones
	1	8
–		7

g $\begin{array}{r} 16 \\ -\ \ 4 \\ \hline \end{array}$

h $\begin{array}{r} 15 \\ -\ 10 \\ \hline \end{array}$

i $\begin{array}{r} 20 \\ -\ 10 \\ \hline \end{array}$

j $\begin{array}{r} 19 \\ -\ \ 9 \\ \hline \end{array}$

k $\begin{array}{r} 27 \\ -\ \ 6 \\ \hline \end{array}$

l $\begin{array}{r} 22 \\ -\ 10 \\ \hline \end{array}$

m $\begin{array}{r} 26 \\ -\ 11 \\ \hline \end{array}$

n $\begin{array}{r} 23 \\ -\ 12 \\ \hline \end{array}$

Challenge! You have $20. You must spend it all at the pet shop. How could you spend the money? Find 3 different ways.

$2 each

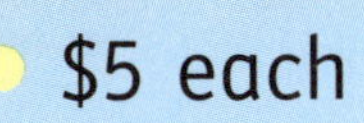

$5 each

$6 each

$12 each

Subtraction from twenty

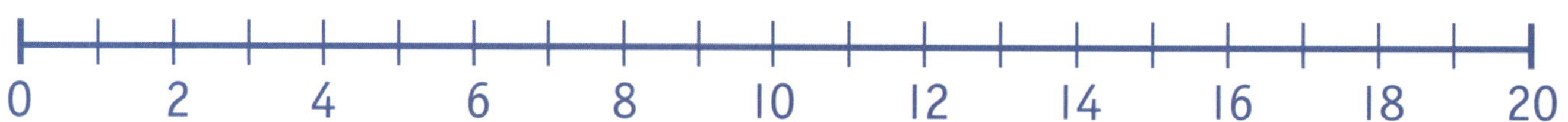

1 Write a number sentence. Then find the change.

a

$20 – $6 = $

b

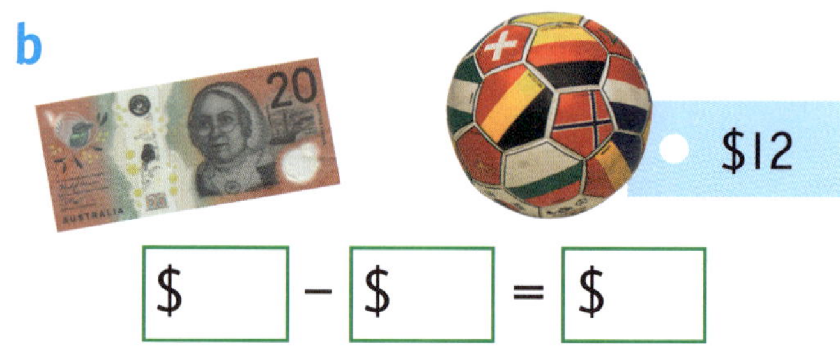

$ – $ = $

c

$ – $ = $

d

$ – $ = $

2 Each pair begins with 20.

a

Furry eats 7. Spot eats 5.

How many carrots left?

b

Jack eats 6. Ruby eats 7.

How many biscuits left?

c

Frog eats 12. Toad eats 6.

How many flies left?

d

Cheeky eats 3. Mango eats 9.

How many bananas left?

AC9M2N06 Number MA1-CSQ-01 Combining and separating quantities B • Represent and reason about additive relations

Difference patterns

The rule is the difference between the numbers.

1 Find the rule. Continue the pattern.

a	48	47	46	45	____	____	____	Rule:
b	98	88	78	68	____	____	____	Rule:
c	845	745	645	645	____	____	____	Rule:
d	567	557	547	537	____	____	____	Rule:
e	759	649	539	429	____	____	____	Rule:
f	673	562	451	340	____	____	____	Rule:

2 Find the rule. Continue the pattern.

a	38	33	28	23	____	____	____	Rule:
b	98	83	68	53	____	____	____	Rule:
c	453	403	353	303	____	____	____	Rule:
d	374	362	350	338	____	____	____	Rule:
e	985	865	745	625	____	____	____	Rule:
f	876	753	630	507	____	____	____	Rule:

3 Write your own difference patterns.

a ____ ____ ____ ____ ____ ____ ____ Rule:

b ____ ____ ____ ____ ____ ____ ____ Rule:

c ____ ____ ____ ____ ____ ____ ____ Rule:

d ____ ____ ____ ____ ____ ____ ____ Rule:

The calculator

Use only these buttons. 5 2 + – =

You can press buttons more than once.

1 Make each number. Draw how you did it.

a 5 + 5 – 2 = 8

b 14

c 9

d 13

e 28

f 23

g 21

Challenge! Press 8 buttons and end up with the number 10 on the screen.

								10

Mastery Checklist

I can:
- [ ] partition by place value to subtract.
- [ ] use an algorithm to subtract.
- [ ] explore difference patterns.
- [ ] solve subtraction problems.

Problem solving

Subtraction

This is a number sentence. **16 – 9 = 7**

This is a story to match it.

Sixteen hens went into the hen house. Nine came out. How many hens stayed in the hen house?

1 Write and draw your own stories to match these number sentences.

15 – 8 = 7

13 – 9 = 4

2 Farmer Jim had 20 sheep on Friday. On Sunday he only had 12 sheep.

Some sheep ran away on Friday night. Some more sheep ran off on Saturday night. How many sheep could have run away each night?

Write and draw your answer.

I'm running away! He he!

I can solve a problem by:

☐ thinking up stories to match number sentences. ☐ writing my own problems.

AC9M2N06 Number **MA1-WM-01** Working mathematically • Apply mathematical techniques to solve problems • Communicate their thinking and reasoning coherently and clearly **MA1-CSQ-01** Combining and separating quantities B • Represent and reason about additive relations • Form multiples of ten when adding and subtracting two-digit numbers • Use knowledge of equality to solve related problems

Capacity in cups

measure capacity in cups

Capacity is how much something holds.

Find four drink containers like these.

1 How many cups does each hold? Colour the number of cups.

a

Container	Number of cups

b

Container	Number of cups

c

Container	Number of cups
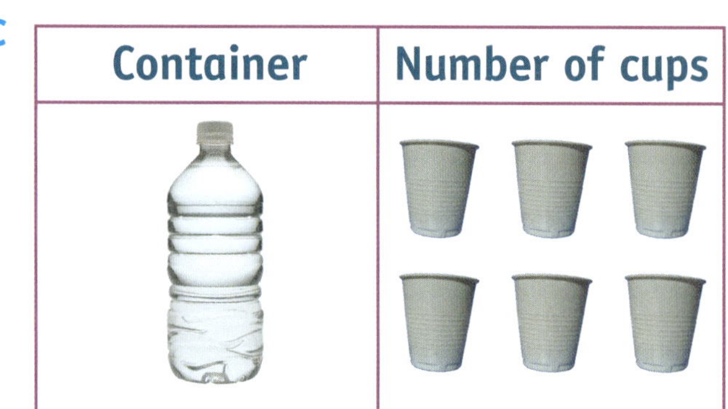	

d

Container	Number of cups
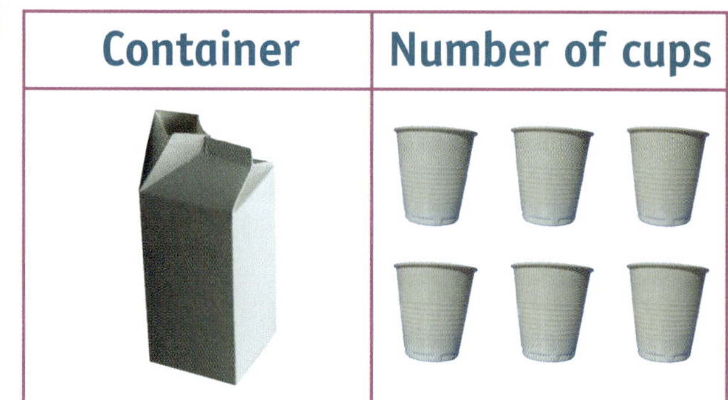	

2 During one week of school:

a Alex drank 10 . How many cups did he drink? ________

b Freya drank 5 . How many cups did she drink? ________

c Ned drank 2  and 3 cups of water. How many cups did he drink? ________

d Karen drank 2  and 3 . How many cups did she drink? ________

Challenge! Jenny makes 2 jugs of cordial a day. Each jug holds 5 cups. How many cups does Jenny make:

a in one week? ☐ **b** in 4 weeks? ☐

Capacity in blocks

1 How many blocks fit in each box?

a

☐ blocks

b

☐ blocks

c

☐ blocks

d

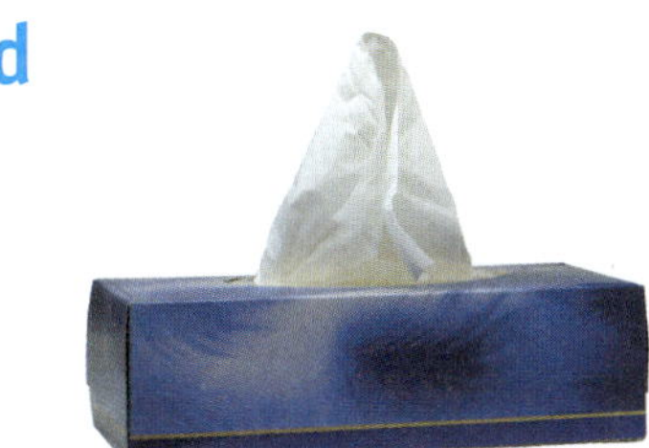

☐ blocks

2 Match each box to a stack of blocks. Fill in the boxes.

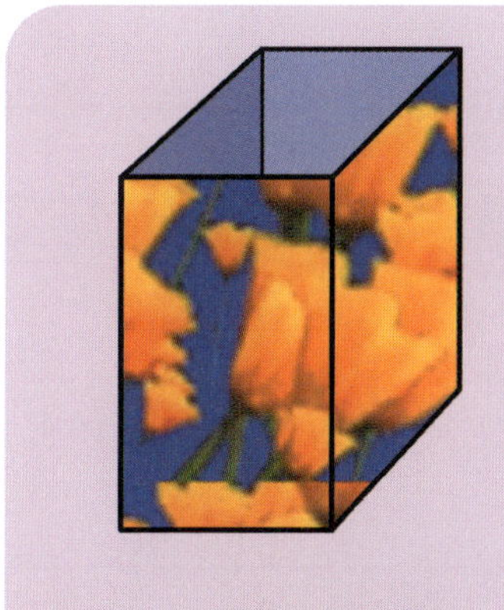

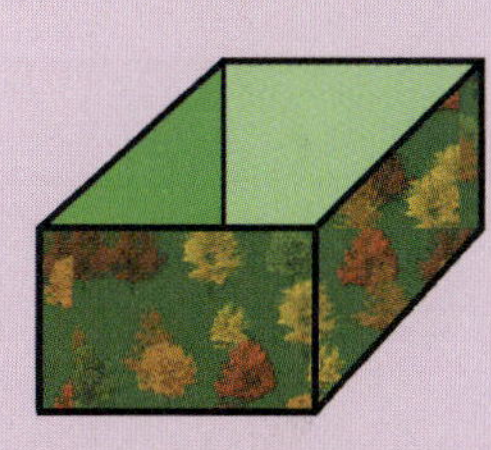

a 2 layers of 9 blocks.

= ☐ blocks

b ☐ layer of ☐ blocks.

= ☐ blocks

c ☐ layers of ☐ blocks.

= ☐ blocks

d ☐ layers of ☐ blocks.

= ☐ blocks

Volume

Volume is how much space an item takes up.

1 How many cubes in this box?

2 How many cubes in this box?

a

b

3 Which box is larger? a or b

4 How do you know?

5 These boxes are the same size.

a How many cubes in this box?

b How many cubes in this box?

c Why is the number of cubes different?

AC9M2M01 Measurement **MA1-3DS-02** Three-dimensional spatial structure B • Volume: Compare volumes using uniform informal units
MA1-WM-01 Working mathematically • Apply mathematical techniques to solve problems • Communicate their thinking and reasoning coherently and clearly

Displacement

1 Half fill a container with water.

Mark the level of the water.

2 Make 2 balls of plasticine, one large and one small.

a Drop each ball gently into the water.

b Draw the new level each time.

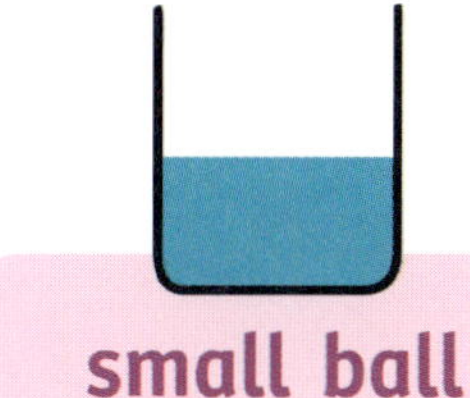

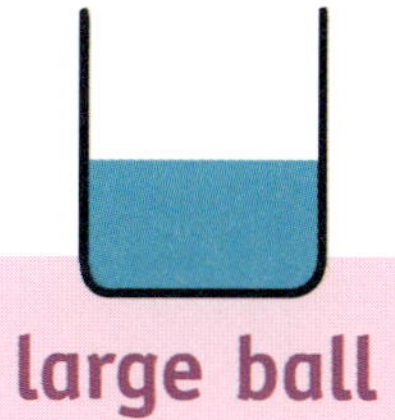

small ball　　large ball

c What happens to the water level? ______________________

3 a Make these 3 models.

A	B	C

b Drop each model into the water. Draw the new level each time.

A	B	C

c Model ______ takes up the most space.

d Model ______ takes up the least space.

4 a Now make 3 different models using 8 cubes in each model.

b Draw the new level each time.

A 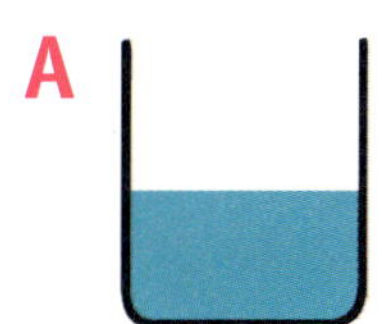 B  C 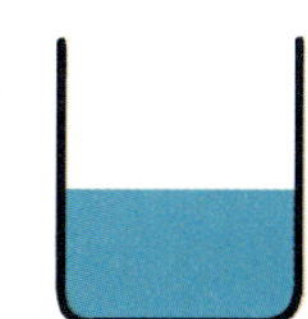

What are you measuring?

1 For each object, what could you measure?
What would you use to measure it?

We can measure:
- length
- area
- capacity
- volume
- mass
- time

Object	I could measure its	I could use a
	capacity mass	cup equal-arm balance

Challenge How many things can you find that measure time?

Draw them here.

Mastery Checklist

I can:
- ☐ measure capacity of boxes in blocks.
- ☐ recognise that units need to be the same size.
- ☐ measure volume by displacement.
- ☐ measure capacity in cups.

Problem solving

Jay's Soup

Jay makes her favourite soup by mixing 3 soups together — 1 bean, 2 chicken noodle and 1 vegetable. Draw and write your answers.

Each can = 1 cup

1 Jay wants to make 8 cups of her favourite soup. How could she make it?

2 Jay is having a dinner for 12 people. Every person will have 1 cup of soup. How could she make her soup for 12 people?

3 She wants to make cordial for them too. The cordial recipe says, "Mix 1 cup cordial with 3 cups of water." How many cups of cordial will she use to make 12 cups?

I can solve a problem by:

☐ calculating capacity in cups. ☐ writing or drawing a diagram.

Thank you class party

Investigation 4

Our class is planning a Thank you party. This party will say thank you to everyone for working so hard all year.

Work with a partner to plan the party.

1 First, count how many people will be at the party.

Children ____________ Adults ____________ Total ____________

Everyone will need a plate.

How many plates will you need? ____________

How many spoons? ____________

How many cups? ____________

2 What food will you have? Choose 5 foods.

____

____

____

____

____

____

3 How much of each food will you need?

____

____

____

____

____

____

4 How many drinks for each person? If each bottle holds 5 drinks, how many bottles will you need? ____________

AC9M2N06 Number **MA1-3DS-02** Three-dimensional spatial structure B • Volume: Compare volumes using uniform informal units
MA1-WM-01 Working mathematically • Apply mathematical techniques to solve problems • Communicate their thinking and reasoning coherently and clearly

Thank you class party

Investigation 4

5 When will the party be held?

At ______________________ on ______________________

How many days until the party? __________

6 Write an invitation to the party. Make sure you include the start time, the date and the place of your party.

7 Write a list of jobs to be done for the party. Don't forget cleaning up!

____

____

____

____

____

To complete these tasks I needed to:

- [ ] count large numbers.
- [ ] plan and decide.
- [ ] make lists of food, drinks, jobs.
- [ ] measure drink (capacity).
- [ ] write time and date.
- [ ] write an invitation.
- [ ] work with a partner.

I enjoyed this task!

☆☆☆☆☆

Revision

1 What is the next number in this pattern?

134, 145, 156, 167, 178, ☐

187	179	198	189
◯	◯	◯	◯

2 What can you do in about 1 minute?

Write a sentence	Drive to school	Water the garden	Eat lunch
◯	◯	◯	◯

3 20 −  = 13

The number that goes in the ☐ is:

6	7	8	9
◯	◯	◯	◯

4 What is the time?

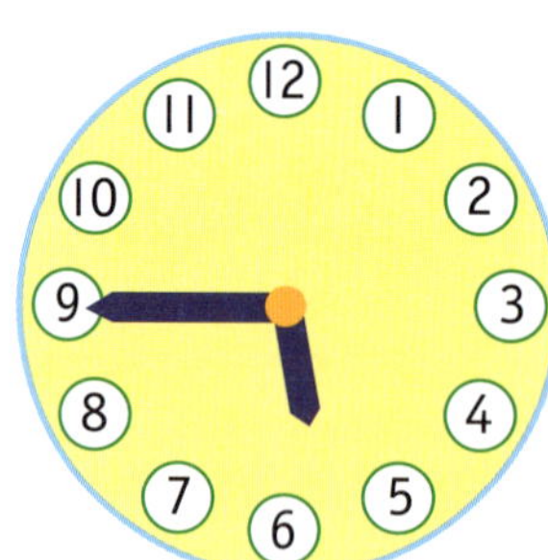

9:30	6:45	8:30	5:45
◯	◯	◯	◯

5 Which one is the same as 8 minus 3 = 5?

3 more than 5 = 8 ◯ 5 − 3 = 8 ◯

5 more than 8 = 13 ◯ 13 less than 18 = 5 ◯

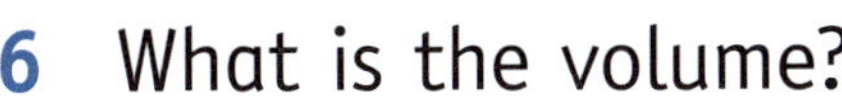

Revision

6 What is the volume?

8 ◯ 12 ◯ 18 ◯ 24 ◯

7 What is the next number in this pattern?

30, 27, 24, 21, 18, ☐

17 ◯ 16 ◯ 15 ◯ 12 ◯

8

$$\begin{array}{r} 18 \\ -\ \ 6 \\ \hline \\ \hline \end{array}$$

8 ◯ 10 ◯ 12 ◯ 24 ◯

9 Which is the closest ten to **134**?

20 ◯ 130 ◯ 135 ◯ 140 ◯

Dividing on a number line

1 How many 3s in 12?

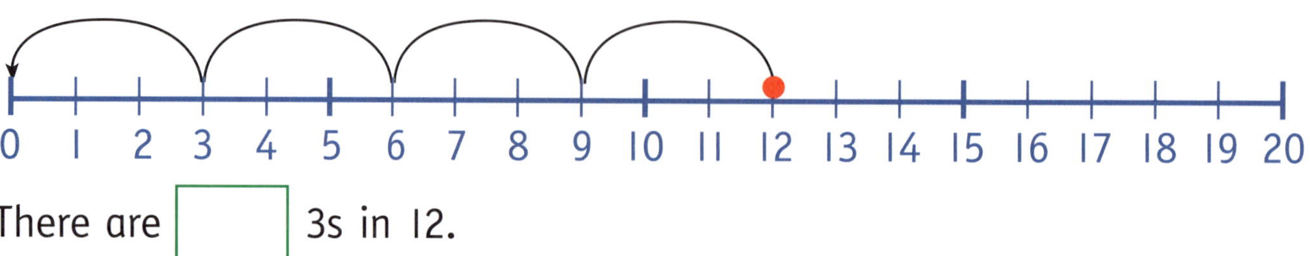

There are ☐ 3s in 12.

2 How many 2s in 14?

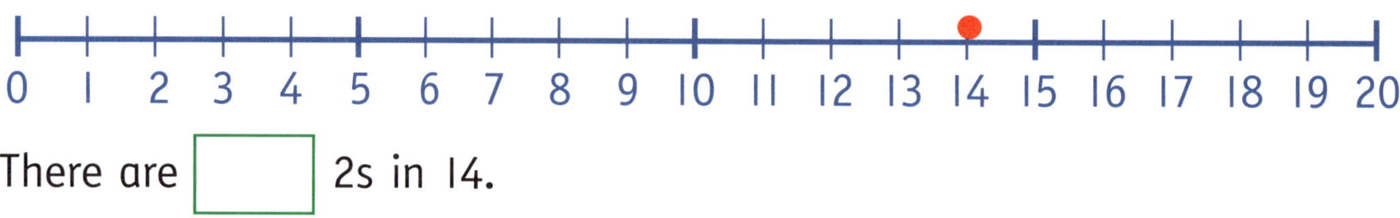

There are ☐ 2s in 14.

3 How many 4s in 20?

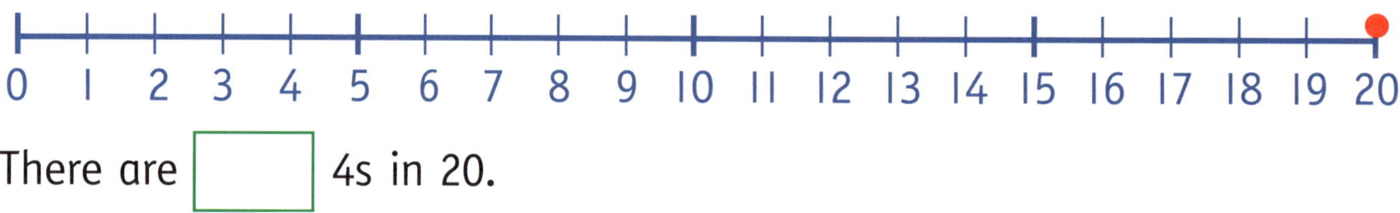

There are ☐ 4s in 20.

4 How many 5s in 15?

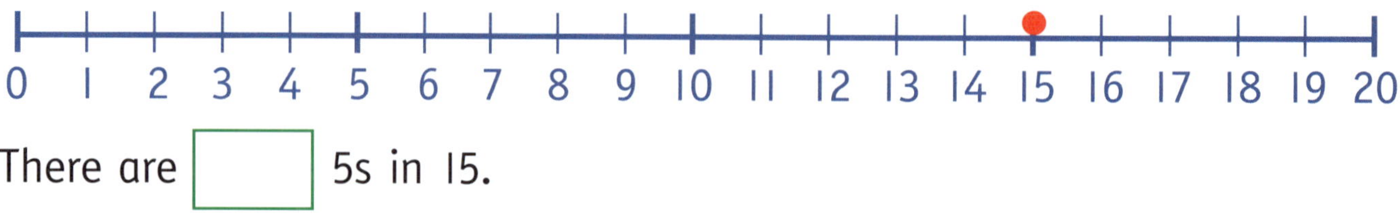

There are ☐ 5s in 15.

5 How many 3s in 18?

There are ☐ 3s in 18.

The division sign

÷ is the sign that tells us to divide.

1 Divide into:

a 2 equal groups.

12 ÷ 2 = ☐

b 4 equal groups.

12 ÷ 4 = ☐

c 3 equal groups.

12 ÷ 3 = ☐

d 6 equal groups.

12 ÷ 6 = ☐

2 Complete.

a 6 ÷ 2 =

b ÷ =

3 Write a division.

a ☐

b ☐

Division

1 Divide equally.

a $8 \div 2 =$ ☐

b $9 \div 3 =$ ☐

c $10 \div 2 =$ ☐

d $15 \div 3 =$ ☐

e $6 \div 2 =$ ☐

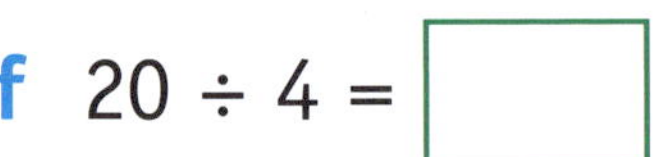

f $20 \div 4 =$ ☐

2 Write a division.

a ☐ ÷ ☐ = ☐

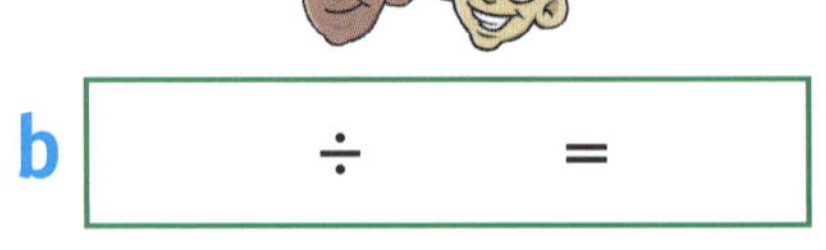

b ☐ ÷ ☐ = ☐

c ☐ ÷ ☐ = ☐

Draw a diagram

16 apples. How many different ways can you share them equally?

Arrays

Groups and rows

Arrays are laid out in **rows** and **columns**.
An array can show **division**.

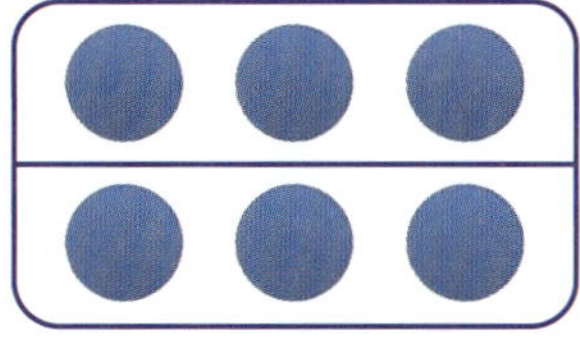

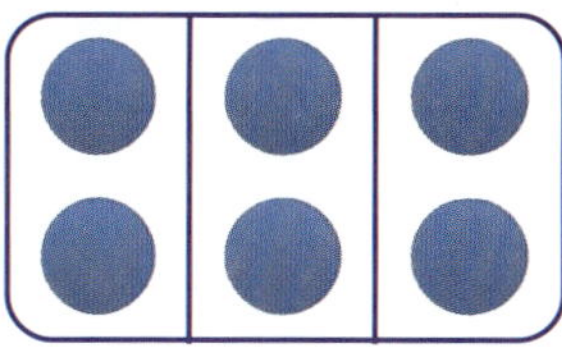

6 ÷ 3 = 2

1 Draw an array.

a 8 oranges divided into 2 rows.

b 12 apples divided into 3 columns.

c 10 ÷ 2 = ☐

d 9 ÷ 3 = ☐

2 Complete the equation.

8 ÷ 2 = ☐

12 ÷ 3 = ☐

3 Write an equation to match the array.

a

b

Remainders

A **remainder** is the number **leftover** when **dividing**.
For example, 7 divided by 2 = 3 and 1 leftover.
Write the remainder after the answer using 'r'.

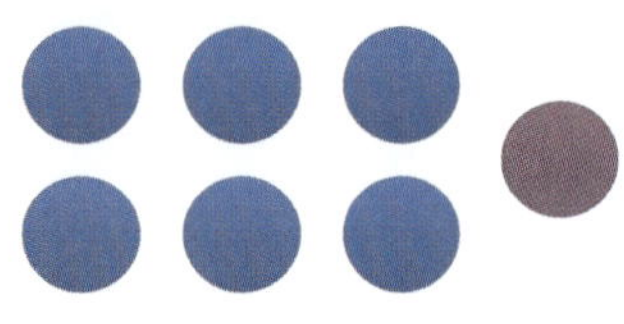

7 ÷ 2 = 3 r 1

1 Draw an array.

a 11 stickers divided into 2 rows.

b 14 marbles divided into 3 rows.

2 Complete the equation.

11 ÷ 2 = ☐ r ☐

14 ÷ 3 = ☐ r ☐

3 Write an equation to match the array.

a ☐ ÷ ☐ = ☐ r ☐

b ☐ ÷ ☐ = ☐ r ☐

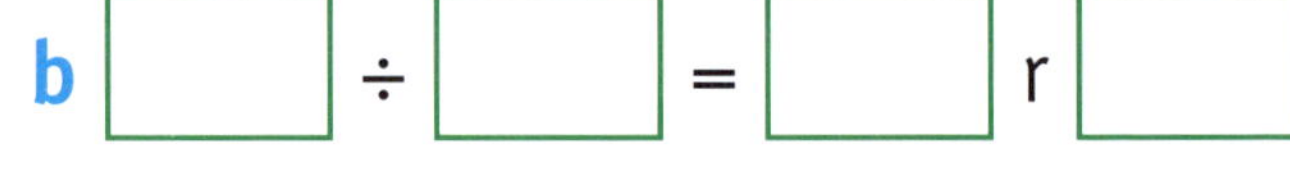

Challenge

3 rows of 5 bananas plus 2 extra bananas. How many in total? ☐

Mastery Checklist

I can:
- ☐ skip count to divide.
- ☐ make groups to divide.
- ☐ use arrays to divide.
- ☐ solve division problems.

Problem solving

Division problems

Draw a picture, number line or array to find the answers.
Write an equation for each problem.

1 Rose has 24 rings. She shares them among her 4 friends.
How many rings does each friend get?

2 Lily made 16 muffins. She eats 2 muffins a day.
How many days do the muffins last for?

3 Iris has 21 seeds. She plants them in 3 rows.
How many seeds in each row?

I can solve problems by:

☐ dividing. ☐ drawing a diagram.

Comparing mass

1 Name things that are:

a lighter

heavier

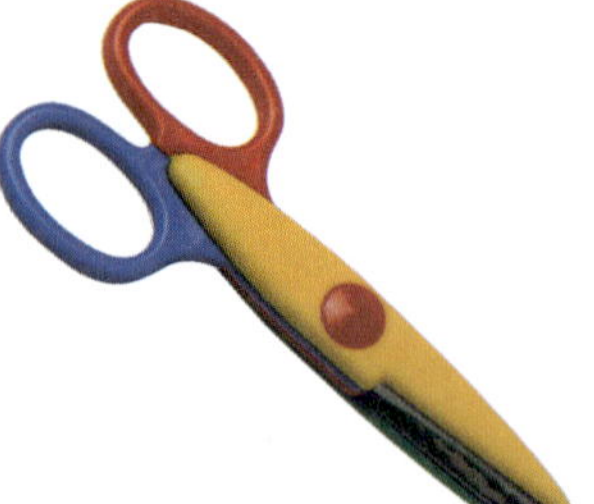

b lighter

heavier

c lighter than you

heavier than you

2 Measure using ,  and 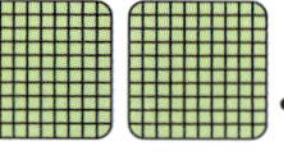.

measure mass on a balance scale

a

b

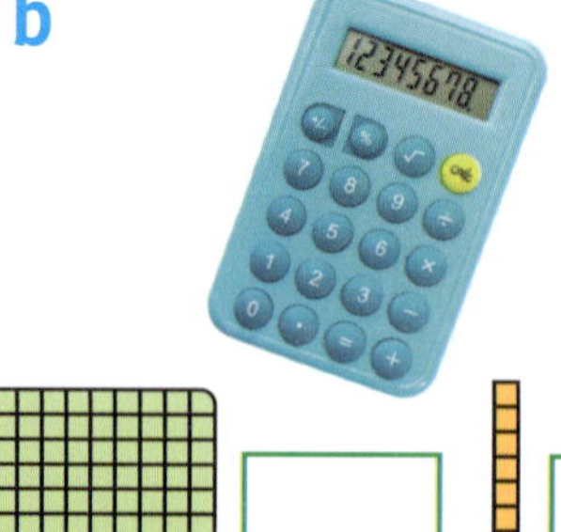

c

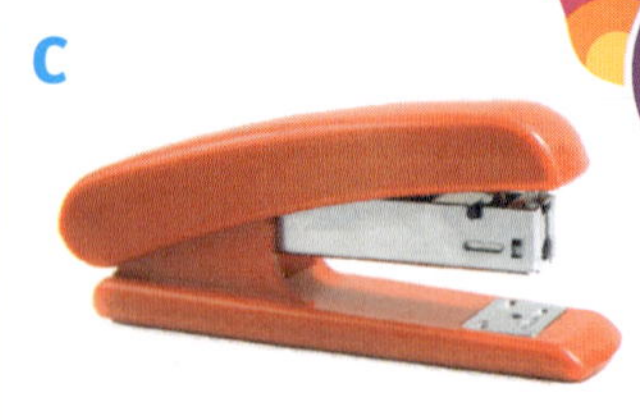

Challenge Who has the heaviest pencil case? The lightest?

______ has the heaviest pencil case.

______ has the lightest pencil case.

Measuring mass

1 Choose the best unit to measure mass using a balance scale.

You could use pencils, blocks, counters, pegs.

measure mass on a balance scale

a The crayon weighs

b The hat weighs

c The tape weighs

d The shoe weighs

e The mug weighs

f The highlighter weighs

g Number from lightest (1) to heaviest (6).

2 Select the best unit to balance.

a 10 blocks weigh the same as ______________________

b 5 pencils weigh the same as ______________________

c 20 counters weigh the same as ______________________

d ______ pencils weigh the same as ______________________

e ______ blocks weigh the same as ______________________

3 a What unit would you use to measure a heavy thing, like a dictionary?

____

b Measure the dictionary using your unit.

The dictionary weighs the same as ______________________

Estimating

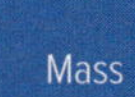

measure mass on a balance scale

1 Estimate how much each item weighs in blocks.

2 Use a balance scale and blocks to check.

a

Estimate: _____ blocks

Measure: _____ blocks

b

Estimate: _____ blocks

Measure: _____ blocks

c

Estimate: _____ blocks

Measure: _____ blocks

d

Estimate: _____ blocks

Measure: _____ blocks

e

Estimate: _____ blocks

Measure: _____ blocks

f

Estimate: _____ blocks

Measure: _____ blocks

3 Finish the sentence by writing 'more' or 'less'.

a The ruler weighs ________________ than the eraser.

b The key weighs ________________ than the 5 pencils.

c The brush weighs ________________ than the 3 crayons.

d The 5 pencils weigh ________________ than the 3 crayons.

4 Estimate using 'more than', 'less than' or 'the same as'.
Use a balance scale to check.

a A dictionary weighs ________________ than 2 textbooks. ☐

b A drink bottle weighs ________________ than a lunchbox. ☐

c A pencil case weighs ________________ than a textbook. ☐

Problem solving

Are mass and volume units the same?

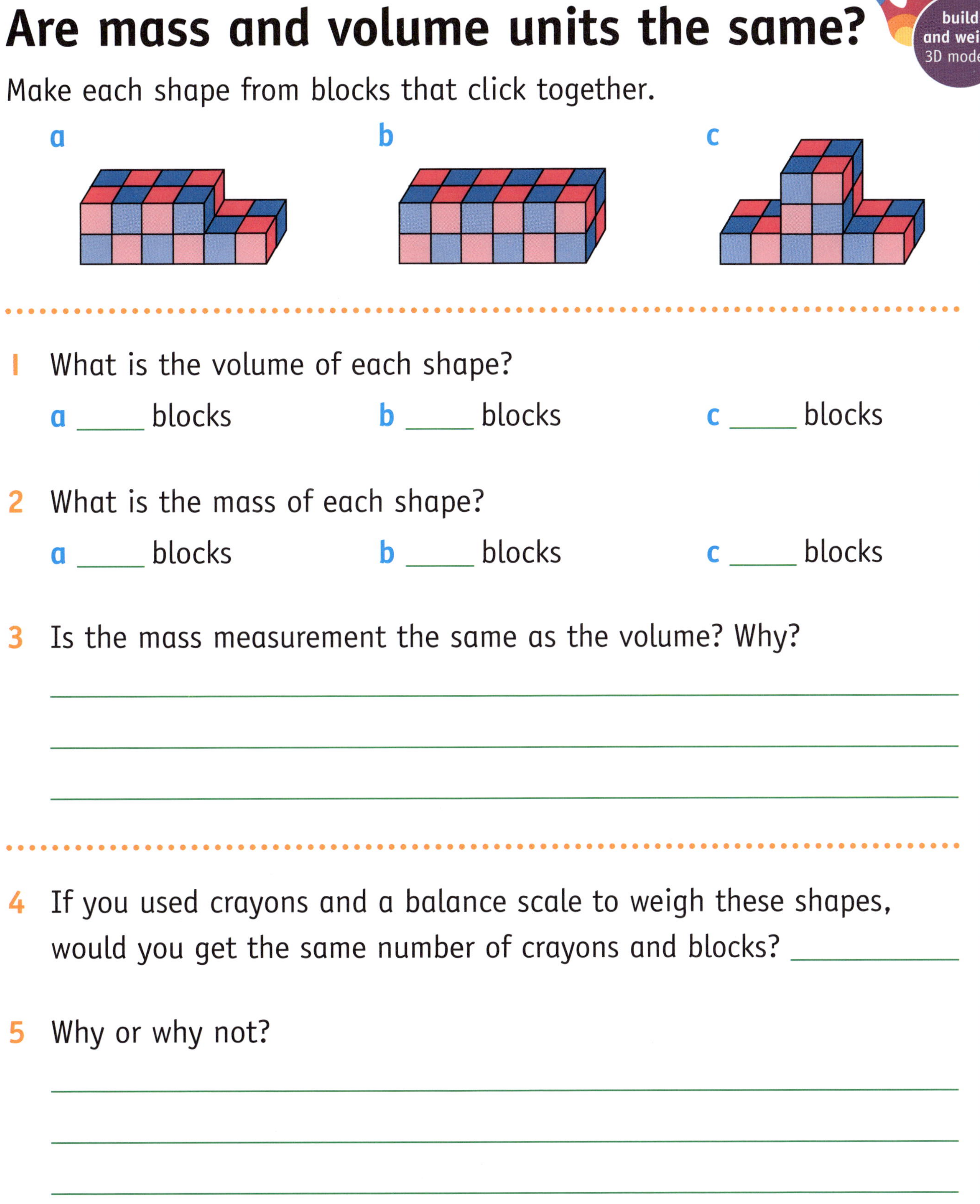

Make each shape from blocks that click together.

a b c

1 What is the volume of each shape?

a _____ blocks b _____ blocks c _____ blocks

2 What is the mass of each shape?

a _____ blocks b _____ blocks c _____ blocks

3 Is the mass measurement the same as the volume? Why?

____

____

____

4 If you used crayons and a balance scale to weigh these shapes, would you get the same number of crayons and blocks? ___________

5 Why or why not?

____

____

____

I can solve problems by:

☐ understanding mass and volume. ☐ measuring and using logical thinking.

Prisms

Prisms have 2 ends that are the same shape. All the other faces are rectangles.

1 a Circle the triangular prisms.

b Write a description. A triangular prism has ______________________________

____

2 Circle the rectangular prisms.

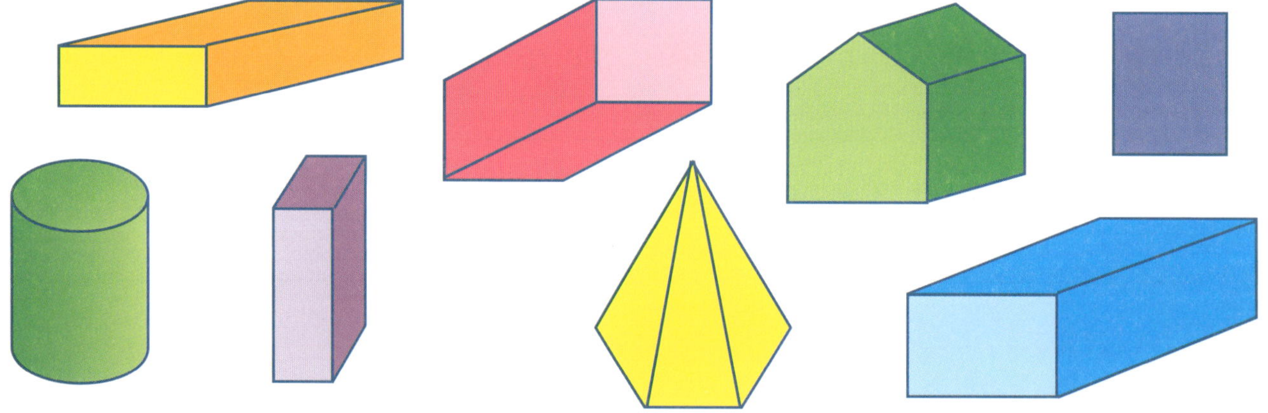

3 Cross out the objects that are not prisms.

Faces, edges and corners

Faces are flat surfaces.

corner, edge, face

1 Look at 3D objects and complete the table.

Shape	Number of faces	Number of edges	Number of corners	Number of curved surfaces
cube				
cylinder				
cone				
rectangular prism				
triangular prism				

Challenge Which 3D objects could you make from these faces?

a

b

Top, front and side view

1 Is the view from the top, front or side?

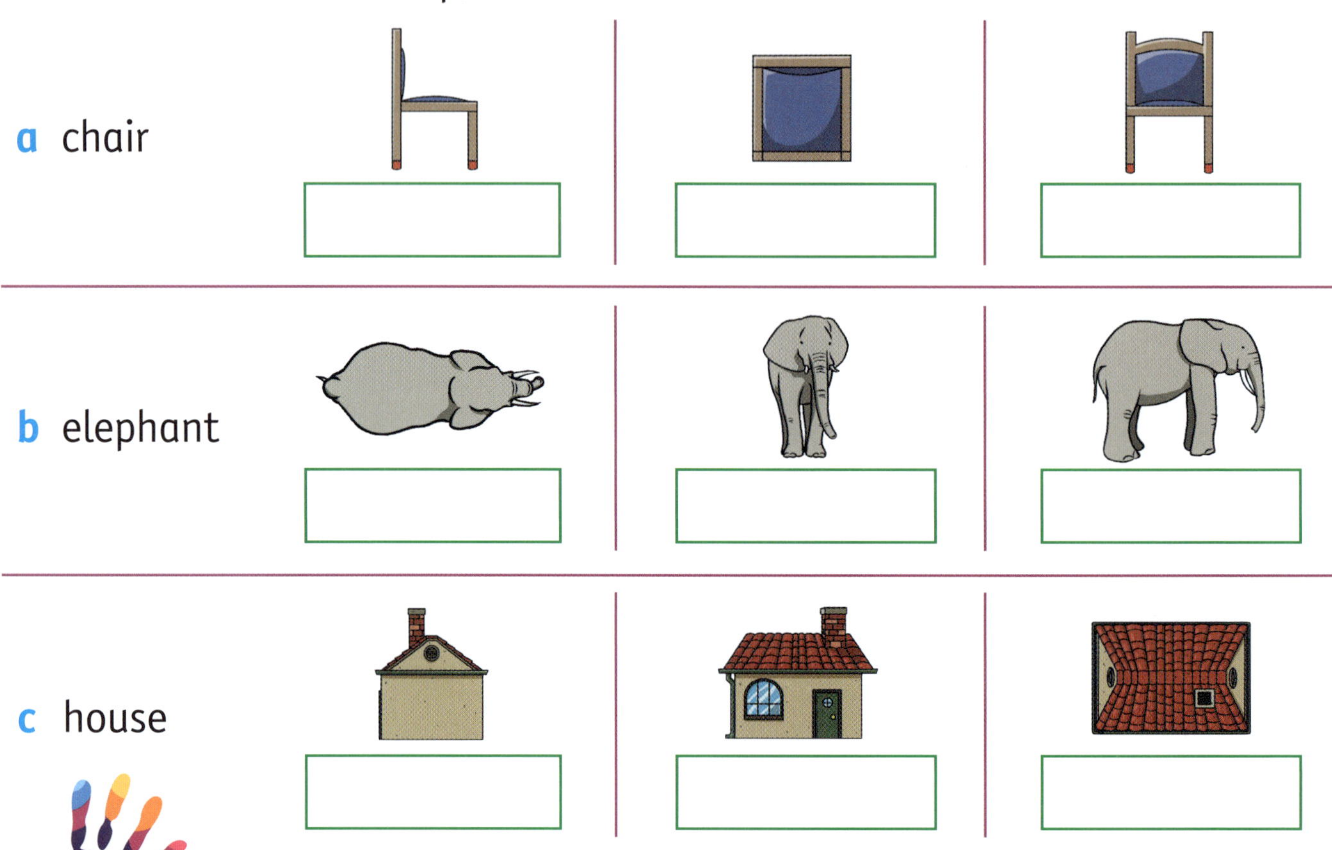

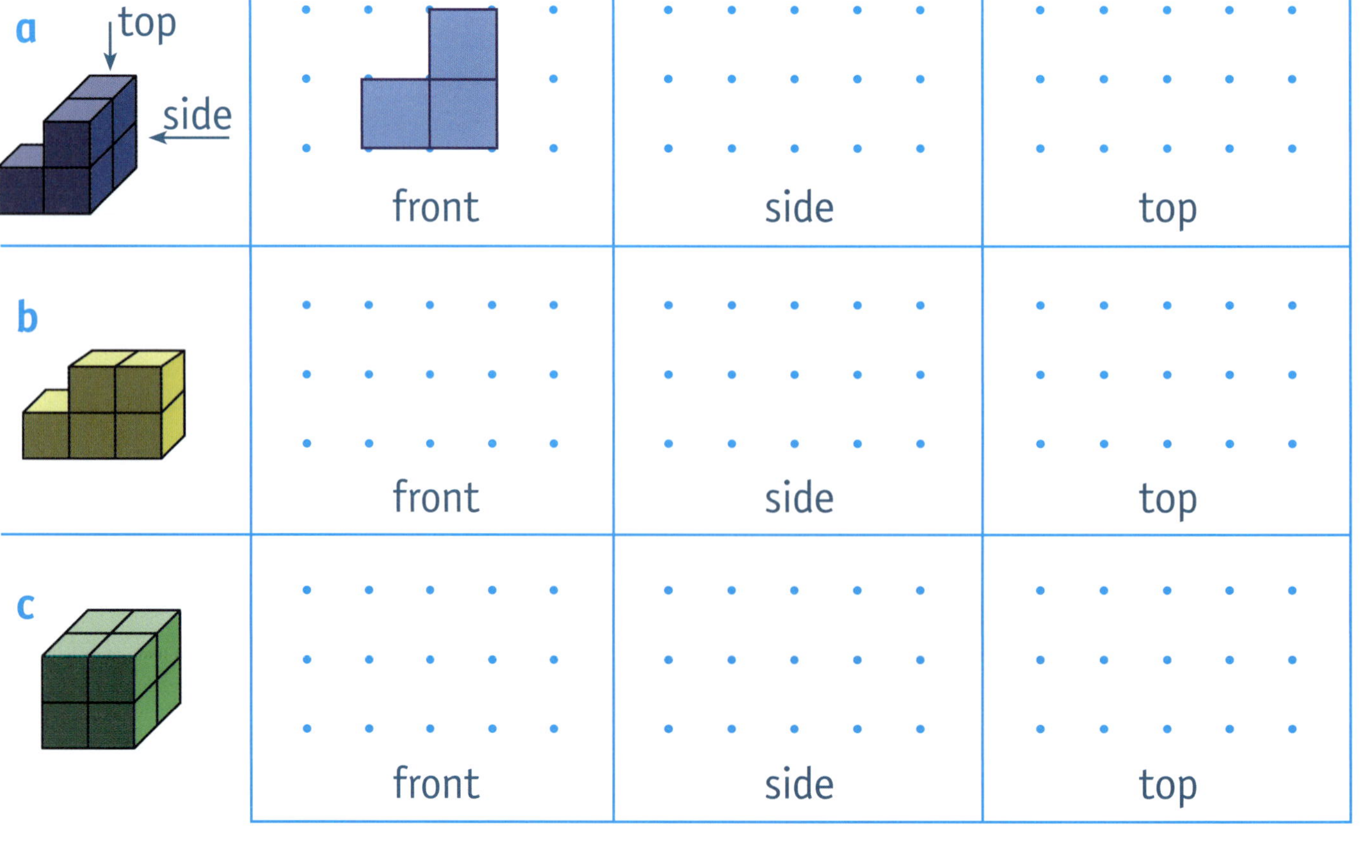

2D faces

1 Draw each view of these 3D objects as a 2D shape.

	front	top	side
(triangular prism)			
(cylinder)			
(square pyramid)			
(rectangular prism)			
(cone)			

Challenge Choose two 3D objects with the same 2D shape from:

the top view.	the front view.	the side view.

Mastery Checklist

I can:
- [ ] compare mass with a balance scale.
- [ ] estimate and measure mass in informal units.
- [ ] identify prisms and the features of 3D objects.
- [ ] recognise different views of items and 3D objects.

Chance and data

Chance

chance experiment

1 Roll 2 dice and add the numbers.
Write all the totals that you can roll.

2 Which 2 totals do you think you are most likely to roll? ☐ ☐

Why? ____________________

3 Now check. Roll two dice and add. Colour a square below for the total.
Keep rolling, adding and colouring squares. Stop when a whole row is full.

Adding the numbers on 2 dice

Totals rolled						
2						
3						
4						
5						
6						
7						
8						
9						
10						
11						
12						

4 Which 2 totals came up most? ☐ ☐

Why? ____________________

AC9M2ST01 • AC9M2ST02 Statistics **MA1-CHAN-01** Chance B • Identify and describe activities that involve chance
MA1-DATA-01 • MA1-DATA-02 Data B • Identify a question of interest and gather relevant data • Create displays of data and interpret them

Interpreting graphs

What could the graph be showing? Write a story to go with each graph. Add labels and numbers.

1

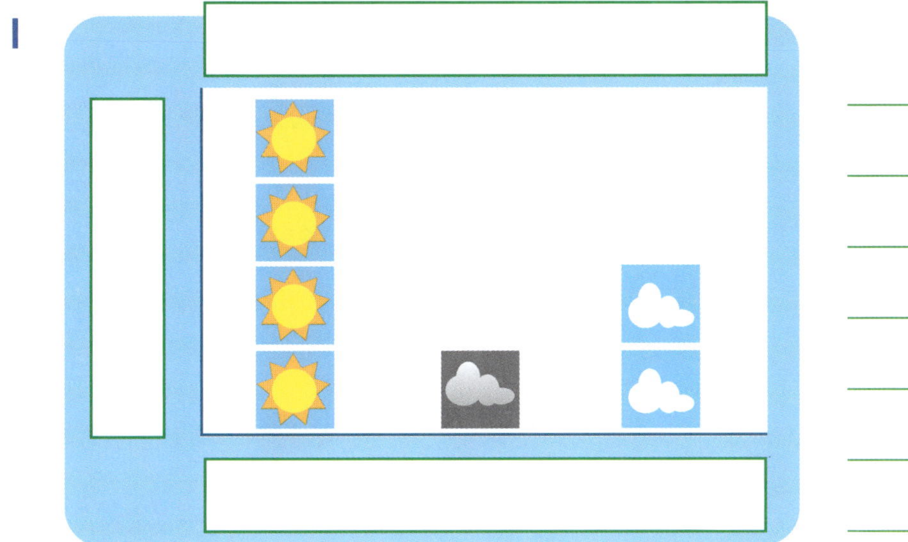

2

3

Chance

Sarah tried to throw a bean bag into a hoop.

Sarah threw the bag 10 times and recorded her results.

inside the hoop	● ●
outside the hoop	● ● ● ● ● ● ● ●

● = 1 throw

1 a How many landed in the hoop? ________

b How many throws missed? ________

c If Sarah has 5 more throws, how many do you think will land:

in the hoop? ______ outside? ______

Draw 5 more dots in the table.

2 Are you 'more likely' or 'less likely' to land the bag in the hoop:

a if the hoop is bigger?	more likely	less likely
b if the hoop is smaller?	more likely	less likely
c if the hoop is closer?	more likely	less likely
d if the hoop is farther away?	more likely	less likely

3 Try it for yourself. Record your results.

Challenge If you were red, which spinner would you choose? [ ]

Why? [ ]

A B

Revision • Term 4

1 Circle:

a the largest number.

235 523 325

b the smallest number.

612 602 620

2 How much to buy 2 of each?

a $4 ______

b $7

3 What is the nearest 100?

a 458 ______

b 548 ______

4 a
```
  1 1
+   4
-----
```

b
```
  1 3
+   5
-----
```

5 a 20 − 3 = ______

b 20 − 9 = ______

c
```
  1 8
−   4
-----
```

d
```
  1 6
−   5
-----
```

6 Finish the division equation.

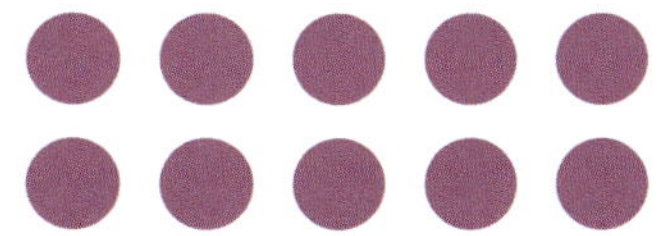

______ ÷ ______ = ______

7 Write 2 multiplications.

a ______ × ______ = ______

b ______ × ______ = ______

8 a

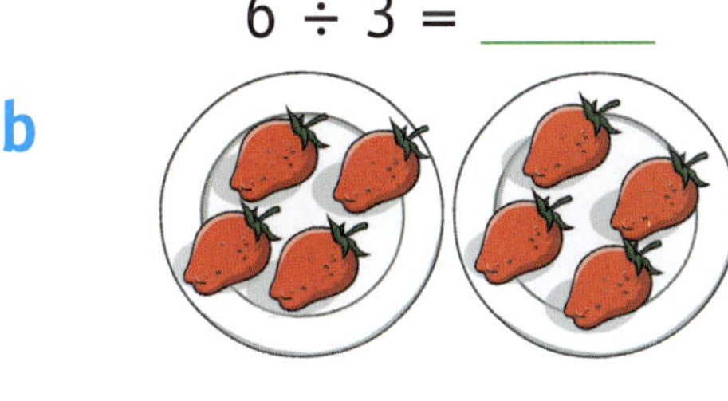

6 ÷ 3 = ______

b

8 ÷ ______ = ______

9 Draw the side view.

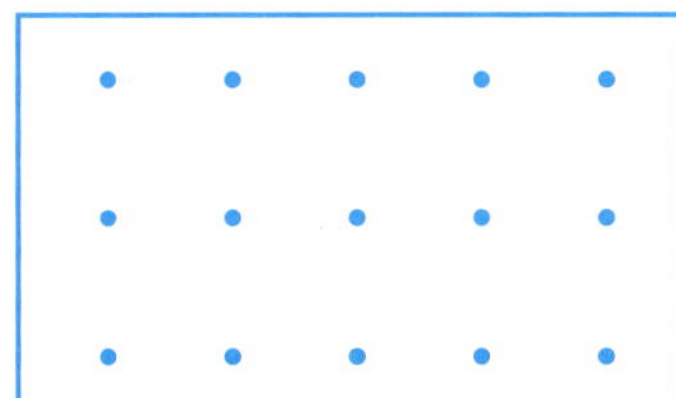

10 Match.

sphere

rectangular prism

cone

Revision • Term 4

11 Match to a label.

half a metre

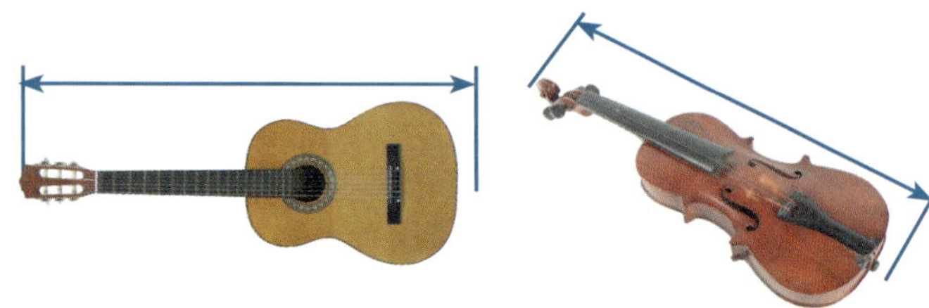

one metre

12 Complete the clocks.
Swimming:

a begins at 1 o'clock.

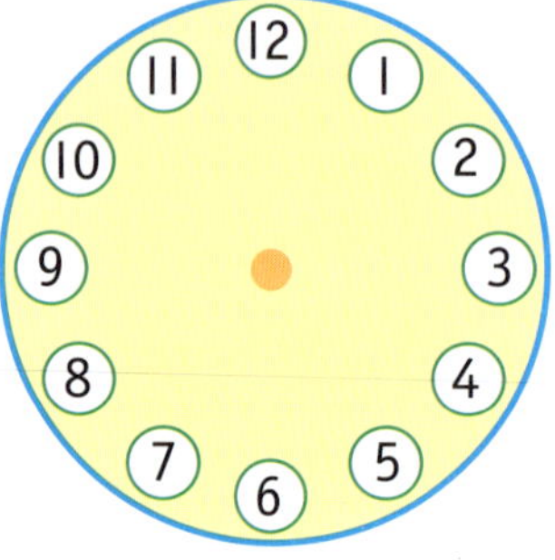

:

b ends at 3 o'clock.

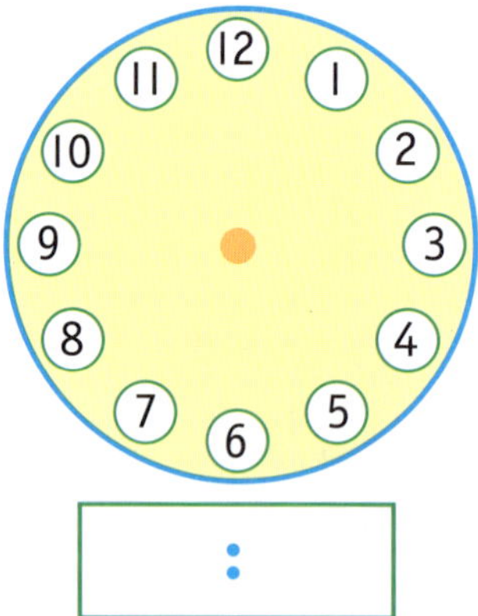

:

c Swimming lasts for ________.

13 Circle your answer.

To measure capacity you could use:

14 How much do they weigh?

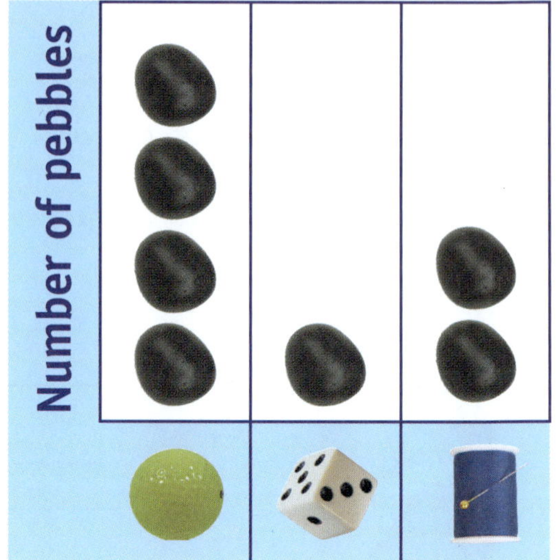

a The thread weighs ________ pebbles.

b The ball is ________ pebbles heavier than the dice.

15 Circle half.

[ ] is half of [ ]

16 Cliff had 12 cards.

He gave half of them to Anna.

Cliff gave Anna ______ cards.

17 Complete the sentence.

It is ________________________

that I will fly to the moon.